GUIDE TO GLOBAL HAZARDS

ROBERT KOVACH AND BILL McGUIRE

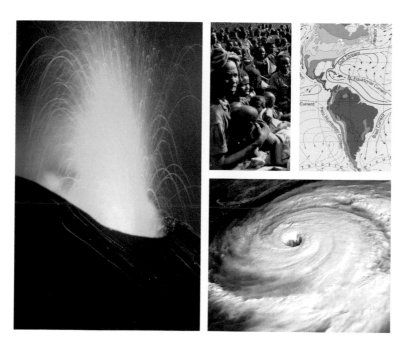

COMMISSIONING EDITOR Christian Humphries

EDITOR Joanna Potts

EXECUTIVE ART EDITOR Mike Brown

DESIGNER Caroline Ohara

PRODUCTION Man Fai Lau

First published in 2003 by Philip's,
a division of Octopus Publishing Group Ltd,
2–4 Heron Quays, London E14 4JP

ISBN 0–540–08388–7

A CIP catalogue record for this book is available
from the British Library.

Printed in China

Details of other Philip's titles and services can be
found on our website at:
www.philips-maps.co.uk

Credits and acknowledgments appear on page 252

FRONT COVER (CLOCKWISE):
top left: Eruption of Stromboli *(Jonathan Blair/Corbis)*
centre: Refugees from the 1984–85 famine in Sudan
(Chris Rainier/Corbis)
right: Map of ocean currents *(Philip's)*
bottom: Satellite image of Hurricane Floyd
(Hal Pierce/GSFC/NASA)

BACK COVER:
right: Ozone concentration in the northern hemisphere
(Greg Shirah/GSFC/NASA)
left: Coastal erosion by wave power *(Philip's)*

Contents

Introduction

There is no doubt that phenomenal disasters are ubiquitous and frequent. We live in an age of catastrophes and calamities, and the number and frequency of disasters may at times overwhelm us, encouraging a profound pessimism that the 'end of the world is nigh'. We must be aware that humans provoke nature. Urbanization and industrialization, together with land mismanagement, the depletion of natural resources, and the pollution of our air, rivers, and oceans may well set the stage for future disasters. In our endless desire for modern consumer goods, one cannot overlook the exploitation of the workers of the world who may or may not realize the causes and effects of unmanaged extraction and utilization of our natural resources because they are more concerned with placing food on their table.

Nevertheless, we continue to build in areas susceptible to hazards. We construct houses in landslide-prone areas; we live in cities vulnerable to earthquakes; and a large percentage of the world's population chooses to live in areas susceptible to hurricanes and tropical cyclones. Coastal flooding is severe during the monsoon season in China, India, and Bangladesh, yet it has the beneficial effect of providing water for agriculture. One is tempted to ask the question, originally posed by the economist Stuart Chase, whether disasters attempt to create a balanced world in which equilibrium is sought between the use of natural resources and human exploitation.

▼ Map showing the distribution of major natural disasters between 1975 and 2001. The map shows disasters in which more than 500 people died. The worst disasters were the 1984 drought in Ethiopia, which killed more than 300,000 people, and the 1976 earthquake in China, which claimed more than 240,000 lives.

⊗   Landslide/avalanche
≋   Flood
🔥   Fire
☀   Drought
🌪   Wind storm
▲   Volcano
▌▐   Earthquake
●   Epidemic

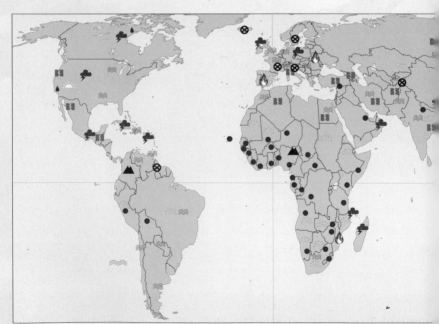

THE WORST NATURAL DISASTERS OF THE 20TH CENTURY				
Location	Country	Disaster type	Date	Killed
worldwide	–	Influenza epidemic	1917	20,000,000
Nationwide	Soviet Union	Famine	1932	5,000,000
–	China	Flood	July 1931	3,700,000
–	Serbia, Poland, Russia	Typhus epidemic	July 1914	3,000,000
Shaanxi, Henan, Gansu	China	Drought	1928	3,000,000
Nationwide	Russia	unknown epidemic	1917	2,500,000
–	China	Flood	July 1959	2,000,000
–	India	Bubonic Plague	1920	2,000,000
–	Bangladesh	Famine	1943	1,900,000
–	China	Bubonic Plague	1909	1,500,000
Calcutta, Bengal	India	Drought	1942	1,500,000
–	India	Drought	1965–67	1,500,000
–	India	Bubonic Plague	1907	1,300,000
Bengal	India	Drought	1900	1,250,000
South Ukraine, Volga	Ukraine	Drought	1921	1,200,000
worldwide	–	Influenza epidemic	May 1957	1,180,200
worldwide	–	Influenza epidemic	1968	666,200

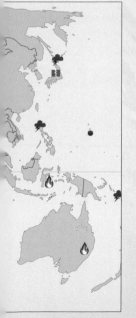

Before discussing the characteristics of individual natural disasters, it is important to define what a hazard signifies. When we speak of a hazard we are referring to the possibility of personal harm, potential losses, and damage to the environment from a natural or human-caused event. Personal harm encompasses death, injury, disease, and physical and emotional stress, while potential losses relate to property damage and disruption of the social and economic fabric of the country. Environmental considerations involve damage to the flora and fauna, the pollution of our land and water resources, and the loss of everyday amenities that we have grown accustomed to.

Identifying the risk

Detection of a natural hazard is a multi-faceted process, which first involves perception and assessment. A hazard is perceived either by individual intuition, awareness, or experience. Awareness of a hazard is strongly dependent on the possibility and ability for detecting it. Perception of the hazard then leads to the concept of risk. What is the specific risk? What are the consequences of the risk in terms of its size, frequency of occurrence, and its economic impact? The final aspect involves an evaluation of the risks. Are they acceptable when compared with the day-to-day risks that society faces? Certainly the public has a right to know what the worst-case outcomes or scenarios of natural hazards might be, and to be able to meaningfully evaluate the risks that directly or indirectly affect their future health and welfare.

Our attitude towards the acceptability of a risk varies among individuals, governments, and societies. But there are only three types of individuals: 1) risk prone; 2) risk averse; and 3) risk neutral. Risk 'prone-ness' is synonymous with risk equity. Broadly-speaking, equity means that it is preferable to spread a total risk (the sum of the individual risks) among as many people as possible – the principle underpinning insurance-underwriting. Risk aversion can be equated with catastrophic avoidance. The likelihood of a major disaster is to be avoided, even at the expense of several smaller ones and possibly more expected fatalities. Risk neutral is equivalent to individual indifference – the head-in-the-sand 'ostrich syndrome'.

Hazard vulnerability
We can regard a hazard as the initial link in a chain of events. A hazard leads to a risk that can ultimately lead to a disaster that can be quantified in terms of loss of life and property damage. However, another consideration needs to be introduced – that of vulnerability. The vulnerability of the population at risk from a specific severe event varies widely on a global basis. Populations are far more vulnerable to the outcomes of natural disasters in less-developed countries compared to developed countries. Part of this is due to their geographic location in relation to regions where potentially damaging natural events take place. Less-developed countries do not have the expertise, financial resources, capital equipment and supplies to cope with and minimize the effects of a disaster. Often these shortcomings are compounded by a lack of

▼ Bar charts of average annual damages (in US dollars) in disasters occurring between 1990 and 2001, and proportion of damages per disaster type. The bar chart on the left reveals that hurricanes caused about US$10,000 million of damages in the Americas. Floods are the single most costly disaster in Europe.

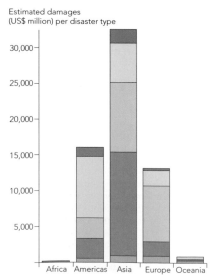

Estimated damages
(US$ million) per disaster type

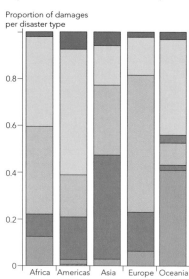

Proportion of damages
per disaster type

IMF: EMERGENCY ASSISTANCE RELATED TO NATURAL DISASTERS, 1995–2003				
Country	Year	Event	Amount (US$ million)	% of quota
Bangladesh	1998	Floods	138.2	25.0
Dominican Republic	1998	Hurricane	55.9	25.0
Haiti	1998	Hurricane	21.0	25.0
Honduras	1998	Hurricane	65.6	50.0
Saint Kitts and Nevis	1998	Hurricane	2.3	25.0
Turkey	1999	Earthquake	501.0	37.5
Malawi	2002	Food shortage	23.0	25.0
Grenada	2003	Hurricane	4.0	25.0

information and the absence of an adequate infrastructure to deal with the aftermath of a damaging event. Unfortunately, the consequences of natural disasters are magnified on the aged and economically disadvantaged who are forced to live in more vulnerable areas.

Our vulnerability to hazards is a double-edged sword. As technology advances, it produces increasing hazards in our day-to-day activities. This, in turn, leads to the heightened exposure of the less advantaged. The reasons for this are lack of resources, limitations on the safety provisions that can be carried out, and the absence of an adequate infrastructure to respond effectively to the crisis at hand. There will always be an element of uncertainty in our assessments of natural and other hazards because of inadequate information and what can be realistically implemented. Another consideration is the irregularity in occurrence of natural disasters. There are certain elements of truth in how a Marxist might view natural hazards: 1) exploitation leads to more natural disasters; 2) the poor suffer the most; 3) disaster-relief maintains the status quo; and 4) high-technology solutions can reinforce under-development, exploitation, and poverty.

Responding to the hazard

At this point it is useful to examine some aspects of personal and group responses to a hazard. Knowledge of the imminence of a natural hazard often leads to warnings and possible evacuation. Warnings can produce either a reaction or in some cases indifference, nonchalance, or stubbornness to 'go down with the ship'. Evacuations are not always easy to implement or even acceptable in many societies. When a disaster strikes, the event produces a number of human reactions such as shock, denial, curiosity, fear, and helplessness. Anger, resentment, guilt, and hopelessness are prevalent. But recovery almost always takes place, beginning with the attempt to regain control of oneself and the situation at hand. A pyramid is built. One takes care of oneself first, then family members, and finally the community as a whole. But different cultures react very differently to the effects of crisis and pain. Mediterranean cultures freely express themselves and cry out for help. North Americans and northern

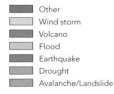

Other
Wind storm
Volcano
Flood
Earthquake
Drought
Avalanche/Landslide

INTRODUCTION

Europeans seem to keep a tight reign on their emotions, with crying often regarded as a sign of weakness.

Bangladesh has continually been struck by a series of terrible famines, cyclones, torrential rains, and floods that kill hundreds of thousands of individuals. On April 29, 1991, a devastating hurricane hit Bangladesh, killing an estimated 139,000 people as a result of its high wind velocities and subsequent storm surge. Mahfuz Ullah, head of the Centre for Sustainable Development in Bangladesh, compiled a remarkable book about survival stories of individuals from cyclones in Bangladesh:

"She told her husband that they should do something to protect themselves from the cyclone ... He did not listen and ... [he] beat her ... She tied her children to bamboo poles ... Next morning she found herself lying naked on the sands ... corpses all around ... She came back home but no one was there to greet her."

Women and children are often angered, irritated, or distressed about poor or poorly conceived rescue attempts in the aftermath of a disaster. This has been repeated time and time again, particularly after mine disasters, even though the main emphasis has been directed to search-and- rescue efforts. Gender may well be a very important ingredient of disaster recovery. Bangladesh is the most densely populated country in the world. When a tropical cyclone strikes, the loss of life is proportionally much higher among women and female children. Bangladeshi women are often marginalized and discriminated against and subjected to a strong social pressure called purdah – the admonition not to leave home when the husband is away. These women have strong survival tendencies and instincts to protect their children and their local source of livelihood. They are reluctant to move to shelters, abandoning their few possessions and the few livestock that they own, for fear that they will lose them either in the disaster itself or in any subsqent looting.

Ethnic differences in natural-hazard perception are an important variable. Some ethnic groups express a greater

▼ *Total number of reported disasters (1991–2000) by continent. The number of hazardous events has increased in recent decades. In the 1960s, there was an average of 53 disasters. In the 1970s, the average number of reported disasters rose to 112. In the 1980s, the number of disasters nearly doubled to 223. As this bar chart shows, since 1997 the number of reported cases has risen on every continent, with the exception of Oceania. The United Nations declared the 1990s, the International Decade for Natural Disasters Reduction.*

■ Africa
■ America
■ Asia
■ Europe
■ Oceania

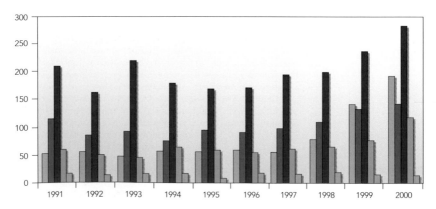

▲ *On September 15, 1999, Hurricane Floyd swept across eastern North Carolina, passing just west of the city of Greenville (shown here). Heavy rains associated with Hurricane Floyd caused the Tar River to burst its banks and led to severe flooding of residential and commercial structures. More than 50,000 people were displaced. Final estimates showed that more than 1,800 homes were damaged by the floodwaters with 55% of those deemed to be uninhabitable.*

fear of earthquakes than others, but this may just reflect the degree of information about the seismic threat. It is possible that a greater technical understanding of earthquakes leads in turn to a heightened climate of fear. On the other hand, the differing ethnic responses to a disaster may only be an expression of an acceptance of the exposure to hazardous day-to-day activities so that they are not viewed as continually life-threatening. In a classic study, R.W. Kates and his colleagues examined a number of social responses following the disastrous 1972 earthquake in Managua, western Nicaragua. A focus on family first was recognized, but an additional aspect – not unknown in many societies –was that of looting. The government, stretched on resources for alleviating the disaster, was overwhelmed. Familial ties were the dominant support mechanism. Looting was justified because of the wide disparity between the haves and the have-nots, and the overwhelming need and justification to take care of one's family as a primary objective.

In late 1995, the Cerro Negro volcano, some 120 km (75 miles) south-east of Managua, Nicaragua's capital, persistently rumbled, but about 12,000 peasant farmers refused to heed evacuation orders. The rationalization was that they preferred to stay and risk the effects of an eruption rather than leave their homes open to looters. This is not an atypical response, perhaps because of previous bitter personal experiences. In many countries such as Nicaragua and the Philippines, for example, a private home is rarely left unguarded or unoccupied. The presumption is that anything presumed to be of value and left unguarded is fair game. It is not surprising that many residents choose not to voluntarily evacuate after the announcement of an imminent natural disaster, such as a flood or volcanic eruption.

In this book we shall examine a wide range of natural hazards and their consequences, including rapid-onset events such as earthquakes, volcanoes, hurricanes, tornadoes, floods, tsunami, and landslides, and slower-onset phenomena such as desertification and drought. Awareness of their location and probable outcomes is an important facet of hazard mitigation. Earthquakes, hurricanes and floods, and volcanic eruptions cause the largest number of fatalities. During the past century there were 1,340,000 earthquake fatalities, 996,000 hurricane and flood fatalities, and 75,000 fatalities as a result of volcanic eruptions. One misleading conclusion is that because of the rapid rise in population the risk per individual of becoming a fatality from a natural disaster on a global basis is declining. The cumulative number of fatalities per year normalized to the population may have decreased, but the number of people affected by natural disasters has grown from 70 million to 200 million since 1970. And the economic losses from disasters have increased from US$1.3 billion to US$6.3 billion per year. In the year 2000, it was estimated that one in 30 people were detrimentally affected by natural hazards.

The trend is particularly ominous with regard to earthquake hazards in urban areas. In the 1950s, 160 million people were concentrated in the world's 50 largest cities. In the year 2000, this number has increased to 500 million, with half this number concentrated in cities of developing countries. Cities in Mexico and Central America are particular examples. Weather-related disasters are another culprit that continues to play havoc in many countries. In 1998 Hurricane Mitch swept across the Yucatán Peninsula into Honduras, resulting in 14,600 fatalities, and setting back economic development in Honduras by at least 20 years.

The stated goal of hazard mitigation and reduction is to halve the number of people affected by disasters by the year 2015. Hazard mitigation has three important facets: 1) physical, 2) engineering, and 3) social. Physical considerations involve making observations and measurements in the field. Observations are integrated into models that attempt to

▼ *On October 12, 2002, many large trees in south-western Louisiana were uprooted by the category 4 Hurrricane Lili. A tree was blown over into this house in Crowley, Louisiana. Hurricane Lili killed 13 people and caused more than US$860 million in damages.*

Dead

Affected population

► *The graph shows that while the number of fatalities in natural disasters has declined since the 1970s, the number of people affected by disasters continues to rise, approaching 2,000 million in 1999.*

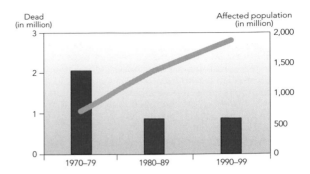

predict the likelihood and outcome of a natural event. We can point to such examples as weather prediction, hurricane warning, eruption prediction, and forecasting flood-stage levels. The engineering aspects are directed towards the design and building of structures that minimize the effects of a natural disaster. Specific examples include the introduction of earthquake-resistant buildings, the building of failure-resistant dams, and the construction of avalanche barriers. Social considerations involve the implementation of land-use planning, the use of scientific predictions, evaluation of the subsequent risk, and cost-benefit analyses.

It might seem surprising, but natural and technological disasters, for all of their detrimental results, can also produce positive effects. We are compelled as a society to attempt to minimize the consequences of a hazard. In fact, one can argue that the hazard itself forces us to introduce measures that mitigate future disasters. The use of pesticides has the goal of reducing food shortages. Construction of flood-control dams can hopefully minimize the effects of drought by water storage as well as the consequences of flash flooding from torrential rains. Earthquakes can have the helpful outcome of pointing out design failures to be avoided in future construction. It is important that we learn lessons from a disaster, so that we can take positive action to prevent or reduce deaths and damage in similar subsequent events. One cannot dispute that disasters can force us to improve our efficiency and response time of relief-efforts for stricken areas. These counter-measures are not sufficiently widespread, however, to overcome the numbing feeling produced by disasters on individuals who might not be directly touched or exposed to the reality of a tragedy in a distant place. Often if we believe that a natural disaster does not directly affect us as individuals, we tend to push it aside. We must guard against apathy as we seek worldwide mitigation of disastrous risks. The purpose of this book is to gain a fuller understanding of natural hazards so that we can become more adept at identifying and evaluating them, and thus make objective decisions about the risks they pose and how to mitigate them.

Earthquakes

An earthquake is a sudden shaking within the Earth caused by the release of accumulated strain in the rocks that make up the Earth's crust. Earthquakes generally take place along a fault, but they can also occur beneath and within volcanoes, or can be triggered by asteroid or comet impacts. There are around 150,000 noticeable earthquakes every year but more than a million a year occur that can be detected instrumentally.

Earthquake effects

The effects of an earthquake may be classified as primary, transient, and secondary. **Primary effects** are permanent features produced by an earthquake, most notably surface ruptures, scarps, horizontal offsets, changes in ground elevation, offsets of fences and roads and twisted railways. Primary effects lead to **transient effects** such as visible ground waves, ground shaking and/or liquefaction, tsunami, and human reactions such as nausea and panic. Shaking is the main cause of earthquake damage and can last from several to tens of seconds. Transient effects produce **secondary effects** such as landslides, slumps, lurches, mudflows, avalanches, seiches (oscillations in lakes and other large water bodies) and, most importantly, building damage.

In the 20th century, more than 1.3 million people died in earthquakes, translating into an average of 13,000 fatalities per year. The year 2001 was a particularly deadly one for earthquakes, accounting for more than 21,000 lives. Earthquakes cannot currently be predicted with any degree of certainty, in the sense of specifying, in advance, the time, place, and size of the event. Seismologists can, however, make broader forecasts,

▼ *The aftermath of the 1999 earthquake in Turkey. The epicentre was located very close to the south shore of the Bay of Izmit, an eastward extension of the Marmara Sea. The earthquake's proximity to the city of Izmit, c. 85 km (52 miles) southeast of the capital Istanbul, contributed greatly to its damaging effects.*

► The damaged Shihkang Dam, near Fengyuen, northwest Taiwan. The 1999 earthquake measured 7.6 on the Richter scale and killed 2,264 people. The fault goes directly under the damaged portion of the dam. The dam was 50 km (30 miles) from the epicentre. The severe damage to the dam cut off the water supply from the reservoir.

which provide information on the probability of an earthquake of a specified size occurring within a given time frame. Earthquakes will continue to occur and the human cost from their effects will remain high. Indeed, death and destruction is likely to increase as more people congregate in poorly constructed urban centres in earthquake-prone regions.

Earthquake geography

The first thing that is evident on a world map of earthquake occurrences is that earthquake locations are primarily confined to narrow bands rather than being randomly distributed around the globe. The point within the Earth where the earthquake rupture initiates is known as the 'focus' or 'hypocentre', while the term 'epicentre' is reserved for the point directly above it on the surface. Earthquakes can be classified according to their depth of focus (focal depth). A **shallow-focus** earthquake occurs at depths ranging from 0 to 65 km (0 to 40 miles) beneath the surface, but those shallow enough to rupture the surface are often the most damaging. **Intermediate-focus** earthquakes have depths ranging from 65 to 280 km (40 to 175 miles), and **deep-focus** quakes range from 280 to 750 km (175 to 465 miles), below which greater earthquakes do not occur. Earthquake activity, as a result, is confined to the outer 12 percent of the Earth's crust, with by far the majority of the seismic energy released in shallow-focus events. Intermediate-focus shocks contribute only about 12 percent, and deep-focus shocks a mere three percent. It would be wrong to assume, however, that intermediate- and deep-focus earthquakes do not cause damage.

The Circum-Pacific belt or 'Ring of Fire'

Eighty percent of all the world's earthquakes occur in the circum-Pacific belt. With its geographic association with most of the world's volcanoes, this zone is commonly known as the 'Ring of Fire'. One of the more active sectors of the circum-Pacific belt is the Aleutian arc, stretching from the Komandorski Islands of north-east Russia into central Alaska. Following the zone southeastward from Alaska to British Colombia, seismic activity falls to a moderate level, but intensifies southward into California, Mexico and Central America. Mexico and Central America possess the highest seismic activity in the western hemisphere together with very high volcanic activity. Shallow-focus earthquakes are most frequent but intermediate focus earthquakes also occur in Mexico. From Guatemala and Honduras, the zone of seismic activity can be traced through the West Indies, looping around into Venezuela and Colombia. The entire Caribbean loop is seismically active and is, in the Lesser Antilles, coincident with frequent volcanic activity.

South America

The western part of South America is highly seismic but the eastern part has a noticeable absence of seismic activity. In terms of seismic geography the western coast of South America is a classic area. Shallow-focus earthquakes occur near the coast with a progression to intermediate- and deep-focus earthquakes eastward beneath the Andes. The South American zone is characterized by the occurrence of very large earthquakes, many of which have produced tsunamis large enough to cross the Pacific Basin.

The Tonga-Kermadec zone

On the western side of the circum-Pacific belt are the Tonga and Kermadec zones, which are very active regions for shallow-focus earthquakes. Half of the world's deep-focus shocks also take place here. Bathymetric measurements (of water depth) have disclosed a deep-sea trench, parallel chains of islands, and the presence of volcanoes in the Tonga-Kermadec zone. Seismic activity continues westward along the New Hebrides-Solomon Island chain to the equator off

▼ *World map showing major earthquakes since 1900 and the locations of mobile land areas and mid-oceanic volcanic ridges. Earthquakes are a series of rapid vibrations originating from the slipping or faulting of parts of the Earth's crust when stresses within build up to breaking up. The world's most devastating quake was at Shaanxi, central China, on January 3, 1556, when an estimated 830,000 people were killed.*

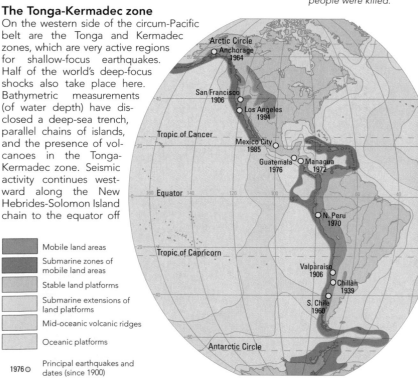

Mobile land areas

Submarine zones of mobile land areas

Stable land platforms

Submarine extensions of land platforms

Mid-oceanic volcanic ridges

Oceanic platforms

1976○ Principal earthquakes and dates (since 1900)

New Guinea. Here the seismic belt divides into two zones that progress northward to Japan – one along the Mariana Islands arc, and the other from the Philippines to Taiwan. Japan and adjacent areas are part of the Kamchatka-Kuril Islands zone, the most active region in the world for shallow- and intermediate-focus shocks. Seismic events occur along the Indonesian arc to Burma (Myanmar) and along the Himalayan belt north of India. North of this belt, into China, the pattern of seismic activity becomes more diffuse. The zone of seismic activity continues westward through Pakistan, Iran, and Turkey into the Mediterranean Sea region. Earthquake-prone Greece, Albania, Romania, and Italy fall within an arc circling the Aegean Sea – an earthquake zone that accounts for about 15 percent of total global seismic energy release. Other regions prominent in the global mosaic of earthquake geography are East Africa, the Gulf of Aden, the Red Sea, and the Dead Sea rift zone.

Two salient observations can be made about global patterns of seismicity. First, seismic activity is greater in the northern hemisphere than in the southern hemisphere. Second, seismic activity decreases rapidly south of the equator, less than 10 percent of large earthquakes take place below latitude 30 degrees south, which constitutes about a quarter of the world's surface.

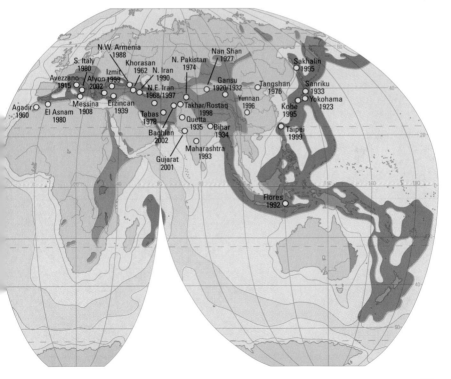

Earthquakes and plate tectonics

Most of the world's earthquakes occur in well-defined belts that divide the Earth's surface into large movable segments called plates, the behaviour of which forms the basis of the theory of plate tectonics. The boundaries of the plates, which underlie the continents and oceans, are defined by these belts of seismic activity. Plate boundaries rarely coincide with the contacts between oceans and continents, and seismic belts also rarely follow these contacts. Differential movement takes place along the plate boundaries generating large, **interplate earthquakes**. These are differentiated from the far less frequent **intraplate earthquakes** that occur within plate interiors. Earthquakes are confined to the planet's rigid outer shell (or lithosphere), which comprises the crust and the uppermost portion of the mantle that make up the tectonic plates. This lithosphere is defined on the basis of rheological (liquid viscosity) rather than chemical considerations. The lithosphere is rocky and characterized by temperatures above the melting temperatures of rock. Its tenacity means that it can endure considerable shearing stresses of hundreds of bars (atmospheres) before it breaks. Lithospheric thickness beneath the ocean basins is about 70 km (45 miles) and beneath the continents it ranges from 100 to 200 km (60 to 120 miles). All earthquakes occur in the lithosphere. Beneath the lithosphere is the asthenosphere, a layer of material that has no lasting endurance to shearing stress, and which therefore easily deforms. The asthenosphere is very hot and partially molten, and although it can sustain slow movement or aseismic creep along a fault, it cannot undergo fracturing, which means that earthquakes cannot originate here.

Plate boundaries

The major plates of the Earth – the Pacific, Indo-Australian, Eurasian, North American, South American, African, and

▼ *World map depicting the position and type of plate boundaries.*

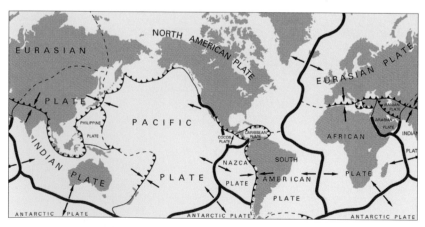

▬▬▬ Divergent plate boundaries (zones of construction)	- - - - - Uncertain plate boundaries
▲▲▲▲ Convergent plate boundaries (zones of subduction and collision)	⟶ Direction of plate movement

Antarctic – were identified decades ago, but as the science of plate tectonics has evolved, increasingly smaller plates have been delineated, such as the Nazca, Caribbean, Philippine, Arabian, and Cocos plates. It is the plate boundaries that are of most interest to us because that is where earthquakes take place. Four main types of plate boundary are recognized: constructive, subduction and collision (both of which are convergent), and transform.

Constructive plate boundaries

The best example of a constructive plate boundary is the ridge that bisects the Atlantic Ocean. New ocean floor is continually being constructed and added along the crest of the Mid-Atlantic Ridge. Segments on either side of the crest move apart as new molten material is injected into the gap, where it solidifies and then is pushed symmetrically away from the crest. As the material cools beneath the Curie point (the temperature at or below which it can retain magnetization), it assumes the present direction of the Earth's magnetic field. The Earth's magnetic field has randomly reversed direction in the geological past. This pattern of reversals can be mapped with magnetic observations, and the spreading rate (typically of the order of centimetres per year) away from the axis of the ridge can be deduced. Shallow earthquakes are associated with divergent or differential movement along this type of plate boundary.

Subduction plate boundaries

Subduction plate boundaries occur all around the boundaries of the Pacific Ocean, including western South America, Alaska, Japan and the Philippines. At this type of boundary a thinner oceanic plate converges with a thicker continental plate. Because the continental lithospheric plate is thicker and less dense than the oceanic plate, the net result is that the oceanic plate is forced, or subducted, beneath the continental plate forming a subduction zone. Where it turns downward it produces an oceanic trench that marks the boundary between the two plates. As subduction continues, intermediate – and deep-focus earthquakes occur along the boundaries or within the interior of the subducting plate. This zone of earthquake activity, named the Benioff zone, can extend to depths of 700 km (420 miles) or so, with a depth progression that increases beneath the continental side of the subduction zone. As the subducting plate is pushed or pulled downward into a zone of higher temperatures, partial melting can occur and molten material or magma can rise to the surface along zones of weakness. The result is a zone of volcanoes parallel to the oceanic trench, but always on the continental side of the subduction zone. Most of the world's earthquakes and seismic energy releases take place in the subduction zones surrounding the Pacific Ocean.

Collision boundaries

At a collision boundary, two continental blocks crash together due to the destruction, by subduction, of the intervening ocean floor. Neither plate has a sufficiently low density to allow it to sink into the asthenosphere, so the lower plate slides between the asthenosphere and the other continental plate, raising the latter to great heights. The result is a mountain range. The best example of a continental collision boundary is the convergence of the Indo-Australian plate with the continental Eurasian plate, which produced the Himalayas. This collision boundary also created a wide zone of deformation and seismic activity where many intermediate-focus earthquakes occur, such as the great 1897 earthquake in Assam, northeast India. Huge, damaging earthquakes continue to plague the Indian subcontinent, including that which struck the Indian state of Gujarat in 2001, killing at least 20,000 people and damaging and destroying as many as 400,000 homes.

Transform boundaries

At a transform boundary, plates slide past each other, neither gaining nor losing material in the process. A classic example is the San Andreas Fault in California (see p. 21), where the Pacific plate to the west is moving north at a rate of six cm/yr relative to the North American plate. The cities of Los Angeles and San Francisco are now located on opposite sides of the San Andreas transform. However, at the current rate of movement, 10 million years from now Los Angeles will become a suburb of San Francisco, and 40 million years from now Los Angeles will be swallowed up in the Aleutian trench. Another notorious transform boundary is Turkey's North Anatolian Fault, movement along which generated the 1999 Izmit earthquake that killed more than 17,000 people.

Earthquakes can be visualized as movements occurring along the boundaries of the plates. The sum of the individual earthquake movements over a long period of time will match the average rate of plate movement. For example, suppose the slip rate along a segment of a plate boundary is three cm (one inch) per year. If earthquakes on the boundary typically result in 300 cm (ten inches) of lateral displacement, then they must occur approximately every century. This simple concept forms the basis of the seismic gap concept. Major earthquakes tend

▼ *Earthquakes occur when crustal plates move against each other. Here, one plate moves under another to create a 'subduction zone'. The movement of the plates causes the earthquake 'shock', spreading outward from the origin. The epicentre is the point on the surface directly above the origin. In this case, the epicentre is in the sea, so a tsunami may occur. Damage on land occurs when the shockwaves reach the surface, with the amount of damage usually decreasing as distance from the epicentre increases.*

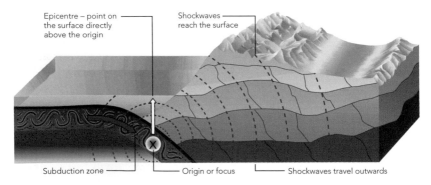

Epicentre – point on the surface directly above the origin

Shockwaves reach the surface

Subduction zone

Origin or focus

Shockwaves travel outwards

to occur in those segments of plate boundaries that have not been subjected to rupture on a timescale of centuries or more. A seismic gap does not mean there has been a cessation of seismic activity in an area, only that the rocks are resisting for a longer period than usual the stresses being placed upon them. The longer that strain and stress accumulates in the rocks, the more violent the eventual earthquake is likely to be.

Intraplate earthquakes

Large earthquakes occur from time to time within the interiors of the tectonic plates far away from their boundaries. These intraplate earthquakes are infrequent but can have deadly consequences because their size can be comparable to those of plate boundary events. In 1811–12, three major earthquakes, possibly registering as high as magnitude eight on the Richter scale and termed the 'New Madrid earthquakes', shook the borders of the US states of Missouri, Arkansas, Tennessee, and Kentucky, a region containing thick deposits of water-saturated, unconsolidated sands and mud deposited by the Mississippi River. Ground shaking from the earthquakes was intensified as a result of the weak sediments, which underwent a process known as liquefaction (in effect the sediments behaved like water). Several long-lasting topographic effects were created. A 240 km (150 mile) -long section alongside the Mississippi River sank, forming a broad depressed area and two new lakes – Lake St Francis, eastern Arkansas, and Reelfoot Lake, north-east Tennessee. Low cliffs were formed and swamplands were elevated into prolific, tillable soils.

The New Madrid earthquakes were felt over much of the North American continent, from Canada to the Gulf of Mexico and as far eastward as the Atlantic seaboard. The quakes shook the underlying, rigid basement rocks, sending seismic energy very effectively across thousands of kilometres. In

MAJOR EARTHQUAKES SINCE 1970					
Location(s)	Country	Richter scale	Date	Killed	Affected
Tangshan, Beijing, Tianjin	China	7.8	July 27, 1976	242,000	–
Gilan, Zanjan provinces	Iran	7.3	June 1, 1990	40,000	605,000
Leninakan, Kirovakan, Spitak	Armenia	6.9	December 7, 1988	25,000	1,642,000
Guatemala City	Guatemala	7.5	February 4, 1976	23,000	4,993,000
Gujarat state	India	7.9	January 26, 2001	20,005	16,066,812
Khorasan province	Iran	7.7	September 16, 1978	20,000	40,000
Izmit	Turkey	7.4	August 17, 1999	17,127	1,358,953
Maharastra state	India	6.4	September 23, 1993	9,782	195,566
Mexico City, Michoacán, Jalisco	Mexico	8.1	September 19, 1985	8,776	130,204
Gulf of Moro, Sulu	Philippines	8	August 16, 1976	6,000	181,348
Kobe	Japan	7.2	January 17, 1995	5,502	1,836,896

terms of area, the New Madrid events were the most widely felt of any earthquake in the continental United States. Due to the sparse population in the 1810s, the impact of the quakes was minimal. A repeat of the events today, however, would have disastrous consequences, both in terms of loss of life and destruction of property and infrastructure.

New Madrid sits in the continental interior far from any plate boundary, yet large earthquakes have occurred here. The reason for this has not been fully explained, but one intriguing possibility is that the New Madrid events were the result of the changing stress-field induced by bending of the lithospheric plate as a result of the deglaciation of North America over the past 20,000 years. It has been suggested that northward retreat of the continental ice sheet may have concentrated seismic strain rate in the region of New Madrid triggering the 1811–12 sequence. Worryingly, the release of accumulated seismic

▶ *Overview of the San Andreas fault near Taft, California, USA. The San Andreas fault is a 1,200 km (750 mile) -long boundary between the Pacific and the North American tectonic plates (see illustration below). The Pacific plate is heading north-westwards at an average 6 cm (2.5 inches) a year. Most of its movement consists of sudden jumps.*

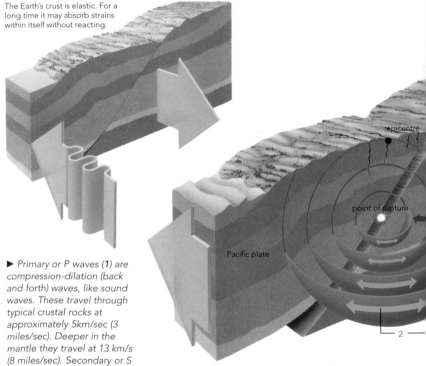

The Earth's crust is elastic. For a long time it may absorb strains within itself without reacting.

epicentre

point of rupture

Pacific plate

2

▶ *Primary or P waves (1) are compression-dilation (back and forth) waves, like sound waves. These travel through typical crustal rocks at approximately 5km/sec (3 miles/sec). Deeper in the mantle they travel at 13 km/s (8 miles/sec). Secondary or S waves (2) travel more slowly, at approximately 3 km/s (2 miles/sec), or 7 km/s (4 miles/sec) deeper in the mantle, and are shear (side-to-side) waves. Both of these* *types of waves radiate in all directions from the focus. Shear waves cannot travel through liquids and so do not penetrate the Earth's molten core. The difference* *in speed between the waves results in a time lapse between their arrival that grows with distance, and allows scientists to pinpoint the focus of a quake.*

strain is not instantaneous and implies a continuously high seismic hazard for this densely populated region.

Other intraplate earthquakes have also occurred in the USA. In the evening of August 31, 1886, a large earthquake – possibly measuring 7.3 on the Richter scale – struck the city of Charleston, South Carolina. This was the largest earthquake to have occurred east of the Appalachian Mountains and, like most quakes in the eastern United States, it was felt over a huge area. As at New Madrid, the underlying rocks in this region of the United States are old and fairly rigid, and seismic waves are easily transmitted to great distances. The Charleston earthquake was an unusual occurrence in several respects. It took place in a region free of notable seismic events since the arrival of the English in 1670, and aftershocks lasted for more than eight years. Reasons for the earthquake occurrence are speculative, but one possibility is that deeply buried faults were activated by compressive stresses applied from the exterior of the continental plate by the opening of the Atlantic Ocean basin.

North American plate

1

Seismic waves

Seismic waves radiating from an earthquake's focus propagate as direct (or body) waves and surface waves. The direct waves propagate as **P-waves** (or push waves) and **S-waves** (also known as shake or shear waves). P-waves travel faster than S-waves and the interval time between their arrivals provides a direct measure of the distance to the earthquake epicentre. Most building damage during a quake results from ground shaking and arises mainly from the side-to-side movement caused by S-waves. The P-waves generate a push-pull motion, rather like a row of wagons being shunted back and forth by a railway engine, and are generally less damaging. In contrast to direct waves, surface waves propagate at the Earth's surface, and in the most powerful quakes, these may travel around the planet many times.

Heavy mass (resists motion)

Paper (moves in direction of arrow)

Pen

Earth motion due to earthquake

Measuring earthquake intensity

The size and effects of an earthquake are measured in terms of intensity and magnitude. Intensities are quantified by subjectively assigning a value to levels of shaking or damage. The common scale in use is the **Modified Mercalli Intensity** (MMI) scale, though there are now several others. The MMI is based upon numerical values ranging from I (no damage and virtually undetectable without a seismograph) to XII (severe shaking causing total destruction). Intensity values ranging from I to V are based on human sensations of shaking whereas the higher values are based on assessments of building damage and fault rupture effects.

Several problems are encountered in assessing earthquake intensity. Intensity maps for earthquakes can be influenced by local geological effects (such as ground liquefaction) and are often biased toward inhabited regions, where the damaging consequences of an earthquake are far more obvious. Most problematic, perhaps is the reliability of the subjective descriptions that form the basis of intensity assessment. In some regions of the United States, for instance, people are so proud of living through an earthquake that they are prone to exaggerate its effects. On the other hand, there are regions of the world where people are inclined to play down an earthquake's effects. For this reason, an earthquake intensity map can only really be trusted, to any serious extent, if constructed by an experienced earthquake engineer or seismologist. Despite their shortcomings, however, seismic-intensity scales can provide a valuable, general map showing the pattern of earthquake damage. Such a map is constructed on the basis of contouring points of equal intensity in order to define so-called 'isoseismals'. These help to pinpoint localized areas of high damage-potential that may reflect the distribution of landfills, unstable hillsides, and sites capable of liquefaction. Seismic intensity studies are also very useful for detecting zones of active faults, even where they are too deep to produce rupture of the ground surface. Furthermore, historical descriptions of damage can provide information about the intensity of historical earthquakes that predate the instrumental catalogue, particularly for countries and regions with a long historical record such as China, the Middle East, and parts of the Mediterranean.

▲ *A seismograph detects the seismic waves generated by an earthquake. The seismograph must be able to move with the shake of the earth, but part of it must remain nearly stationary. This is achieved by isolating the recording device (such as a pen) from the rest of the Earth using the principle of inertia. In this simple model, the pen is suspended by a spring. The spring and the heavy mass remain remain virtually motionless, while the paper moves with the earth and records the vibrations. The first seismograph was invented in China in* AD 136.

Measuring earthquake magnitude

In contrast to intensity scales, magnitude determinations are not based on subjective estimates of damage but on the ground motion generated during an earthquake or the amount of energy released, as recorded by seismographs. Again, a number of magnitude scales are now in use, but the original **Richter scale** is based on the simple premise that each unit of magnitude increase produces a ten-fold increase in the observed amplitude of the seismic waves. Thus, an earthquake of magnitude 8 produces amplitudes 10 times greater than an event of magnitude 7. Since the scale is logarithmic there is no mathematical bottom or ceiling to the magnitude scale. In terms of the amount of energy released, however, each unit increase in magnitude signifies a 31.5 percent increase. In purely descriptive terms, earthquakes with Richter magnitudes greater than 7.5 are said to be 'great', those with magnitudes ranging from 6.5 to 7.5 are referred to as 'major', and those with magnitudes of 5.5 to 6.5 are classified as 'large'.

One of the shortcomings of the conventional Richter scale is that the scale saturates for very large earthquakes – those with magnitudes exceeding eight. Conventional earthquake magnitudes are determined from measurements by seismographs that are limited in terms of their bandwidth (in this context the range of frequencies detected by the seismograph). Very large earthquakes radiate a significant amount of energy at low

(MODIFIED) MERCALLI INTENSITY SCALE

Average peak velocity (cm/s⁻¹)	Intensity value and description	
	I	Not felt, except by a very few under especially favourable circumstances.
	II	Felt by only a few persons at rest, especially on upper floors of buildings
	III	Felt quite noticeably by people indoors, especially above the ground floor. Not immediately recognizable as an earthquake. Standing motor cars may rock slightly. Vibrations like a passing truck. Duration estimated.
1–2	IV	Felt indoors by many, outdoors by few. At night, some awakened. Dishes, windows, doors disturbed. Sensation like heavy truck striking building. Standing cars rock noticeably.
2–5	V	Felt by nearly everyone; many woken up. Some dishes, windows broken. Unstable objects overturned. Pendulum clocks may stop.
5–8	VI	Felt by all, many frightened. Some heavy furniture moved; damage slight.
8–12	VII	Damage negligible in buildings of good design and construction; slight to moderate damage in well-built structures; considerable damage in poorly built or badly designed structures; some chimneys broken.
20–30	VIII	Damage slight in specially designed structures; considerable damage in ordinary substantial buildings with partial collapse. Damage great in poorly built structures. Fall of chimneys, factory stacks, columns, monuments, and walls. Heavy furniture overturned.
45–55	IX	Damage considerable in specially designed structures; well-designed frame structures thrown out of plumb. Damage great in substantial buildings, with partial collapse. Buildings shifted off foundations. Rails bent.
>60	X	Some well-built wooden structures destroyed; most masonry and frame structures destroyed with foundations. Rails bent.
	XI	Few, if any, masonry structures remain standing. Bridges destroyed. Rails bent greatly.
	XII	Damage total. Lines of sight and level are distorted. Objects thrown into the air.

EARTHQUAKES

◄ *Damage from the 1960 Chilean earthquake. On May 22, 1960, an earthquake occurred off the coast of south-central Chile. A Pacific-wide tsunami was triggered by the earthquake, which had a surface-wave magnitude of 8.6, an epicentre of 39.5° S, 74.5° W, and a focal depth of 33 km (20 miles). The number of fatalities associated with both the tsunami and the earthquake has been estimated to be between 490 and 2,290.*

frequencies that are not easily captured by conventional seismographs. For these events, seismologists now use a so-called 'moment-magnitude value' that is based on observations or parameters more directly related to the size of the earthquake, such as the area of fault rupture and the amount of fault offset.

The 1960 Chilean earthquake

The world's largest instrumentally recorded earthquake was the Chilean quake of May 22, 1960, which registered 9.5 on the Richter scale. The event was associated with an 800 km (500 mile) -long fault rupture with an offset of 21 metres (70 feet). The first large shock of the series, on May 21, 1960, caused many casualties and extensive property damage at Concepción, Chile's main industrial centre, and the surrounding area. Due to its submarine origin, the quake generated tsunamis up to nearly 30 metres in height that devastated much of the coast of Chile and Peru, and claimed lives as far away as Hawaii and Japan. The effects were noticeable along shorelines throughout the Pacific Ocean area. The southern Chilean cities of Valdivia and Puerto Montt suffered devastating damage because of their closeness to the centre of such a massive quake. A quarter of all the world's seismic energy released between 1904 and 1986 was released in this single, giant quake, which resulted from the eastward movement of the Eastern-Pacific Nazca plate beneath the thicker South American plate. Although there was significant loss of life, Chile escaped even greater tragedy because of the warning provided by the initial smaller quakes. Most inhabitants had left their homes as a result of the first shocks saving many lives as a result. Total damage costs for Chile alone were estimated at around US$550 million. In addition to the loss of many towns and villages, Chile itself was forever changed by the enormous amount of energy released in the earthquake. Huge landslides, massive flows of debris and rock, were sent tumbling down the mountain slopes of the Andes. Some landslides were so enormous they changed the course of major rivers or dammed them up creating new lakes. The land along the coast of Chile, particularly in the city-port of Puerto Montt, subsided as a result of the movement of the ground during the quake and the coastal city was flooded with ocean water. The earthquake was also responsible for the eruption of the Puyehue volcano on May 24.

The San Andreas Fault: Californian earthquakes

The San Andreas Fault in California represents the main boundary between the Pacific and the North American plates (see illustration p.20, and photo p.21). The Pacific plate is moving northwestward at an average rate of six cm/yr, and much of this movement consists of sudden jumps such as that which triggered the famous 'Great San Francisco Earthquake' of April 18–23, 1906. This earthquake (measuring 8.3 on the Richter scale) and its ensuing fires claimed an estimated 3,000 lives, and razed to the ground a substantial part of the mainly wooden city. The quake ushered in a new era of earthquake studies in the United States, and research contributed greatly to our understanding of how earthquakes occur.

What was initially surprising about the 1989 Loma Prieta earthquake was the amount of damage in the Marina District of San Francisco, located about 160 km (100 miles) northwest of the epicentre. The Marina District is located on the north shore of the San Francisco Peninsula and is one of the most desirable and expensive locations of the city. Much of the area is built on landfill and rubble from the 1906 earthquake. The collapse of buildings and secondary fires was extensive because of amplified ground shaking, liquefaction of the fill material, and failures because of poorly supported first storeys. Street parking in San Francisco is scarce, so it is common to find the ground floor of a residence has been cleared of supports and obstructions in order to build a garage. As a result, the buildings easily 'pancake' and collapse vertically. This is a common mode of building failure in many countries where apartments and living quarters are built above a ground-floor shop.

▼ Troops walk east along Market Street, San Francisco, after the devastating earthquake of April 18, 1906. The 12-storey Call skyscraper burns in the distance. Many buildings not damaged by the force of the earthquake itself were destroyed by the subsequent fires.

Five years later, one of the costliest earthquakes of all time also occurred in California. The Northridge earthquake (January 17, 1994) was the first event in more than 50 years to occur directly below a major population centre in California, but like Loma Prieta it produced no rupture of the surface. In fact, the earthquake occurred on a hidden fault known as a blind thrust, which has no surface expression. More and more 'blind thrusts' are being found in California but the worry is that others will rupture before

their existence is verified. The Northridge quake claimed 61 lives and property damage was enormous, totalling US$44 billion and making the event the costliest natural disaster in US history. Twenty-thousand people were made homeless and there was substantial damage to freeway overpasses, a major dam, electric power facilities and gas pipelines. What this earthquake emphasized, above all else, is that – even with stringent seismic building codes in place – an earthquake does not have to be a magnitude 8 event to cause significant damage if positioned directly beneath a metropolitan area.

The Great Tangshan earthquake

The deadliest earthquake in recent times took place at Tangshan, northern China, on July 28, 1976. Regional stresses produced by the ongoing northward collision of the Indian subcontinent with the Eurasian plate caused one of the many faults in the area to rupture at a depth of 10 km (6 miles) below the city. With little enforcement of building codes in the region, this quake, measuring 7.8 on the Richter scale, had a devastating impact on Tangshan, an industrial city and coal mining centre of one million people. The earthquake struck at 3.42am, when many residents were asleep in their mud-brick houses that were bonded with mortar and covered with heavy mud and lime roofs. About 93 percent of the homes collapsed and 78 percent of the industrial buildings failed, resulting in nearly a quarter of a million deaths – more than one in four of the city's population. Miners working the night shift survived because they were thousands of metres underground when the quake struck.

Preparing for earthquakes

It is often stated that around eight million people were killed by earthquakes during the last millennium. This is not strictly true because, as earthquake engineers are particularly fond of repeating, it is buildings not earthquakes that kill people. Where once considerable time, effort, and money was spent on trying to forecast earthquakes, to date without any suc-

▲ *A Marina District apartment building that was heavily damaged in the 1989 San Francisco earthquake. Many buildings in the Marina district were built on the rubble from the 1906 San Francisco earthquake. The loose foundations were responsible for much of the destruction in the area. October 18, 1989, San Francisco, California, USA.*

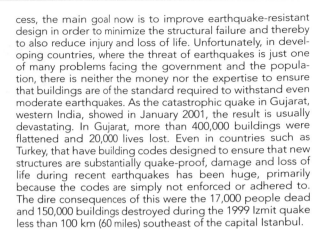

cess, the main goal now is to improve earthquake-resistant design in order to minimize the structural failure and thereby to also reduce injury and loss of life. Unfortunately, in developing countries, where the threat of earthquakes is just one of many problems facing the government and the population, there is neither the money nor the expertise to ensure that buildings are of the standard required to withstand even moderate earthquakes. As the catastrophic quake in Gujarat, western India, showed in January 2001, the result is usually devastating. In Gujarat, more than 400,000 buildings were flattened and 20,000 lives lost. Even in countries such as Turkey, that have building codes designed to ensure that new structures are substantially quake-proof, damage and loss of life during recent earthquakes has been huge, primarily because the codes are simply not enforced or adhered to. The dire consequences of this were the 17,000 people dead and 150,000 buildings destroyed during the 1999 Izmit quake less than 100 km (60 miles) southeast of the capital Istanbul.

Earthquake-resistant design

Given sufficient money, buildings can be engineered well enough to withstand even catastrophic earthquakes. The key is to ensure that buildings are strong yet flexible, so that they can handle the transverse shaking that is the key culprit in damaging buildings. Modern skyscraper designs rely on frame and X-bracing to minimize the effects of lateral swaying and the distribution of applied earthquake forces. Some skyscrapers in San Francisco sit on bearings made of layers of steel and rubber that allow the buildings to shift with ground movements. A shock-absorbing-building design was utilized as long ago as 1916 by US architect Frank Lloyd Wright (1869–1959). His design of the Imperial Hotel in Tokyo, Japan (see page 29), was radical for its time – allowing for flexure in all directions and creating a foundation that was shallow but acted as a shock absorber because it was uniformly loaded. To guard against the possibility of walls separating and dropping the floors, a common mode of failure during earthquakes, the floors were balanced at the centre. More importantly, the key principles of earthquake-resistant design – symmetry and regularity – were not violated. As testament to the strength of Wright's design, the Imperial Hotel was not severely damaged in the Great Kanto earthquake that struck Tokyo in 1923, killing up to 200,000 people and razing much of the city to the ground.

In 1994 the costliest earthquake in US history – at US$44 billion – rocked southern California, centring on Northridge. One of the major surprises of the event was the number of concrete structures and steel-

▼ Evacuation of a child's body, Gujarat, western India. The earthquake, measuring 7.9 on the Richter scale, struck on January 28, 2001. It killed more than 20,000 people and left 600,000 homeless. Within one week of the earthquake, police in Ahmedabad filed nearly 40 cases of culpable homicide and criminal conspiracy against the builders, architects and engineers of poorly contructed buildings that collapsed in the devastating earthquake.

27

framed buildings that were damaged. Local building codes had focused on the mandatory strengthening of masonry structures but had largely ignored to what extent improvements should or must be made to older concrete buildings and steel-framed buildings, a procedure known as retro-fitting. This is both costly and time-consuming, and often encounters resistance from the owners of existing buildings who lack the funds or the will to undertake the strengthening work required. While legislators press for safety, insurers may decline to underwrite and banks may refuse loans. Estimates for seismic strengthening of existing hospitals, schools and other buildings in California ran as high as US$35 billion prior to the occurrence of the Northridge earthquake. Retro-fitting is a perennial problem in many urban centres prone to large earthquakes, and an insufficient strengthening of older properties may lead to serious damage in potential future quakes at, for example, Tokyo and Istanbul.

The human cost of urban earthquakes

The terrible consequences of a combination of poor construction and an absence of seismic building codes were graphically demonstrated during the 1988 Armenian earthquake. Here seismic waves were amplified as they entered soft sediments, causing the ground to shake eight times more violently, bringing down dozens of recently built apartment blocks and killing more than 25,000 people. The huge death toll owed much to deficiencies in design and seriously flawed construction techniques, which incorporated floors constructed of individual hollow-core precast planks that were poorly tied together and barely connected to the walls. A common failure was the collapse of the middle floors of buildings, leaving almost no space for trapped people to survive. In 1995, a similar situation led to wholesale building collapse and serious loss of life when a

▼ *A crowd of people stand around in the rubble that was once their homes. They were among the survivors of a devastating earthquake that struck northern Armenia in 1988. Many of the buildings destroyed by the quake were newly built apartment blocks.*

▶ *Victims search for belongings in the rubble left after the 1995 earthquake at Kobe, central Honshu Island, Japan. The earthquake killed an estimated 5,502 people. One month after the earthquake, 226,000 people were still being housed in evacuation centres.*

powerful earthquake, measuring 7.5 on the Richter scale, struck the Russian island of Sakhalin, north of Japan. The quake hit at 1.03 am, when most of Sakhalin's 600,000 population were asleep. In the late 1960s, the Soviets had built a settlement at the oil-producing town Neftegorsk, near the northern end of the island. Many of Neftegorsk's total population of 3,200 lived in

▲ *The Imperial Hotel, Tokyo, Japan, was designed (1916–22) by Frank Lloyd Wright. Wright's design included many original features to help the building withstand an earthquake. On its opening day of September 1, 1923, the Great Kanto earthquake struck. The earthquake caused widespread destruction in Tokyo, but the hotel was scarcely damaged. In 1968 the Imperial was demolished. The main entrance hall and lobby were rebuilt (seen here) at the Meiji Mura Museum, Inuyama, Honshu, Japan.*

the 17 Soviet-built five-storey buildings with 80 apartments each, known in Russian as *khrushchoby*, which were hastily constructed with prefabricated slabs of unreinforced concrete and set up on sandy soil sites. In the 1995 quake, the total collapse of all 17 apartment blocks killed about 2,000 people.

The Great Hanshin earthquake

In 1995 a powerful earthquake, struck the industrial city of Kobe, central Honshu Island, Japan, causing the costliest natural disaster of all time – with economic losses estimated at US$130 billion. The so-called 'Great Hanshin Earthquake' was the strongest quake to hit Japan since the Great Kanto quake of 1923. Oddly, it struck on the anniversary of the Northridge earthquake a year earlier. Both occurred during the early hours, when most people were asleep, and both earthquakes were about the same magnitude (Northridge 6.7, Kobe 6.8) but there the similarity ends. While just 57 people died during the Northridge event, some 5,500 died at Kobe and 140,000 buildings were damaged or destroyed. Although the Hanshin quake involved just 20 seconds of violent shaking, the shallow depth of the quake (just 14 km/9 miles) and its proximity to Kobe (about 20 km/12 miles), resulted in great destruction. Devastation in the central part of Kobe and parts of neighbouring Osaka was severe. Surprisingly, the earthquake was barely felt in Tokyo, some 450 km (280 miles) away. Kobe is not considered to be a major centre of earthquake activity but

active faults do run through the region, and a significant strike-slip fault (a fault with predominantly horizontal movement) runs directly through downtown Kobe. The average horizontal displacement from the Great Hanshin quake was about 130 cm (51 inches), significantly shorter than that observed during the Great Kanto earthquake 72 years earlier.

One of the reasons for the particularly damaging outcome of the Hanshin quake was the excessive confidence in technology. Most shocking was the collapse of elevated freeways and the Shinkasen railway that link western Japan with the northeast of the country. The elevated highways were widely believed to be able to withstand earthquakes, but nine bridges on the Hanshin expressway, which connects Kobe and Osaka, buckled and collapsed, and the famous Shinkasen bullet-train from Tokyo was halted. Bridges collapsed because bolts and steel plates connecting girders failed. There is no doubt that the degree of destruction of supposedly quake-proof structures was a surprise to Japanese engineers, politicians and rescue officials, and a debate about differences in design-philosophy continues as a result of this earthquake. Japanese architects and engineers had placed great emphasis on the massive strength of their modern structures rather than allowing for ductility and flexibility. Adding shock-absorbing systems to buildings, a technique known as base isolation, is able to insulate a structure from earthquake ground-motions by sandwiching layers of rubber and steel in the foundation. Base isolation may ultimately improve the ability of Japanese buildings to withstand future large quakes, but the cost is exorbitant.

Earthquakes in developing countries

Earthquakes continue to devastate developing countries, where – due to the poor quality of building construction – the

▲ *The city of Kobe, central Honshu Island, Japan, burns amid the rubble of collapsed buildings following the 1995 earthquake. The devastation caused by the quake was a shock to many who considered Japan a world leader in earthquake mitigation.*

scale of damage and loss of life are often hugely dispropor-
tional to the size of the quake. At Agadir in southern Morocco,
for example, an earthquake measuring just 5.9 on the Richter
scale claimed more than 14,000 lives in 1960. In 1993, an earthquake measuring 6.4 on the Richter scale struck 400 km (250
miles) southeast of Mumbai (Bombay) in the state of Maha-
rashtra, western India. The quake buried nearly 10,000 sleeping residents beneath the rubble of their mud-and-brick
homes. Although the shaking lasted for barely 20 seconds, the
earthquake was strong enough to be felt more than 1,300 kilometres (800 miles) away in Chennai (Madras), on the southeast
coast of India. The quality of the building stock is not the only
reason why the scale of earthquake damage may be high in
India: much of the country is covered by thick soils and alluvial
deposits that amplify the effects of seismic shaking.

The collapse of unreinforced dwellings continues to be a
serious problem in those parts of developing countries that
are prone to large earthquakes. In January 2001, an earthquake measuring 7.7 on the Richter scale devastated the
Bhuj region of Gujarat, western India, killing 20,000 people
and destroying 400,000 homes. With the rapid growth of
huge urban conurbations in quake-prone regions, some –
like Mexico City, central Mexico, and Karachi, south-east
Pakistan – with populations likely to exceed 20 million in the
next decade or so, future death tolls in excess of a million
people have been forecast by some seismologists.

Liquefaction and landslides

The severe ground-shaking experienced in large earthquakes is
often associated with the liquefaction of thick soils, unconsolidated sediments, alluvium, and landfill. These materials begin

▶ *Map of Japan
indicating the plate
zones and location of
the Great Hanshin
earthquake in 1995.
Kobe is located further
away than many other
cities in Japan from the
dangerous intersection
of three tectonic plates:
the Pacific, Eurasian,
and Philippine. The
Pacific plate is
subducting under the
Eurasian plate beneath
Japan at the rate of
about 10 cm per year,
creating several deep
oceanic trenches with
associated earthquake
activity. Kobe is located
north of where the
Philippines plate is
subducting beneath the
Eurasian plate. These
plates put a sideways
strain on the Eurasian
plate, which has
fractured creating the
median tectonic line.
This new line strains the
crust behind it and
becomes the Arima-
Takatsuki tectonic line.
Movement in this newly
created fault zone was
the cause of the Great
Hanshin earthquake.
An earthquake of this
size in this zone can be
expected once every
1,000 years.*

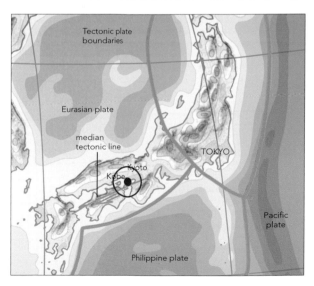

to behave like water, causing any structures built on the land to founder or collapse. Liquefaction played an important role in the building failure during the 1988 earthquake in northern Armenia, and seven years later during the quake on the Russian island of Sakhalin. In the 1989 Loma Prieta earthquake that struck the San Francisco Bay area of the western United States, liquefaction was also responsible for the collapse of part of the Nimitz Freeway in Oakland and severe damage to buildings in the Marina District of San Francisco. Soft sediments are also very effective at magnifying the effects of seismic waves as they pass through them. In the devastating earthquake, measuring 8.1 on the Richter scale, that struck Mexico City in 1985, most damage occurred in an area of underlying ancient lake sediments, which amplified the ground motion and set buildings with heights of 10–15 storeys swinging like pendulums. Despite the fact that the earthquake's epicentre was more than 300 km (190 miles) away, the augmented shaking led to more than 8,000 deaths, left 50,000 peple homeless, and caused property damage amounting to US$4 billion.

Severe ground-shaking during earthquakes is also very effective at destabilizing slopes and triggering landslides. On January 31, 2001, an earthquake measuring 7.6 on the Richter scale occurred off the coast of El Salvador, about 100 km (60 miles) south-southeast of the capital San Salvador. This subduction-zone earthquake was felt as far north as Mexico City, as well as Nicaragua, Honduras, and parts of Costa Rica and Panama. In El Salvador, the earthquake killed about 700 people, injured a further 2,500, and nearly 45,000 people had to be evacuated from damaged homes. The quake hit the Las Colinas suburb of San Salvador particularly hard, as ground-shaking triggered a landslide that claimed the lives of 265 people and left 285 people unaccounted for. Prior to the earthquake, developers had cut into the slope above Las Colinas to build luxury homes. After the disaster, arguments raged that the hillside had been weakened by residential developments, and the incident clearly highlights

◀ The 2001 earthquake in El Salvador triggered a devastating landslide in the Las Colinas district of the capital San Salvador. The slide killed about 700 people and left many thousands of people homeless. After the landslide, many citizens blamed developers for building homes on land known to be vulnerable to earthquake.

▲ *A crowd of people watch as buildings blaze in the aftermath of the Great Kanto earthquake in Tokyo, Japan (September 1, 1923). The fires that followed the Great Kanto earthquake claimed an estimated 200,000 lives and left Tokyo in ruins.*

the increasing problem of building on unsuitable land in regions of high seismicity.

The El Salvador incident pales into insignificance when compared to other seismically triggered landslides. In 1970, an earthquake measuring 7.7 on the Richter scale occurred off the coast of Peru, triggering the collapse of part of the Nevados Huascarán mountain and sending billions of tons of rock and ice crashing onto the towns below. The landslide claimed the lives of more than 18,000 people in an instant. In 1556, probably the greatest seismic catastrophe of all time occurred when a powerful earthquake hit Shaanxi province, north-central China. The quake triggered the liquefaction of sediments into which the local population had dug to build their homes and buried alive an estimated 800,000 people. *See also* **Landslides**, pages 142–51

Fire

In urban centres, one of the most destructive consequences of a major earthquake is the fire that follows. Nowhere has this been more apparent than after the Great Kanto quake that struck Tokyo in 1923. The earthquake itself was immensely destructive, but the fires were even worse. Over-turned charcoal stoves started tens of thousands of small fires that soon merged to form giant tongues of flame that licked across the ruins, feeding on the wooden buildings that constituted much of the city architecture. Survivors found no protection from the firestorms that raged for two days, and tens of thousands were immolated as they crowd-ed into parks and other open spaces that were overwhelmed by the conflagrations. Quake and fires together claimed up to 200,000 lives and destroyed 360,000 buildings, leaving Japan's capital a smouldering ruin. Great post-quake fires also played a major role in the destruction of Lisbon, Portu-gal (1755), and San Francisco, United States (1906), and they remain a serious threat in the aftermath of a quake. In 1995 fires caused considerable damage in Kobe, Japan, and the million or so wooden buildings remaining in Tokyo suggest that fire will once again be a serious problem when the next big earthquake strikes sometime in the next few decades.

Tsunami

Offshore earthquakes may not cause as much building damage through ground shaking but they can inflict terrible destruction through the generation of the giant sea waves known as tsunami. These are generated when a submarine earthquake imparts a sharp jolt to a large area of sea floor, sending waves radiating rapidly from the source. In deep water, tsunami can travel at velocities in excess of 800 km/h (500 mph) – meaning, for instance, that they can cross the entire Pacific Basin in slightly more than 20 hours. Although barely detectable in deep water, earthquake-generated tsunami can build to heights in excess of 20 metres (66 feet) as they approach land. As they have typical wavelengths of the order of hundreds of kilometres, rather than just a few tens of metres for wind-driven waves, they keep driving inland for several minutes and take the same time to retreat, leaving total devastation in their wake. During the past 100 years or so, more than 50,000 people living in countries around the Pacific Rim have lost their lives to tsunami, many of which caused deaths in more than one country. Waves generated in the great Chile earthquake of 1960 took just 15 hours to reach Hawaii, where they claimed 60 lives and destroyed 500 homes. Five hours later, the waves crashed into Japan where they still had sufficient energy to destroy property and take a further 180 lives. One of the most recent destructive tsunami occurred in Papua New Guinea in 1998, when an earthquake just off the island's coast gave no warning time to residents of Aitape and surrounding villages. Waves up to 17 metres high poured across the narrow strip of sand upon which the villages were built, killing almost 3,000 people.

See also **Tsunami**, pages 62–73

Prediction or protection?

Large, damaging earthquakes often overwhelm local resources and place unplanned financial burdens on countries and agencies. It is important to learn from past earthquakes in order to reduce future losses. In simple terms, this means that efforts need to be increased to produce accurate seismic hazard and risk maps of hazardous regions, particularly those in urban areas. Society needs to focus more on the effects of earthquakes and the potential severity of the hazard. Areas of anticipated high levels of ground shaking, liquefaction and seismic landslides need to be identified in advance. At the very least, this information needs to be conveyed in a clear, cogent fashion to local governments so that the authorities and the local population are at least aware of the threat. For the level of property damage and loss of life to be reduced effectively, however, building codes need to be devised and adhered to.

► **Earthquake-proof buildings** *The shock of an earthquake on an unprotected structure causes the building to sway, risking complete collapse. The building on the right uses a base-isolation system. By isolating the effects of an earthquake through shock-absorbers made of layers of rubber and steel, the structure is made more sound.*

General building

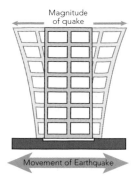

Base-isolation system building

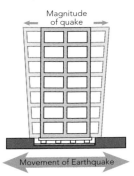

The axiom that earthquakes don't kill people but buildings do is undoubtedly a truism, and the risk of building collapse can be reduced substantially – even in developing countries – by relatively simple measures. Common reasons for building failures are lack of connection ties of walls and floors, use of poor construction materials such as adobe and unreinforced masonry, lack of internal supports, and excessively heavy roofs. In developed countries, this has led to the demand for seismic retrofitting of older structures. However, the seismic overprice is high and, especially in developing countries, has to be balanced against other societal needs. In some instances, retrofitting is fought by conservationists who want to preserve historic adobe, brick and stone buildings for their cultural heritage. All of these aspects are compounded by the observation that human interest in the consequences of disasters has repeatedly been shown to diminish over time until the next disaster strikes.

While nobody would deny the critical importance of building for safety in active seismic zones, many seismologists now doubt our ability to usefully predict earthquakes. There is no doubt that some earthquakes are preceded by certain events, such as the release of gases like radon from the ground, variations in the level of water in wells, small foreshocks, and even unusual animal behaviour. Unfortunately, these signs do not always occur and sometimes they are observed without there being an ensuing earthquake. As such, they are unsuitable for earthquake prediction. A team of Greek scientists, known as the VAN Group, claim they have been able to predict recent earthquakes by detecting what they call seismic electrical signals, but this remains to be validated. While the Japanese government still hopes to detect warning signs before the next 'big one' strikes Tokyo, the state authorities in California have decided to focus on protection rather than prediction. Here, the focus is on building for safety during earthquakes – so that when the 'big one' strikes, the buildings stay up and the people inside stay alive.

Volcanoes

A volcano is a landform that develops around a weakness in the Earth's crust from which molten magma, disrupted pre-existing volcanic rock, and gases are ejected or extruded. Volcanoes may be of the **central-vent** type, where eruption takes place from a single pipe, or the **fissure** type, where magma is extruded along a linear fracture. They may also form large, low-lying craters known as calderas, created as a result of subsidence or collapse following an eruption. Central-vent volcanoes typically form cones or domes, while eruptions from fissures build plains or plateaux. Volcanoes can be classified as active, dormant, or extinct; but this loose, generic description of a volcano's status should be used with caution.

Eruption frequencies
Volcanoes display a wide spectrum of eruption histories. Stromboli, one of the Lipari Islands north-east of Sicily, is almost always in eruption, while Mount Etna, a few hundred kilometres to the south in eastern Sicily, and Kilauea in south-east Hawaii typically erupt every few years. Oshima, a volcanic island off the south coast of Honshu, Japan, and the volcanoes

▼ World map of volcano locations and tectonic forces. Volcanoes most frequently occur on the boundaries of tectonic plates, where magma can escape from the Earth's interior.

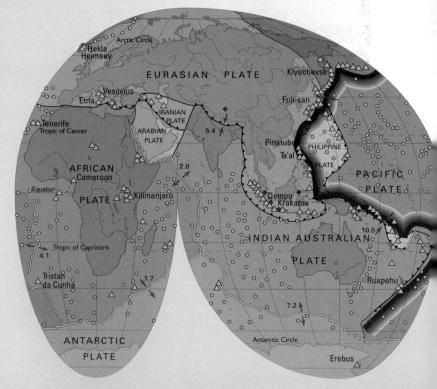

of Iceland have eruption frequencies of hundreds of years, whereas gaps of thousands or tens of thousands of years separate the huge caldera-forming eruptions that characterize the Taupo Volcanic Zone of central North Island, New Zealand, and Campi Flegrei in the Bay of Naples, southern Italy. Interestingly, 75% of the greatest eruptions of the last 200 years were the first recorded eruptions of the volcanoes concerned, highlighting the fact that long-repose times typically go hand in hand with more violent eruptions.

Volcano locations

Volcanoes are not distributed randomly across the face of the planet, but are concentrated in restricted zones where the supply of magma from the Earth's interior is facilitated. Most of these coincide with the margins of the tectonic plates that make up the outermost, rigid shell of the planet, but occasionally volcanoes also occur above hotspots within plate interiors. Both the Hawaiian island volcanoes and those that formed the giant Yellowstone calderas are associated with hotspots. At plate margins, volcanoes form both where plates are moving apart (**constructive margins**) and where one plate is diving down beneath another (**destructive margins**). The former include the predominantly lava-producing volcanoes of Iceland, while examples of the latter are the violently explosive volcanoes of the Pacific rim, most notably Mount St Helens (Washington State, USA), Popocatapétl (Mexico), and the Soufrière Hills volcano on the Caribbean island of Montserrat.

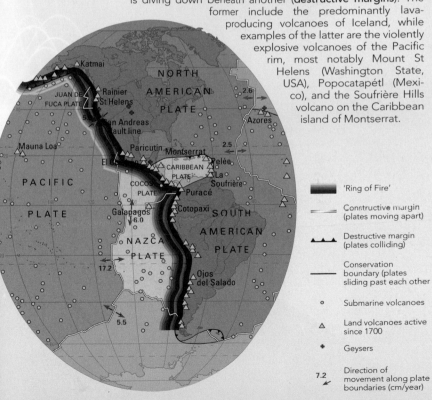

'Ring of Fire'

Constructive margin (plates moving apart)

Destructive margin (plates colliding)

Conservation boundary (plates sliding past each other

○ Submarine volcanoes

△ Land volcanoes active since 1700

✦ Geysers

7.2 Direction of movement along plate boundaries (cm/year)

How volcanoes erupt

Magma forms in the hot plastic layer of the Earth's upper mantle known as the asthenosphere. Here temperatures are high enough, and pressures still sufficiently depressed, to allow mantle rock to partially melt. At deeper levels in the Earth, temperatures are higher but so too are pressures, thereby inhibiting the melting of rock. Magma originates beneath constructive plate margins, where the convection processes bring hot, mantle rock into lower-pressure regimes. It is also formed at destructive margins, due to the increasing temperatures encountered by the plate as it plunges back into the interior. The molten lava generated in the asthenosphere rises by buoyancy. Once the magma reaches the brittle layer (the lithosphere) that makes up the plates, it makes room for itself by exploiting channels of weakness or breaking the overlying rock.

How violently the magma eventually breaches the surface depends largely on the behaviour of the gas it contains. If the eruption is violent, the magma will be torn into fragments, collectively known as **tephra**, ranging in size from blocks the size of automobiles to fine ash. In contrast, the effusion of lava, perhaps combined with spectacular lava fountaining, characterizes quieter eruptions. All volcanic eruptions are driven by rapidly expanding gases within the

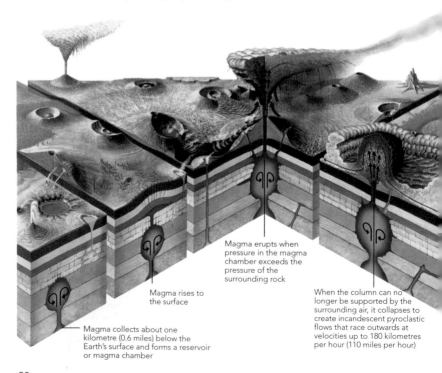

Magma erupts when pressure in the magma chamber exceeds the pressure of the surrounding rock

Magma rises to the surface

When the column can no longer be supported by the surrounding air, it collapses to create incandescent pyroclastic flows that race outwards at velocities up to 180 kilometres per hour (110 miles per hour)

Magma collects about one kilometre (0.6 miles) below the Earth's surface and forms a reservoir or magma chamber

► *Lava fountains at Mauna Loa, Hawaii. This discontinuous row of lava fountains, 15–30 metres (50–100 feet) high, occurs along a rift at 2,800 metres (9,186 feet). The eruption, which began on March 25, 1984, fed several lava flows, one of which threatened the city of Hilo. In early April, the flows stopped about 6.4 kilometres (4 miles) short of the outskirts of the city.*

◄ *Volcanic forces begin deep in the Earth. Mantle material swells up and becomes partly molten. As it rises, the decrease in pressure causes it to melt further and to melt the surrounding rock. If the magma is viscous and the pressure drop is rapid, dissolved gases (mainly water vapour) explode out of the solution. This blows the rock apart and sends fragments (known as pyroclasts) high into the air, forming a massive eruption column composed of hot gases and pumice and ash. The particles heat up the surrounding air, causing convection currents that buoy them even higher – up to 50 kilometres (30 miles) in the greatest eruptions.*

magma, so the two factors that determine the violence of an eruption are the amount of dissolved gases and how easily it can escape.

Magma composition

It is the magma's viscosity that controls how the gas escapes, and it is the composition of the magma that determines, to a large extent, its viscosity. The important constituent is silica, polymerizing chains of silicon and oxygen atoms that help to bind the magma together. The relatively free-flowing basalt magma that issues from Kilauea volcano, south-east Hawaii, has a low silica content, of around 50 percent. In contrast, more viscous andesite magma, containing about 60 percent silica, feeds explosive volcanoes such as Montserrat's Soufrière Hills. The most violent blasts, such as the explosion 73,500 years ago that opened the 100 kilometre (60 mile) - long Toba caldera in Sumatra (Indonesia), are fed by rhyolitic magma that may contain more than 70 percent silica.

The lava fountaining typically associated with eruptions on Iceland and Hawaii, and frequently on Sicily's Mount Etna, involves low-silica, low-viscosity magma with a low gas content. As magma rises through the crust, the low viscosity enables the gas to escape freely. Close to the surface, the bubbles form an expanding foam that drives the magma upwards through the vent or fissure, forming a fountain of liquid rock. These relatively quiet, effusive eruptions of lava gradually build up gently sloping mountains, known as shield volcanoes. Kilauea, Hawaii, is a good example of a shield volcano. Magma that has a high silica content, with high viscosity and high content of dissolved gas, behaves very differently. As the magma rises, gas bubbles start to form, but their growth is hindered by the high viscosity so that they have an internal pressure that can be as much as several hundred atmospheres. Once the surface is breached and the much lower pressure of the atmosphere is reached, the pressurized bubbles expand instantaneously, ripping the magma apart in an explosive blast. The resulting ash and magma fragments are hurled into the atmosphere in a so-called **pyroclastic eruption**. The tephra produced in such an eruption falls back to earth and accumulates around the vent, forming a volcanic cone. Many volcanoes, including Mount Etna, eastern Sicily, and Mount Fuji, Honshu, Japan, are constructed from alternating and interleaving layers of pyroclastic material and lava flows, forming strato-volcanoes. **Strato-volcanoes** dominate the Pacific 'Ring of Fire', marching across the High Andes, through Central America and up the west coast of the United States. Others dominate Alaska, Russia's Kamchatka Peninsula, and the Japanese islands.

Scales and styles of volcanic eruption

The reported size of historic volcanic eruptions is subjective because it is based on the vantage point of an observer, and therefore is typically unreliable. Nevertheless, a Volcanic Explosivity Index (VEI) has been developed that uses a range of parameters, such as the total volume of material ejected and the height of the eruption column, to provide a relative measure of the scale of individual eruptions. Like the Richter scale for earthquakes, the VEI is open-ended,

CLASSIFICATION OF VOLCANIC ERUPTIONS

Type of eruption	Volcanic explosivity index (VEI)	Eruption rate (kg/sec)	Volume of ejecta (m^3)	Eruption column height (km)	Duration of continuous blasts in hours	Troposphere/ stratosphere injection	Qualitative description
Hawaiian	0 Non-explosive	10^2–10^3	$<10^4$	0.8–1.5	<1	Negligible/ none	Effusive
	1 Small	10^2–10^4	10^4–10^6	1.5–2.8	<1	Minor/ none	Gentle
Strombolian	2 Moderate	10^4–10^5	10^6–10^7	2.8–5.5	1-6	Moderate/ none	Explosive
Vulcanian	3 Moderate-large	10^5–10^6	10^7–10^8	5.5–10.5	1-12	Great/ possible	Severe
	4 Large	10^6–10^7	10^8–10^9	10.5–17.0	1->12	Great/ definite	Violent
Plinian and ultra-Plinian	5 Very Large	10^7–10^8	10^9–10^{10}	17.0–28.0	6->12	Great/ significant	Cataclysmic
	6 Very Large	10^8–10^9	10^{10}–10^{11}	28.0–47.0	>12	Great/ significant	Paroxysmal
	7 Very Large	$>10^9$	10^{11}–10^{12}	>47.0	>12	Great/ significant	Colossal
	8 Very Large	–	$>10^{12}$	–	>12	Great/significant	Terrific

▼▶ *The Paricutín*
eruption in west-central
Mexico began on
February 20, 1943. Within
24 hours, the Strombolian
-type eruption had
generated a 50 metre
(164 feet) -high cinder
cone. By the end of the
eruption in 1952, the
height of the cone was
424 metres (1,391
feet).This photo was
taken shortly after the
initial eruption in a
cornfield. By August
1944, most of the villages
of Paricutín and San Juan
Parangaricutiro were
covered in lava and ash.
All that remained of San
Juan were two church
towers that stood above
a sea of rugged lava.
Although no people
died directly from the
eruption, three people
were killed when struck
by lightning generated
by pyroclastic eruptions.

and involves assignment of a number that increases, broadly speaking, with increasing violence. The scale starts at 0 for quiet, effusive eruptions, such as those characteristic of Icelandic and Hawaiian volcanoes, and has yet to record anything greater than an 8, used to classify the cataclysmic super-eruptions of Toba and Yellowstone. The VEI is logarithmic, which means that each point on the scale relates to an eruption ten times more violent than one on the point below. Consequently, the great 1815 VEI 7 eruption of Tambora, Sumbawa, Indonesia, was ten times more violent that the 1991 blast at Mount Pinatubo, Luzon, Philippines, and one hundred times more violent than the VEI 5 eruption of Mount St Helens, Washington, USA, in 1980. The VEI does have its drawbacks, principally the manner in which it measures very large effusive eruptions. For example, the voluminous 1783 Laki fissure eruption in Iceland registered only a 4 on the index, because the eruption was relatively non-violent and did not generate a large eruption column. Nevertheless, the

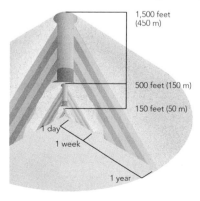

1,500 feet
(450 m)

500 feet (150 m)

150 feet (50 m)

1 day
1 week
1 year

huge volumes of gases released during the event had a serious impact on Europe's weather.

As well as scale, the style of eruption can also be used to differentiate volcanic activity. A number of styles exist, and the most widely known are discussed below. They are named after a particular volcano that typically demonstrates that type of activity, but a single volcano may display several styles during the course of a single eruptive episode.

Icelandic

Icelandic eruptions are often referred to as fissure eruptions. These involve the relatively quiet extrusion of lava from a long fracture rather than from a central vent. Lava flows as great sheets, often to both sides of the fissure, and may travel for tens of kilometres. On cooling, the flows typically form flat-lying plateaux. The greatest of these, such as the Columbia River Plateau in north-west United States, the Deccan 'Traps' in western India, and the flood basalts in Siberia, cover hundreds of thousands of square kilometres, and were formed by eruptions on a scale not seen for more than 60 million years. Historic eruptions of the Icelandic type are largely confined to Iceland, which forms a land segment of the highly fissured zone of the Mid-Atlantic oceanic ridge system. Mantle-derived magma is continually being extruded along this ridge system and eruptions from fissures have, on average, taken place at five-year intervals. It has been estimated that about one-third of all lava produced on Earth over the past 500 years has been extruded on Iceland.

▼ *Pu`u `O`o cone of Mount Kilauea, south-east Hawaii, pictured early in the Hawaiian-style eruption of September 1983. In June 1983, the activity became localized at the Pu`u `O`o vent, which straddles the boundary of Hawaii Volcanoes National Park. For the next three years, Pu`u `O`o erupted about every three to four weeks, usually for less than 24 hours at a time. These eruptive episodes were characterized by spectacular lava fountains that catapulted lava as high as 470 m (1,540 feet) above the vent.*

▲ *Eruption of Stromboli volcano at night. The volcano spews fiery cinders from one of three active cones along its west side. Stromboli is one of the Lipari Islands off the north-east coast of Sicily. The Strombolian type of eruption is named after the volcano island. The ancient Greeks referred to Stromboli as the 'Lighthouse of the Mediterranean'.*

Hawaiian

Hawaiian-style eruptions involve the steady extrusion of basaltic lava from fractures or fissures several kilometres long that are located on the flanks of a central-vent volcano. Low gas content and low magma viscosity conspire to ensure that eruption is quiet, with little in the way of explosive activity or the production of tephra. Great floods of lava contributed to the formation of gently sloping volcanic shields down the flanks of the Hawaiian volcanoes of Mauna Loa and Kilauea.

Strombolian

The Strombolian type of eruption is named after the island-volcano of Stromboli, the most northerly of Italy's Lipari Islands, off the north-east coast of Sicily, southern Italy. Small, discrete, explosions, every few minutes, release a 'firework display' of incandescent fragments of basaltic lava accompanied by a white cloud that contains minimal volcanic ash. Stromboli appears to be unique among the world's volcanoes in that it has been in a state of perpetual eruption for some 2,500 years. It seems that material ejected from Stromboli rolls into the surrounding sea rather than falling back into the vent, which would stop activity until accumulated pressures could remove the debris.

◄ *Spectacular view from the International Space Station of the vigorous eruption of Mount Etna, north-east Italy, on October 30, 2002. Three days earlier, a series of earthquakes triggered the eruption. The photo shows an ash plume curving out toward the horizon, as well as smoke from fires ignited by the lava as it flowed down the 3,320 metre (10,900 foot) - high mountain. Ashfall was reported in Libya, more than 550 km (350 miles) away.*

Peléean

The 1902 eruption of Mount Pelée on the Caribbean island of Martinique spawned this style of explosive eruption, which is a common feature of volcanoes whose magmas are viscous and gas rich. Peléean eruptions are characterized by the violent sideways expulsion of ground-hugging clouds of incandescent ash and gas, known as *nuées ardentes* or pyroclastic flows. On May 8, 1902, the eruption of Pelée obliterated the town of St Pierre, leaving two survivors out of a population of about 30,000. Just the day before, a further 1,500 people lost their lives during a similar eruption on the neighbouring island of St Vincent.

Vulcanian

The Vulcanian style of eruption is named after the island of Vulcano, a neighbour of Stromboli in Italy's Lipari Islands. Vulcanian blasts are violent, often due to an accumulation of gases that blasts apart a crust of congealed crust formed over the vent. The ejecta typically comprises blocks of pre-existing rock rather than molten magma blebs (small, usually rounded ejecta), and some of these may be as large as cars and carried distances of several hundreds of metres. At certain times in their eruptive cycles Vulcanian explosions are common features of many volcanoes, particularly when

▲ *Cast of a Pompeiian body, preserved exactly where the person was overcome by pyroclastic flows from Mount Vesuvius, southern Italy, in AD 79. A plinian style eruption caused the destruction of the Roman towns of Pompeii and Herculaneum. Concrete casts like this were made by archaeologists; the bodies left exact moulds in the hardening ash and mud.*

magma comes into contact with groundwater. They have been recorded at Paricutín, west-central Mexico; Lassen Peak, northern California, USA; Etna, eastern Sicily; and Soufrière Hills, Montserrat.

Plinian

This most energetic style of eruption bears the name of Roman administrator Pliny the Younger (AD 62–114), who recorded the events surrounding the devastating eruption of Mount Vesuvius in AD 79, which destroyed the Roman towns of Pompeii and Herculaneum. Plinian eruptions eject an enormous ash column that extends 30 km (19 miles) or more into the stratosphere, where it spreads to form a 'pine-tree' like canopy from which a continuous rain of ash falls. Typically, the eruption column cannot sustain its own weight and ash and debris fall back to the surface, where they form pyroclastic flows that pour down the flanks of the volcano. More recent Plinian eruptions were generated in 1980 at Mount St Helens, Washington, USA, following the collapse of the north flanks of the volcano, and at Mount Pinatubo, Luzon, Philippines in 1991.

The style of an eruption can be related to the Volcanic Explosivity Index. Here, Icelandic and Hawaiian eruptions normally score 0, Strombolian eruptions 1–3, and Vulcanian and Peléean blasts 2–5. Plinian eruptions occupy the top end of the scale, with typical scores of 5–7; the extreme value of 8 only being achieved a couple of times every hundred millennia.

▼ *On July 22, 1980, voluminous plumes of volcanic ash and rock blasted from the side of Mount St Helens, southwest Washington state, USA. The eruption of Mount St Helens is a recent example of the Plinian style of eruption.*

VOLCANOES

Volcanic hazards and risk

The most important factors in assessing potential hazard at an active volcano are the scale, style, and frequency of eruption. Risk assessment is, however, a much more complex procedure and depends, for example, on the population density in the vicinity, the presence or absence of monitoring and alert systems, and the ability of the civil authorities to engender appropriate responses from the local population during a crisis. Specific factors that may determine the level of destruction and loss of life include eruption duration, and the timing and length of the eruption climax. Volcanic hazards continue to plague society because of the growth of urban centres near active volcanoes – more than 500 million people (about one in 12 of Earth's population) now live in the danger zones around active and potentially active volcanoes. Many regions and countries are at risk, including Italy, Japan, the west coast of the United States, Mexico, Central America, the islands of the Caribbean, Philippines, and Indonesia. Vulnerability is likely to increase. Overcrowding and land shortage is forcing increasing numbers of people to live near a volcano, often believing it to be dormant. Some people choose to live on the slopes of a volcano for its often better climate, richer soil, and even its scenic beauty. While volcanic eruptions are far less lethal than floods or earthquakes, they nevertheless continue to claim a significant number of lives. More than 250,000 people have died in volcanic eruptions since the start of the 18th century. In the 20th century, more than 80,000 people lost their lives. In any single decade, up to a million people may be detrimentally affected by volcanic activity, a figure that is likely to rise as vulnerability increases in populations living close to volcanoes.

MOST DEADLY VOLCANOES OF THE 20TH CENTURY			
Country	Name of volcano	Date	People killed
Martinique	Mount Pelée	May 8, 1902	30,000
Colombia	Nevado del Ruiz	November 13, 1985	22,800
Guatemala	Santa Maria	October 24, 1902	6,000
Indonesia	Mount Kelud	1909	5,500
Indonesia	Mount Kelud	May 1919	5,000
Guatemala	Santiaguito	1929	5,000
Papua New Guinea	Mount Lamington	January 15, 1951	3,000
Cameroon	Nyos	August 21, 1986	1,746
Indonesia	Mount Agung	January 3, 1963	1,584
St Vincent & Grenadines	Mount Soufrière	May 7, 1902	1,565
Indonesia	Mount Merapi	1930	1,369
Philippines	Mount Ta'al	January 31, 1911	1,335
Indonesia	Mount Merapi	December 13, 1931	1,300
Indonesia	Mount Merapi	1951	1,300

▶ *Damaged houses along the channel of the River Abacan, Luzon, Philippines. Several houses were carried away by lahars caused by the eruption of Mount Pinatubo in 1991. During and immediately after the eruption, lahars resulting from the passing of the typhoon Yunya were drained through the former valley of the River Abacan, causing destruction in the city of Angeles.*

▲ *House covered by volcanic ash on the flanks of Mount Pinatubo, Luzon, Philippines. This photo was taken on June 28, 1991, 13 days after the major eruption of Pinatubo. Within 3 km (2 miles) of the rim of the caldera, 1–2 metre (3–6.5 foot) -thick deposits of ash covered the ground.*

Volcanic eruptions produce a wide variety of hazards that can kill and injure people and destroy property. Large explosive eruptions can endanger people and property hundreds of kilometres away and even affect global climate. Furthermore, some volcanic hazards, such as landslides, can occur even when a volcano is not erupting.

Tephra

An explosive eruption blasts solid and molten rock fragments (tephra) and volcanic gases into the air with tremendous force. The largest rock fragments (bombs or blocks) usually fall back to the surface within a few kilometres of the vent. Most tephra, however, is composed of tiny particles (less than 2 mm/0.08 inch across) of volcanic glass, minerals, and rock that form ash. These particles rise high into the atmosphere within huge, billowing eruption columns that may attain heights of 20 km (12 miles) in less than 30 minutes, forming an eruption cloud. Such ash clouds can pose a serious threat to aviation, and during the past 15 years about 80 commercial jets have been damaged by inadvertently flying into ash clouds, some coming close to crashing due to engine failure. Large eruption clouds can extend hundreds of kilometres downwind, resulting in ash fall over enormous areas. Ash from the May 18, 1980, eruption of Mount St Helens, for example, fell over an area of more than 50,000 km^2 (19,000 feet^2) in the western United States. Even more impressively,

47

the great Tambora eruption of 1815 on Sumbawa, Lesser Sunda Islands, south-east Indonesia, blasted out sufficient ash to blanket an area of about 2.5 million square kilometres (1 million square miles). Heavy ash fall causes many problems, including roof collapse. Ash can accumulate at up to 15 cm (6 inches) in just 10 minutes and almost one metre (3.3 feet) in an hour. When wet, only about 30 cm (12 inches) of ash is required to bring down poorly constructed roofs. Falling ash can also bring down power cables and telephone lines, make driving near impossible, damage crops, contaminate water supplies, degrade electronics, and cause health problems in humans and animals.

Volcanic gases

Volcanoes emit enormous quantities of gas during eruptions, and even when a volcano is not erupting, cracks in the ground allow gases to reach the surface through small openings, known as fumaroles. More than 90 percent of all gas emitted by volcanoes is water vapour (steam), most of which is heated groundwater (underground water from rainfall and streams). The balance is made up from carbon dioxide, sulphur dioxide, hydrogen sulphide, hydrogen, nitrogen, fluorine and carbon monoxide. Sulphur dioxide gas can react with water droplets in the atmosphere to create acid rain, which causes corrosion to buildings and damages vegetation. Carbon dioxide is heavier than air and can be trapped in depressions at concentrations that are deadly to people and animals. Fluorine, which in high concentrations is toxic, can be attached to volcanic ash particles that later fall to the ground. The fluorine can then poison livestock grazing on ash-coated grass and also contaminate domestic water supplies. Following the 1783

▲ *Congealed lava flow near Kalapana, south-east Hawaii. Between 1983 and 1990, lava from the Kilauea volcano repeatedly invaded communities along Hawaii's southern coast, destroying more than 180 homes, roads, and important historical and archaeological sites. In November 1986, lava flows briefly entered the town of Kalapana. In 1990, they moved through the entire community.*

Laki eruption in southern Iceland, fluorine poisoning destroyed 75 percent of the island's sheep and horses and half of its cattle, leading to mass starvation and the death of 20% of Iceland's population. Cataclysmic eruptions, such as the June 15, 1991, eruption of Mount Pinatubo, Luzon, Philippines, inject huge amounts of sulphur dioxide gas into the stratosphere, where it combines with water to form an aerosol (mist) of sulphuric acid. By reflecting and absorbing incoming solar radiation, such aerosols can lower the Earth's average surface temperature for extended periods of time by up to 1°C (2°F). They also contribute to the destruction of the ozone layer by altering chlorine and nitrogen compounds in the upper atmosphere.

Geysers and geothermal reservoirs

The eruption of water that has been superheated by magma from below is called a geyser. Geysers are found in Iceland, Chile, Yellowstone National Park in the United States, New Zealand, and the Kamchatka Peninsula of Russia. In these areas water from snow, rain, streams and lakes filters downward through a network of fractures and connecting voids where it encounters heat from a near-surface body of magma, absorbs some of the heat, and then erupts. An eruption of a geyser is triggered by a reduction in pressure. As the superheated water rises into reservoirs of greater volume some water will flash to steam. Bubbles of steam rise to lower pressure levels and finally overwhelm the water resulting in a large, spectacular eruption.

When a heat source such as convecting magma is relatively near the surface it can come in contact with circulating groundwater giving rise to two types of geothermal systems: vapour-dominated systems and hot-water systems. Vapour-

▼ *A plume of hot water and steam, a geyser is the result of the boiling of water by volcanic heat in a series of interconnecting chambers in the depths of the Earth (A). The expansion of steam produced drives the water and steam above it out at the surface (B), and this is followed by a period of refilling and heating making it a so-called periodic phenomenon (C).*

A

B

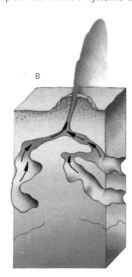

C

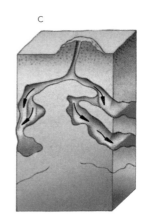

VOLCANOES

◄ Two dome fountains on Mauna Ulu ('Growing Mountain'), a satellite volcano of Kilauea, south-east Hawaii. Lava-dome fountains were visible for hours during this eruption sequence on June 29, 1970. Domes grow to several hundred metres high and can wreak terrible destruction when they collapse.

dominated systems are not very common but three are present in the United States. These are at the Geysers, north of San Francisco, Mount Lassen National Park in northern California, and Yellowstone National Park in Montana, Idaho, and Wyoming. A famous vapour-dominated system is found at the Larderello area of Tuscany, north-east Italy. One of the most studied liquid-dominated systems is found at Wairakei, central North Island, New Zealand.

Oceanic ridge systems (accretionary plate boundaries) and convergent plate boundaries, where mountains are being uplifted and volcanic arcs are being formed, are areas where the escape of heat from the Earth's interior is very high. It is no coincidence that geothermal reservoirs are found in areas of active volcanic activity.

Lava flows and domes

The ability of lava to flow is to a large extent dependent upon its viscosity, which, as previously mentioned is a reflection of its chemical composition. Low-silica basalt lava can form fast-moving (20–50 km/h or 12–30 mph) streams or can spread out in broad thin sheets up to several kilometres across. Since 1983, the Kilauea volcano in south-east Hawaii, has erupted basalt lava flows that have destroyed nearly 200 houses and severed the nearby coastal highway. Similarly, the frequent lava eruptions generated at Mount Etna, eastern Sicily, have damaged roads and property, inundated farmland, and threatened a number of towns and villages over the last 30 years. In contrast, flows of higher-silica andesite and dacite lava tend to be thick and sluggish, travelling only short distances from a vent. Dacite and rhyolite lavas often squeeze out of a vent to form irregular mounds called lava domes. The huge Soufrière Hills andesitic lava dome on the Caribbean island of Montserrat has grown and collapsed many times since its appearance late in 1995, and continues to pose a serious threat today. As they are constantly being fed by new lava, such domes are easily destabilised to form hot landslides that disaggregate spontaneously to form pyroclastic flows. Both the Soufrière Hills dome and that which developed at Mount St Helens,

Washington, United States, between 1980 and 1986, are impressive structures, standing several hundred metres high and having diameters in excess of one kilometre (0.6 miles).

Pyroclastic flows

These high-speed avalanches of hot ash, rock fragments, and gas can move down the sides of a volcano during explosive eruptions or when the steep side of a growing lava dome collapses and breaks apart. Pyroclastic flows typically have temperatures of 600–900°C (1,112–1,652°F) and are capable of moving at velocities in excess of 100 km/h (60 mph). They tend to be topographically controlled, and will follow valley floors, although their more gas-rich upper levels may become detached and travel up and over valley sides. A pyroclastic flow is extremely destructive, knocking down and burning anything in its path. Most recently, such phenomena took thousands of lives at El Chichon, southern Mexico, in 1982, and destroyed the capital Plymouth on Montserrat in 1997. Lower density, gas-dominated pyroclastic flows, known as surges, are also highly destructive and lethal. In 1997, 19 farmers burned to death in a small surge on the island of Montserrat. On May 18, 1980, during the climactic eruption of Mount St Helens, a huge pyroclastic surge flattened mature forests up to 20 km (12 miles) from the volcano. Pyroclastic flows and surges have also been the bane of those living on the flanks of Vesuvius, killing as many as 2,000 people in Pompeii during the AD 79 eruption and about 4,000 in a smaller eruption in 1631. With 600,000 people now residing in the danger zone around Vesuvius, coping with the pyroclastic flow threat forms a critical part of contingency plans for dealing with a future eruption.

▼ Cars trapped in lava at the Royal Gardens subdivision of Mount Kilauea, south-east Hawaii. The cars are all that remain after this section of the volcano was overrun by lava during the eruption of Mount Kilauea on October 7, 1987.

Volcano landslides

A landslide or 'debris avalanche' is a rapid downhill movement of rocky material, snow, and/or ice. Volcano landslides range in size from small movements of loose debris on the surface of a volcano to massive collapses of an entire summit or sides of a volcano. Steep volcanoes are susceptible to landslides because they are built up partly of layers of loose volcanic rock fragments. Some rocks on volcanoes have also been altered to soft, slippery clay minerals by circulating hot, acidic groundwater. Landslides on volcano slopes are triggered when eruptions, heavy rainfall, or large earthquakes cause these materials to break free and move downhill. At least five large landslides have swept down the slopes of Mount Rainier, Washington, during the past 6,000 years, while the largest volcano landslide in history triggered the Mount St Helens, Washington, eruption on May 18, 1980. At least four volcanic landslides occur every century and can be particularly destructive if they fall into water, generating the giant sea waves known as tsunami. In 1792, the collapse of the flank of the Unzen volcano, Nagasaki, Japan, resulted in a tsunami that killed more than 14,000 inhabitants of adjacent coastal villages. More recently, in 1888, part of the Ritter Island volcano, located in the Dampier Strait off the east coast of Papua New Guinea, dropped into the sea, creating a tsunami that claimed around 3,000 lives and destroyed villages on nearby islands, including Umboi and New Britain.

See also **Tsunami**, pages 62–73, **Avalanches**, pages 136–41, **Landslides**, pages 142–51

Lahars

Mudflows or debris flows formed on the flanks of a volcano are called lahars. These flows of mud, rock, and water can rush down valleys and stream channels at speeds of 35 to 75 km/h (22–47 mph) and can travel distances of more than 80 km (50 miles). Some lahars contain so much rock debris (60 to 90% by weight) that they look like fast-moving rivers of wet concrete. Close to their source, these flows are powerful enough to rip up and carry trees, houses, and huge boulders kilometres downstream. Further downstream, they entomb everything in their path in mud. Historically, lahars have been one of the deadliest volcano hazards, and can occur both during an eruption and when a volcano is quiet. The water that creates lahars can come from melting snow and ice (especially water from a glacier melted by a pyroclastic flow or surge), intense rainfall, or the breakout of a summit crater-lake. Large lahars are a potential hazard to many communities downstream from glacier-clad volcanoes, such as Mount Rainier, Washington, which is situated just 35 km (22 miles) away from the Seattle-Tacoma metropolitan area.

Nevado del Ruiz eruption, Colombia, 1985

Lahars contributed to the worst volcanic catastrophe of recent times, when pyroclastic flows melted the ice and snow cap of the Nevado del Ruiz volcano, west-central Colombia,

▶ *Rescue-workers attempt to free a boy caught in the lahars of Nevado del Ruiz, west-central Colombia, 1985. The heat of the erupting volcano melted the snow at the summit, sending a 40 metre (130 foot) -high mix of snow and hot mud hurtling into the town of Armero. The eruption of Nevado del Ruiz and resulting lahars claimed 22,800 lives and demolished Armero.*

in 1985. In January 1985, changes in the behaviour of the volcano began with the ejection of thin ash layers from the summit and an increase in seismic activity. Despite such early warning signs, the Colombian government was reluctant to act. The first small lahar began in September, travelling 27 km (17 miles) at 10–30 km/h (6–19 mph). The increased volcanic activity prompted scientists to send an unofficial map of the area to local residents, indicating the areas at risk. The government dismissed the scientists' actions as unnecessarily alarmist, and most residents decided to stay. On November 13, an explosive eruption melted ice and snow in the summit area. The resulting deluge of water, mud and debris reached the town of Armero in just two hours, overwhelming it in a 40 metre (130 foot) -high wall of mud and taking 22,800 lives. Lahars also caused major disruption after the 1991 eruption of Mount Pinatubo, Luzon, Philippines. For many years afterwards, Luzon's rivers were clogged, farmland inundated, and fisheries damaged. A future lahar threat faces the inhabitants of Seattle and Tacoma, who live at the foot of the Mount Rainer volcano, including around 100,000 people who now

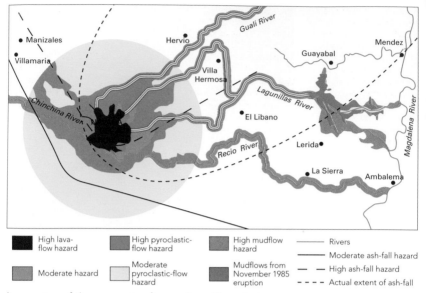

■ High lava-flow hazard	■ High pyroclastic-flow hazard	■ High mudflow hazard	——— Rivers
■ Moderate hazard	☐ Moderate pyroclastic-flow hazard	■ Mudflows from November 1985 eruption	——— Moderate ash-fall hazard
			— — High ash-fall hazard
			- - - - Actual extent of ash-fall

live on top of the remnants of several mudflows that swept down the mountain thousands of years ago. Mount Rainier with its four cubic kilometre (one cubic mile) ice-cap has the potential to generate a massive lahar – an eruption 5,000 years ago spawned a lahar 60 times greater than the one which devastated the Colombian town of Armero.

Forecasting volcanic eruptions

More than 1,500 volcanoes have erupted in the last 10,000 years and are classified as active. To these may be added around the same number of long-dormant but not extinct volcanoes. There is simply neither the funding nor the expertise to monitor the c.3,000 potentially destructive volcanoes, and presently barely 150 are monitored to any useful extent. This makes forecasting future eruptions problematic, particularly for the many dangerous volcanoes in developing countries. Even in Europe, Japan, and the United States, accurately predicting the timing, nature, and scale of an eruption remains difficult. Volcanologists have an advantage over seismologists, however, as no volcano will erupt without warning signs. These signs typically take the form of swarms of small earthquakes and a swelling of the ground surface, which together reflect the passage of magma to shallower depths prior to eruption. This may also be accompanied by gas discharges that may damage vegetation and kill wildlife. Monitoring such geophysical and geochemical eruption precursors, especially in the early stages, requires expensive kit, including Global Positioning System (GPS) receivers (for detecting ground swelling) and seismographs (for recording earthquake characteristics). These are in place around many

▶ *Volcanologists sample gases from the fumarole field atop Vulcano island in southern Italy. The levels of carbon dioxide released by a volcano can give an indication of how soon it may erupt.*

◄ *The eruption of the Nevado del Ruiz volcano in west-central Colombia caused widespread damage and loss of life through a deadly combination of pyroclastic flows, lahars, and ashfall. This map depicts the extent of the damage. Many of the towns and villages affected were situated alongside rivers – the path of most of the lahar flows.*

European and Japanese volcanoes, while US Geological Survey (USGS) scientists are closely monitoring activity at the most dangerous US volcanoes.

Earthquakes and ground surface deformation

Monitoring seismicity (earthquake occurrence) and ground surface deformation continue to form the basis of eruption forecasting, as they have done for more than a century. Pre-eruption earthquakes start deep within the crust, often below 10 km (6 miles), and rise progressively toward the surface. Initially, the earthquakes are similar in form to those associated with movements along faults, and in a similar way they are the result of rock fracturing as it is stressed by the rising magma. Once a passage has been opened, a mixture of magma and gas is able to travel through it, vibrating the walls of the fracture or conduit, and resulting in distinctive seismic signals known as 'harmonic tremor'. This is commonly an immediate precursor of an eruption. Volcano-deformation monitoring focuses on measuring the inflation of the ground surface as it is stretched above a filling magma reservoir. A range of techniques are now available, one of the most effective being the Global Positioning System (GPS). The establishment of roving GPS receivers above permanent benchmarks distributed across a volcano can fix their positions to just a few centimetres. This allows changes in their height and distance

► *A geologist examines the dome above a global positioning system (GPS) receiver in the Long Valley caldera, central California, USA. Different systems are being used to see how much the ground moves on and near various earthquake faults. By registering any movement beneath a caldera, geologists can predict its instability.*

April 10–May 13 June 15–July 25

August 23–Sept 30 Dec 5–Jan 16

<10⁻³   10⁻²   >10⁻¹
AEROSOL OPTICAL DEPTH

to be determined, relative to neighbouring bench-marks, providing a picture of how the surface is deforming. This information can be used to estimate the depth and volume of magma that might feed a future eruption. The core methods of seismic and ground-deformation monitoring are increasingly supplemented by other techniques. These include surveillance of the local gravity field, which can provide information on the mass and density of fresh magma emplaced beneath a volcano. Similarly, observing variations in the local magnetic and electrical fields can also help to detect a fresh mass of magma as it rises from deeper in the crust. Studying the composition of volcanic gases and groundwater may also reveal geochemical signals that support other observational evidence for the generation of new magma.

Although precursory activity ensures that an eruption is rarely unexpected, accurately predicting the start, climax, duration, and size of an eruption remains very difficult. New research, focusing on identifying accelerations in precursory activity such as rate ground-swelling or earthquake numbers, looks promising in terms of pinpointing the start of an eruption – at least for some types of volcanoes. Accurate prediction of the remaining variables remains, for the time being at least, a distant hope.

◀ *On June 15, 1991, Mount Pinatubo exploded, injecting about 15 million tonnes of sulphur dioxide into the stratosphere, where it reacted with water to form a hazy layer of aerosol particles. Over the next two years, strong stratospheric winds spread these aerosol particles around the globe. Because they scatter and absorb incoming sunlight, aerosol particles exert a cooling effect on the Earth's surface. The eruption increased aerosol optical depth in the stratosphere 10–100 times the normal level measured prior to the eruption. Over the next 15 months, scientists recorded a drop in the average global temperature of about 0.6°C (1°F).*

◀ *The first major eruption of Pinatubo on June 12, 1991. After more than two months of increasing seismicity, localized deformation, and emission of small plumes, on June 12 a series of strong explosions and a tephra column heralded the start of the major pyroclastic phase. The tephra column rose to about 20 km (12 miles).*

▼ *The peripheral areas of the Pacific Ocean Basin, containing the boundaries of several plates, are dotted by many active volcanoes that form the so-called 'Ring of Fire'. The 'Ring of Fire' provides excellent examples of plate-boundary volcanoes, including Mount St Helens, USA.*

Successful predictions

Two eruptions every quarter of a century could be said to have been forecast, although in neither case was the precise timing of the start of eruption predicted. In March 1980, deep earthquake swarms were observed at Mount St Helens, Washington, north-west United States, warning monitoring volcanologists that the volcano was entering an active phase. By mid-April a significant topographic bulge was detectable beneath the north flank of the volcano, representing the emplacement of a large volume of magma within this part of the volcano. The eruption came on May 18, 1980, when ground-shaking, arising from an earthquake, initiated the collapse of St Helens' north flank. The ensuing giant landslide removed the rock overburden above the new magma body, causing the gas contained therein to explosively decompress, generating a powerful blast of super-heated steam and magma to be released northward and upward. The blast flattened mature forests up to 20 km (12 miles) away but, due to successful early warnings and evacuation, only claimed 57 lives. Barographs around the world recorded the fluctuations in air-pressure from the blast, which took 33 hours to reach the other side of the world.

In early April 1991, a seismic swarm similar to that recorded during the early stages of activity at Mount St Helens was recorded beneath Mount Pinatubo in Luzon, Philippines. Having lain dormant for more than 500 years, little was known about the threat from Pinatubo, and a race developed better to understand the type and extent of potential hazards before an eruption. Volcanologists from the US Geological Survey (USGS) and the Philippine Institute of Volcanology and Seismology (PHIVOLCS) initiated a monitoring programme, while at the same time mapping the nature and

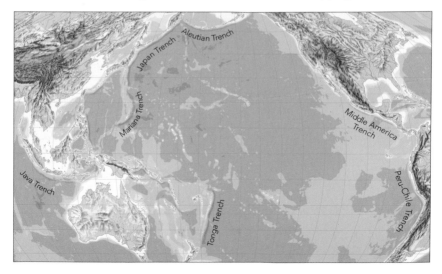

extent of the deposits of past eruptions. A system of alert levels was developed, and the public educated in how to respond to these. As activity accelerated, an 'Alert Level 3' was triggered – eruption likely within two weeks. In mid-June, an 'Alert Level 4' was declared – eruption likely within 24 hours. When the climactic eruption came on June 15, close to 60,000 people had been evacuated from the immediate vicinity of the volcano, leading to a death toll of just a few hundred (although hundreds more would die in the months ahead due to continued lahar formation).

Restless calderas

Not all volcanoes behave as predictably as Pinatubo, and sometimes precursory signs are not immediately followed by eruption. This is particularly well demonstrated at Mammoth Mountain, eastern California – a ski and holiday resort on the western edge of Long Valley caldera (a giant, low-lying, volcanic crater) where there is well-documented evidence of volcanic eruptions over the past two million years. Earthquake-swarm activity began in the 1980s, prompting residents to worry whether these episodes of activity were

▶ A radar image of Ta'al volcano on the island of Luzon in the northern Philippines. Ta'al is a restless caldera and has erupted on numerous occasions since the 18th century. The black area in the left-centre of the photograph is Ta'al Lake, which nearly fills the caldera. The large island in Ta'al Lake, which itself contains a crater lake, is known as Volcano Island.

◀ An aerial view of Long Valley caldera, on the eastern slopes of the Sierra Mountains, California, USA. It is a restless caldera and regularly exhibits signs of activity, such as seismic movement and the expulsion of gases. However, eruption may not happen for hundreds of years. It is estimated that this entire valley exploded approximately 700,000 years ago, about the same time that the volcanic landscape of Yellowstone National Park was formed.

forewarnings of a future eruption. During the 1990s, carbon dioxide emissions began to kill trees on the flanks of the mountain and intensified concerns about the imminence of an eruption. Still, as of early 2003, no eruption has occurred, but this is not entirely surprising. Long Valley is known as a 'restless caldera', one that is constantly experiencing some form of geophysical or geochemical activity, such as seismic activity, surface deformation, or gas discharge. This does not mean imminent eruption, and such restless caldera systems – Yellowstone National Park, western United States, and Campi Flegrei, Bay of Naples, southern Italy, are two other examples – may show this activity for decades or even centuries with no ensuing eruption. Nevertheless, Mammoth Mountain does seem to have been primed in recent decades and an eruption in the not too distant future would not be a surprise to the monitoring scientists.

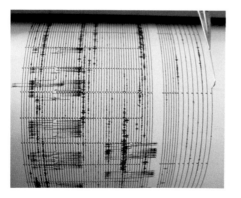

▼ A seismograph shows the 1992 seismic activity of Volcano Island inside the Ta'al Lake caldera, northern Philippines.

One restless caldera that has erupted recently is Rabaul in New Britain, Papua New Guinea. Here, earthquake swarms and ground swelling in the mid-1980s led to worries about a forthcoming eruption, but the situation quietened down again within a few years. In 1994, severe seismic shaking accompanied by uplift of the ground in excess of 1 metre (3.3 feet) was followed in less than 24 hours by a major eruption. Fortunately, the local population had been well educated about the potential eruptive threat during the crisis in the mid-1980s, and self-evacuation meant that only four people died directly as a result of the eruption. The rapid onset of the Rabaul eruption after an apparently disconnected episode of unrest is worrying, and is concerning scientists both at Mammoth Mountain and at Italy's Campi Flegrei, where periods of pronounced unrest occurred in the 1970s and again a decade later.

Volcanoes to watch

A number of volcanoes are currently showing signs of unrest, in addition to those mentioned in the previous section. In the Caribbean, seismic swarms have been recorded beneath the island of Dominica, which experienced major eruptions during prehistoric times. Ground swelling has also been reported in recent decades at the Colli Albani (Alban Hills) close to Rome, Italy, and at Three Sisters volcano in Oregon, north-west United States. Sixty kilometres (40 miles) south of Manila, Luzon, Philippines, another volcano may be set for eruption. Ta'al volcano consists of a central volcanic crater-lake, Lake Ta'al, which surrounds an island of an area of about 26 square kilometres (10 square miles), known as Volcano Island. Ta'al is one of the landmarks of the Philippines, sometimes called the 'Killer Volcano' of the Philippine islands. Extensive agricultural lands in its vicinity produce rice, corn, and sugar. Cattle raising and fishing are important industries. Ta'al has had 32 massive eruptions since the first documented eruption in 1752. Its volcanic eruptions are

▼ *Lake Ta'al on the Ta'al Volcano, Luzon, Philippines. Despite a history of violent eruptions, the area surrounding the volcano is being developed for tourism.*

► *Mount St Helens, Washington, USA, erupted in 1980. Constant monitoring of the volcano ensured that almost no lives were lost. In contrast, there is no preparation scheme for the inevitable eruption of Ta'al in the Philippines. After May 18, 1980, five more explosive eruptions of Mount St. Helens occurred during 1980, including this spectacular event of July 22. This eruption sent pumice and ash 10–18 km (6–11 miles) into the air, and was visible in Seattle, Washington, 160 km (100 miles) to the north.*

disruptive, leading to wholesale and permanent resettlement of townships, yet today it is being exploited and developed at an alarming rate. Past eruptions have been violent, discharging boulders, ash, sand and mud laced with sulphuric acid. In 1911, Ta'al violently erupted in an explosion that was heard 180 km (110 miles) away. The eruption was phreatomagmatic, meaning that it involved the mixing of magma and water. It killed around 1,300 people and injured a further 200 people. The volcano subsequently lay dormant until 1965, when a new crater opened on the south-west flank of the main crater, killing several hundred people. Today, a visit to Ta'al emphasizes the shortness of human memory. Housing developments are being constructed along the shores of Lake Ta'al, and hotels and tourist facilities are built on the rim of the volcanic crater itself. This increased vulnerability is made worse by an influx of around 4,000 squatters and illegal immigrants to Volcano Island. With today's population density, an eruption similar to the eruption of 1911 could easily kill between 4,000 and 6,000 people. A disaster preparedness scenario for Ta'al is frightening. There is an inadequate road network for escape, and population growth is uncontrolled. The situation is particularly worrying as seismic unrest during the early 1990s suggests that fresh magma may once again be accumulating at shallow depths, prior to another eruption.

Tsunami

The most destructive waves on Earth are driven not by wind but rather are generated by a violent displacement of the ocean bed. Tsunami (the word is both plural and singular) are large, long, water waves caused by underwater earthquakes (seaquakes), submarine volcanic eruptions or landslides. They are often incorrectly called 'tidal waves', for their formation has nothing whatsoever to do with the tides. One of the peculiar things about these fearsome waves is that they are barely noticeable far out at sea because their wave height in deep water is insignificant. It is their wavelength (the crest to crest distance) that gives tsunami their remarkable speed and energy. When one of these monstrous waves strikes a coastline, people standing onshore typically see the sea-level rise above the highest tide level, then suddenly retreat far below the lowest water level – only to rear back and strike the shore at astonishing speed and with towering height. The impact on a populated coastline can be calamitous. In 1896, when a tsunami struck the Sanriku coast of north-east Honshu, Japan, some 400 km (250 miles) north of Tokyo, the first thing people noticed was the sea making a peculiar hissing sound as it was sucked out far beyond the limit of low tide. For a while there was a strange silence. Then, with a tremendous roar, the sea returned to strike, rising as high as 25 metres (80 feet) and surging inland, drowning 30,000 people and destroying entire villages. Less than an hour earlier, an earthquake had rocked the seabed some 700 km (435 miles) north-east of Sanriku – an indication of the speed at which these waves can travel.

▼ A tsunami occurs when a submarine earthquake causes a sudden shift in the seafloor along a fault line. The upheaval creates a bulge that breaks down into a series of waves travelling at speeds of up to 750km/h (450mph). The map shows the hourly procession of the 1946 tsunami that originated in the Aleutian Islands.

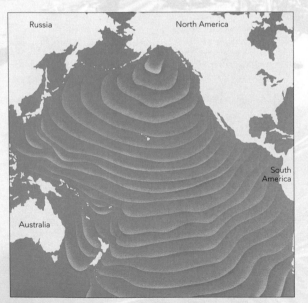

Russia

North America

South America

Australia

Intensity	Run-up height (m)	Description of tsunami	Frequency in Pacific Ocean
THE SCALE OF TSUNAMI INTENSITY (SOURCE: SOLOVIEV, 1978)			
I	0.5	Very slight. Wave so weak as to be perceptible only on tide gauge records	One per four months
II	1	Slight. Waves noticed by people living along the shore and familiar with the sea. On very flat shores waves generally noticed.	One per four months
III	2	Rather large. Generally noticed. Flooding of gently sloping coasts. Light sailing vessels carried away on shore. Slight damage to light structures situated near the coast. In estuaries, reversal of river flow for some distance up stream.	One per eight months
IV	4	Large. Flooding of the shore to some depth. Light scouring on made ground. Embankments and dykes damaged. Light structures near the coast damaged. Solid structures on the coast lightly damaged. Large sailing vessels and small ships swept inland or carried out to sea. Coasts littered with floating debris.	One per year
V	8	Very large. General flooding of the shore to some depth. Quays and other heavy structures near the sea damaged. Light structures destroyed. Severe scouring of cultivated land and littering of the coast with floating objects, fish and other marine animals. With the exception of large ships, all vessels carried inland or out to sea. Large bores in estuaries. Harbour-works damaged. People drowned, waves accompanied by a strong roar.	Once in three years
≥VI	16	Disastrous. Partial or complete destruction of manmade structures for some distance from the shore. Flooding of coasts to great depths. Large ships severely damaged. Trees uprooted or broken by the waves. Many casualties.	Once in ten years

The Pacific Ocean

Tsunami are particularly common in the Pacific Ocean because the majority of the world's earthquakes take place along the circum-Pacific belt known as the 'Ring of Fire'. Most vulnerable are Japan (the word 'tsunami' is Japanese for 'harbour wave'), Hawaii, Alaska, Indonesia, and the Pacific coast of South America. A tsunami can strike any coastline, but because of their particular positions on the circum-Pacific belt (where 80 percent of all earthquakes take place) and the configuration of their coastlines (it is the angle of incidence relative to the shoreline that determines how serious the damage will be), these regions are most susceptible to devastating tsunami. The Hawaiian islands owe their vulnerability to their location in the heart of the Pacific Ocean – as well as being hit by local tsunami, the islands are struck by 85 percent of all tsunami generated in the Pacific Basin. Japan has also been badly affected by tsunami: over the last 1,200 years more than 70 tsunami have taken in excess of 100,000 lives in Japan. This number of fatalities may in fact have been succeeded in 1703 alone by the arrival of a single, devastating tsunami generated somewhere in the eastern Pacific. The eastern coast of the Japanese island of Honshu is especially vulnerable, and on average is struck by a 10 metre (33 foot) - high tsunami every decade or so.

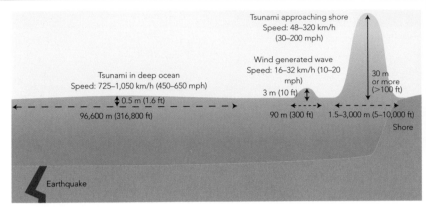

Tsunami approaching shore
Speed: 48–320 km/h
(30–200 mph)

Wind generated wave
Speed: 16–32 km/h (10–20 mph)

3 m (10 ft)

30 m or more (>100 ft)

Tsunami in deep ocean
Speed: 725–1,050 km/h (450–650 mph)

0.5 m (1.6 ft)

96,600 m (316,800 ft)

90 m (300 ft)   1.5–3,000 m (5–10,000 ft)

Shore

Earthquake

The Atlantic Ocean

Compared with the Pacific, tsunami are relatively rare in the Atlantic Ocean, and only around two percent of recorded tsunami occur here. Two particular tsunami are worthy of note: the first generated by the 1755 earthquake off the coast of Portugal, and the second triggered by an offshore quake in the area of the Grand Banks, north-east Canada, in 1929. The size and destructiveness of this latter tsunami owed something to the fact that its formation resulted not just from the displacement of the seafloor due to fault movement, but also from an associated submarine landslide triggered by the quake at the edge of the continental shelf. The resulting wave, with a run-up in excess of 10 metres (33 feet), killed around 30 people on the sparsely populated coast of Newfoundland.

▲ The development of a tsunami-sized wave following an ocean-based earthquake. Seismic movement creates a swell in the water. The wave grows and gathers speed as it reaches shore. The nearest coast experiences the full force of the tsunami, although the effects can often be seen throughout the world as a general coastal water-level rise.

The Mediterranean Sea

Due to its long history of civilization, the eastern Mediterranean has the most complete catalogue of tsunami. Since 450 BC, more than 250 earthquakes have triggered around 80 tsunami, 25% of which were destructive. One tsunami, generated in c. 1640 BC by a massive volcanic eruption on the Greek island of Santorini, is reported to have devastated the north coast of Crete, dealing a severe blow to the Minoan civilization.

The Caribbean Sea

The Caribbean Sea has had its share of devastating tsunami, particularly in the north and east where major earthquakes in 1867, 1918, and 1946 all generated tsunami. The destruction caused by these events was confined to the Caribbean and loss of life was relatively small. The 1867 earthquake in the Anegada Passage (between the US Virgin Islands of St Croix and St Thomas) measured 7.5 on the Richter scale. It created a tsunami with run-up heights up to 7 metres (23 feet), which killed 12 people and damaged boats and coastal properties. The 1918 earthquake between Hispaniola and Puerto Rico measured 7.5 on the Richter scale. It generated a tsunami up to 6 metres (20 feet) high, which claimed up to 100 lives and caused significant damage. Most worryingly, sonar imagery of the deep Puerto Rico trench has revealed the presence of huge landslide scars, several kilometres across, that indicate the past occurrence of giant submarine landslides. Should collapses on such a scale occur in the future, they could have the potential to generate widespread tsunami similar to those in the Atlantic Basin.

Tsunami characteristics

Tsunami are most commonly triggered by submarine earthquakes, which cause a sudden vertical offset in the seafloor. This abrupt offset of the seabed displaces a large volume of water, producing a depression in the level of the sea surface. Water, being incompressible, rushes in to fill the depression and spreads out at right-angles to the axis of the offset. Oscillatory wave motion is created, and waves of large wavelength move away from the point of disturbance. Wind-driven waves that crash onto beaches typically have wave periods (the time taken for a single wavelength to pass a fixed point) of several seconds and wavelengths of a few to several tens of metres. In marked contrast, the wave period of a tsunami varies from 20 minutes to several hours and its wavelength can be hundreds of kilometres long. Both length and speed depend on water depth. In the central Pacific Ocean, where water depths are 5 km (3 miles) or more, a tsunami can travel at 700 km/h (435 mph). Its height may be just a metre or two, or even a few tens of centimetres, but the wavelength will be of the order of 480

▼ In 1958, Lituya Bay in Glacier Bay National Park, south-east Alaska, was struck by one of the largest tsunami ever recorded. An earthquake, measuring 8.3 on the Richter scale, caused a massive landslide on the eastern wall of Gilbert Inlet (shown here), and the rocks crashed into the sea, producing a wave 525 m (1,720 feet) high. A giant tsunami, at least 30 m (100 feet) high, swept across the bay.

km (300 miles) giving a wave period of 40 minutes. The long wavelength and low wave-height explain why ships on the open seas do not feel the passage of a tsunami. The Japanese fishing-fleet, out at sea during the 1896 Sanriku tsunami, did not know anything unusual had happened until they returned to their wrecked port and found human bodies floating in the harbour waters.

As a tsunami approaches the shoreline, its speed, like that of all waves, decreases because of the upward-sloping sea bottom and its wavelength is compressed. The enormous amount of energy that has been stored in the very long wavelength is transferred to wave height, with terrible consequences. As wave-height rises in shallow water – in some instances, to 30 metres (100 feet) or more – the tsunami curls over to strike with incredible force. Gulfs, bays, and estuaries are the coastlines most vulnerable to tsunami. These funnel-shaped inlets focus a tsunami, amplifying it into a bore – a vast wall of seawater weighing billions of tonnes that crashes inland with destructive power almost beyond belief. The height of a tsunami is measured above mean sea-level and is referred to as the run-up. This regularly exceeds 10 metres (30 feet) and – in rare cases – may reach or surpass 40 metres (130 feet). Although other factors are also important, higher run-ups generally equate to greater damage. Another characteristic that contributes to the destructive power of tsunami is that they often take the form of not one wave, but a series of waves – the greatest of which may not be the first. These wave 'trains' magnify damage potential, with later waves breaking-up structures weakened by earlier ones and claiming the lives of those fortunate enough to survive the earlier impacts.

The Lisbon tsunami, Portugal, 1755
On November 1, 1755, the great Lisbon earthquake in Portugal produced one of the worst tsunami tragedies. The 'calamity of

MOST DEADLY TSUNAMI OF THE 20TH CENTURY					
Location of origin	Country	Date	Run-up*	Intensity	Killed
Moro Gulf	Philippines	August 16, 1976	5.0	2.5	8,000
Sanriku	Japan	March 2, 1933	29.3	3.5	3,000
–	Papua New Guinea	July 17, 1998	17	–	2,180
Tokaido	Japan	September 1, 1923	12.1	3.0	2,144
Nankaido	Japan	December 20, 1946	6.6	2.0	1,997
–	south-central Chile	May 22, 1960	25.0	4.0	1,260
Flores	Indonesia	December 12, 1992	26.2	2.7	1,000
Ryukyu trench	Japan	December 7, 1944	20.0	2.5	998
Makassar Strait	Indonesia	February 23, 1969	4.0	2.0	600
Lomblen Island	Indonesia	July 18, 1979	10.0	0.0	540

The maximum water height above sea level in metres for this event. The run-up is the height the tsunami reached above a reference level such as mean sea level.

▲ Debris and subsidence along the shore in Degirmendere, north-west Turkey, following the tsunami caused by the 1999 Izmit earthquake. The town of Degirmendere was very close to the epicentre of the quake, and felt the strongest shaking. Fatalities were numerous in the surrounding area, and many buildings were destroyed. The shoreline subsided about 2 metres (6.5 feet), and the water-line advanced 50 metres (165 feet) inland from its location prior to the earthquake. The scarp, left by subsidence, was approximately 2 metres (6.5 feet) tall. Prior to August 17, the area in the centre of town was the location of a restaurant, park, and a four-storey hotel. After the quake, the entire centre was beneath the waters of Izmit Bay.

the century' began in the morning with an alarming noise that witnesses described as sounding like grating thunder beneath the Earth. This first shock was followed by an eerie silence. In the second, much bigger shock, columns, walls, roofs, and spires of shops, homes, and churches came tumbling down. After the third shock, fires broke out, devouring a good part of the city. By this time, the people of Lisbon were terror-stricken. But they had not yet faced the worst. As aftershock upon after-shock reverberated through the city and a suffocating cloud of dust enveloped it, people rushed down to the harbour, intent on escaping by boat. They were met by a towering tsunami about 15 metres (50 feet) high, generated by the sudden displacement of the seafloor off the coast of Portugal. The first wave was followed by subsequent waves. About 60,000 people were killed in the disaster, many by drowning, and others by fire. This tsunami raised waters all along the coastline of Europe and as far away as the West Indies. In Martinique and Barbados, where normally wave-heights are less than 1 metre (3.3 feet), the waves rose above 6 metres (20 feet). Oscillations of land-locked bodies of water, known as seiches, occurred in northern Germany, Sweden, Scotland, and as far away as Canada.

The Krakatoa tsunami, Indonesia, 1883

Although most tsunami result from submarine seismic distur-bances, some have other causes. Tsunami can also be gen-erated by impacts from space, submarine landslides and rock avalanches into the ocean, and by submarine volcanic eruptions. The most notable volcano-instigated tsunami occurred during the cataclysmic 1883 eruption of Krakatoa – one of the most violent natural explosions in 3,000 years. Krakatoa is a volcanic island located in the Sunda Strait between the Indonesian islands of Java and Sumatra. The volcano was quiescent for two centuries until 1877, when a series of eruptions began. The biggest eruption started in May 1883, and continued through July and August. Krakatoa itself was uninhabited and people on surrounding islands had learned to take its spectacular explosions in their stride. Then on the morning of August 27, the whole northern and lower portions of the volcano were blown apart in a climactic paroxysm. The explosion was heard as far away as Rodriguez Island, nearly 5,000 km (3,100 miles) to the west in the Indian Ocean. The enormous discharge of volcanic ash and dust darkened the skies as far as 250 km (150 miles) away. Volcanic debris transported by air currents diffused for years over a latitude band from 30° N to 45° S, ultimately affecting North and South America, Europe, Asia, southern Africa, and Australia. Spectacular sunrises and sunsets were observed around the world as atmospheric ash filtered solar radiation.

The most serious consequence of the disintegration of Krakatoa, however, was the generation of a long-period water wave (tsunami) and shorter-period, higher amplitude sea waves (up to 15 metres/50 feet high). Colossal waves struck all along the coasts of Java and Sumatra, inundating towns and villages and killing 36,000 people. Such was the power of the waves that the Dutch warship *Berouw* was carried more than 2.5 kilometres (1.5 miles) inshore, where it was left stranded some 10 m (30 feet) above sea level. Racing across the seas, the tsunami ultimately reached Cape Horn, South America (about 13,000 km/8,000 miles away), and was detected – very much reduced – on tide gauges in the English Channel (some 17,500 km/10,900 miles away). As with the Lisbon quake almost 130 years earlier, seiches were observed in closed and semi-closed bodies of water halfway across the planet.

▼ *A woman sits amid damaged boats and debris left by the tsunami that swept through the town of Masachapa, Nicaragua, on September 3, 1992. The tsunami ravaged the fragile Nicaraguan coastal towns, taking the lives of 170 people.*

▲ In 1998 a tsunami devastated the coastal villages of Papua New Guinea. Many of the more than 2,100 victims of the tsunami drowned in the Sissano Lagoon behind the sand spit in this photograph. Two Arop villages once stood on this sand spit in north-west Papua New Guinea. The wave removed all trace of the several hundred houses that stood on the sand spit, except for the remains of a septic tank seen in the foreground of this image.

The Flores Island tsunami, Indonesia, 1992

More than a century after Krakatoa, tsunami continue to exact a toll in south-east Asia. On December 12, 1992, an earthquake, measuring 7.8 on the Richter scale, struck the northwest coast of the Indonesian island of Flores, 1,800 km (1,100 miles) east of Jakarta. The death toll of the combined earthquake and resulting tsunami was more than 2,000, with over 500 people seriously injured and 90,000 left homeless. About 30,000 houses and other structures were destroyed. The maximum run-up height was a terrifying 26.2 metres (86 feet) at the small village of Riangkroko, 100 km (60 miles) east of the epicentre. The waves also caused severe coastal erosion, exposed eroded coral complexes, and left sand deposits up to 1 metre (3.3 feet) thick. Just a few months earlier, another destructive tsunami had struck on the other side of the world.

The Nicaragua tsunami, 1992

The term 'tsunami-earthquake' is used to describe those quakes that generate tsunami disproportionately large for their assigned Richter magnitudes. One such example was the magnitude 7.0 earthquake of September 1, 1992, that occurred in the Pacific Ocean, about 120 km (75 miles) west-south-west of Nicaragua's capital, Managua. Wave heights between 8 and 15 metres (26–49 feet) struck 26 towns along 250 km (150 miles) of Nicaragua's Pacific coast, centered on the town of El Transito. The tsunami reached 1 kilometre (0.6 miles) inland, took more than 100 lives, and left 10,000 people homeless. The tsunami struck in the early evening when fishing boats were docked. Damage to tourist facilities and port infrastructure was severe. Another unfortunate aspect was the damage to the coastal ecology. The force of the waves and the salinity of the seawater destroyed plants and the habitats of fish and turtles. The unusual destructiveness of the tsunami was striking, and its ferocity may have been a reflection of the severe rupture of the seafloor and the long duration of the earthquake. In one respect, the residents of El Transito and neighbouring settlements were lucky. It seems that the tsunami wave-trough reached the coast first, leading to relatively gentle inundation by a great, slow-moving swell rather than by a violent, crashing breaker.

The Papua New Guinea tsunami, 1998

One of the most recent tsunami catastrophes took place on July 17, 1998, along the north coast of Papua New Guinea. The earthquake, measuring 7.0 on the Richter scale, and its accompanying submarine landslide occurred in the New Guinea trench, along a plate boundary segment between the Pacific plate and the Australian plate. The resulting deaths of 2,180 people made this the third-deadliest tsunami of the 20th century. Run-up heights up to 17 metres (56 feet) were reached along 25 kilometres (15.5 miles) of coastline and the surge-flow velocities were 15–20 metres (49–66 feet) per second. The scale of the tsunami and their concentration along a short strip of coastline are a reflection of the augmentation and focusing effects of the submarine landslide triggered by the quake. The great loss of life can also be largely explained by the proximity of the quake to the coast, resulting in the tsunami taking just 30 minutes to reach the shore. Most of the tsunami's energy was centred on a 40 km (25 mile) -long strip of coastline, a portion of which was backed by a shallow-water lagoon. The tsunami was described as consisting of three waves, the first being a withdrawal or depression. The subsequent waves arrived at two-minute intervals. Papuan survivors recounted tales of an underwater source of fire. One eyewitness reported that the tsunami was an "infernal wall of water with fire sparks flying" and many of the dead had the appearance of being severely burned. It appears that

▼ *In 1998 a massive tsunami, caused by an earthquake in the New Guinea trench, struck the north-west coast of Papua New Guinea. The villages of Sissano and Arap I and Arap II were worst affected.*

● Epicentre of earthquake

— Area affected

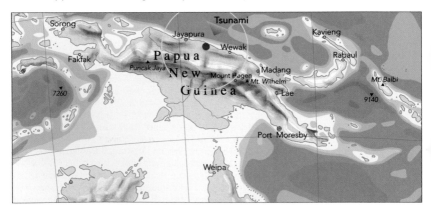

▲ *Mother and daughter among the ruins of the destroyed village of Sissano following the tsunami that struck north-west Papua New Guinea on July 21, 1998. The tsunami killed 2,180 people, many of whom were children studying at seaside schools.*

the rapid rise of sea level at sundown initiated luminescence, known as 'sea-fire', in which tiny marine dinoflagellates emit light when stirred. This bioluminescence may have given the appearance of flying sparks as the wave struck. The reported burns on the bodies resulted from friction and abrasion as the victims were pulled for several hundreds of metres through debris amidst churning sand-charged water.

Tsunami monitoring and mitigation

Although towering concrete tsunami defences have been constructed along parts of Japan's Pacific-facing coast, these remain to be tested. Other physical measures include growing plantations of trees to help break up the waves and dissipate their energy, and constructing properties on strong elevated piles. The best defence, however, relies upon a combination of ensuring an effective warning system is in place, that evacuation procedures are established and understood by the population, and that construction of property along threatened shorelines is prevented.

When the eruption of Krakatoa took so many lives in 1883, no warning system existed that could provide sufficient warning of tsunami to save the lives of people in vulnerable coastal areas. But after a brutal tsunami swept Hawaii in 1946, an effective monitoring system was set up to watch for signs of a tsunami every time a large earthquake shook the Pacific region. Strategically located observatories in the United States, Japan, Taiwan, Chile, New Zealand and other countries relay data to the network's centre on Honolulu, Hawaii, which then alerts countries all around the Pacific. A tsunami travels at very high speeds, but distances are so great in the Pacific Ocean that this warning system works quite well. The transit time to Hawaii of a tsunami produced by an earthquake disturbance somewhere around the Pacific Rim ranges from five to 15 hours. A tsunami-

◀ Inhabitants of Hilo, eastern Hawaii, flee the 1946 Aleutian tsunami, just visible in the background. Hilo was hit by a series of six or seven large tsunami waves arriving at 15–20 minute intervals.
The highest of the waves had a run- up of 8.1 metres (27 feet) above sea level.
The waves destroyed Hilo's waterfront, killing 159 people.

warning system would not be as effective in smaller bodies of water, such as the Caribbean and Mediterranean Seas, because the travel-time distances would be much shorter.

In developing countries, there is currently no means of getting warning messages to threatened populations immediately after a large offshore earthquake. In order, therefore, to attempt to minimize the level of potential destruction and loss of life, scientific investigators made several recommendations to the local population following the Papua New Guinea tragedy. They stressed that new homes should not be constructed on the narrow and very exposed strip of sand between the sea and lagoons, and new hospitals and schools should be located at least 400 metres (1,300 feet) inland. They also suggested that Casuarina trees, a local variety, should be systematically planted in front of coastal communities: these trees having withstood the onslaught of the 1998 tsunami far better than coconut trees. To allow rapid evacuation, every family should have a designated tree with a ladder or carved steps to provide a safe refuge.

Mega-tsunami

In recent years, one focus of tsunami research has been so-called 'mega-tsunami'. These are giant waves with run-up heights that may exceed 100 metres (330 feet) and which are formed very infrequently by the collapse of ocean island-volcanoes or segments of the continental shelf, or by asteroid impacts in the sea. Attention has concentrated in recent years on the potential for imminent collapse – at least in terms of the geological timescale – of the western flank of the Cumbre Vieja volcano on the Spanish island of La Palma in the Canaries, off the north-west coast of Africa. In 1949, an eruption displaced as much as 200 km³ (48 miles³) of rock, which slid 4 metres (13 feet) seawards before grinding to a halt. In the 1990s, ground-deformation monitoring suggested that the mass may still be creeping downslope at around 1 cm (0.4 inches) a year. It is virtually certain that eventual catastrophic collapse – when it eventually happens – will occur during the

▶ The village of Teles, between Malol and Aitape, north-west Papua New Guinea, was on the outer edge of the devastating 1998 tsunami. The damaged house is an example of the form of housing seen below (top). When the wave struck, the house buckled. Reinforced as illustrated below (bottom), the house would have better withstood the force of the wave.

dynamic situation of a future eruption. The problem is, nobody has any idea when this might occur.

The collapse of ocean island-volcanoes and the generation of giant catastrophic landslides is common, and the debris of more than 70 huge collapses form an apron around the Hawaiian islands. Others cover the seafloor around La Palma and other islands in the Canaries, and have been detected around volcanoes elsewhere in the Indian and Pacific Oceans. Fortunately, however, no collapses have occurred during historic times, so the nature and scale of the tsunami such a collapse might generate is not precisely known. A recent model of a future Cumbre Vieja collapse forecasts an original water bulge almost 1 kilometre (0.6 miles) high that rapidly subsides to 100 metre (330 feet) -high waves that crash onto the neighbouring Canary Islands. Within the next 12 hours, tsunami radiate out in all directions across the Atlantic Basin, impacting on north-west Africa, United Kingdom, southern Europe and north-east South America. The brunt of the waves are predicted to be felt in the Caribbean and along the eastern seaboard of North America, where run-up heights in excess of 20 metres (66 feet) are expected to cause severe destruction and loss of life.

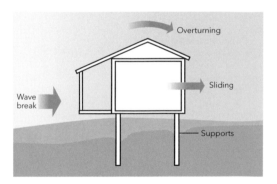

Overturning

Sliding

Wave break

Supports

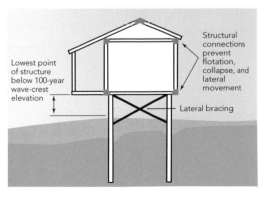

Lowest point of structure below 100-year wave-crest elevation

Structural connections prevent flotation, collapse, and lateral movement

Lateral bracing

Waves

Waves are a familiar sight, caused mainly by the wind blowing over a fetch, or open stretch of water, and often persisting in the form of a swell, long after the forces that created them have subsided. All waves, including those that reach the shore, are the product of interactions between the swell from distant weather systems, oceanic currents, and prevailing winds. The swell that reaches the Californian coast could have come from as far away as the stormy region south of New Zealand, and waves that began off Cape Horn, South America may crash against the coasts of Western Europe, 10,000 km (6,200 miles) distant. Ocean waves are major transporters of energy around the world.

Waves move across the surface of the ocean in much the same way as a sailing ship, with the wind behind the wave pushing it across the ocean surface. The energy transferred from the wind to the surface of the water can itself be transferred from one wave to another. Waves in the process of generation are called 'forced waves'. As they move from the source area, they travel as long-crested 'swell waves'. The awesome power of waves releases a considerable destructive force as they break against a shoreline. Waves in the open ocean are typically not hazardous, but there have been some exceptions when 'freak' or giant waves are created due to steepening as a result of opposing currents. One source of such freak waves, which can pose a serious threat to shipping, is the so-called 'Roaring Forties' off the south-east coast of Africa. Here, the supertanker *Gigantic* is believed to have been sunk by such a wave during the late 1970s.

Types of wave

Waves are of several different types, which differ in their length, the distance separating wave crests, and their periodicity (the elapsed time between successive wave crests). Wave height, the vertical distance between the trough and crest of a wave, is determined by the fetch (distance over

▼ *Waves are caused by the friction of the wind on the water surface and by ocean currents. Ocean currents are primarily dependent on wind patterns. Wind patterns depend partly on seasonal changes in temperatures in the northern and southern latitudes.*

January Temperature
and Ocean Currents
(Northern Hemisphere –
Winter)

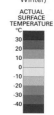

ACTUAL
SURFACE
TEMPERATURE
°C
30
20
10
0
-10
-20
-30
-40

Ocean currents
Cold Warm Speed (knots)
⟵ ⟵ Less than 0.5
⟵ ⟵ 0.5 – 1.0
⟵ ⟵ Over 1.0

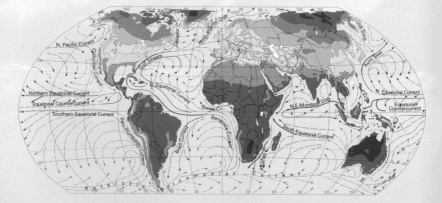

which the wind blows), the duration of the wind, and the wind speed. In the Pacific Ocean, which has the greatest fetch of any ocean, wind-driven waves reach their greatest height.

Surface tension is the main determinant of wave shape, and gravity only becomes important when the wavelength exceeds 1.74 centimetres (0.685 inches). Capillary waves have wavelengths less than 1.74 centimetres (0.685 inches) and a periodicity of less than one second, and are created by wind blowing gently across the water surface. Such waves are characterized by rounded crests and pointed troughs. Once wavelength exceeds 1.74 centimetres (0.685 inches), gravity becomes the dominant influence on wave form, with waves becoming more pointed and troughs more rounded as wavelength increases. The wind reinforces the wave shape by pressing down on the windward side and eddying over the crest to reduce pressure on the leeward side. When the crest of a wave steepens to an angle of 120°, it becomes unstable and breaks, producing a white-capped breaking wave characteristic of strong wind conditions. Orbital movement of water particles at the surface has a diameter equal to the wave height, but reduces to zero at a depth equal to half the wavelength. In shoaling water, characterised by a depth of less than half the wavelength, the waves heighten and the wavelength shortens.

Breakers and surf

As waves approach the shore, their height becomes greater and their wavelength becomes shorter, until they eventually break as surf on the shore. The breaking results from the orbital movement of the water particles inside the wave and the friction caused by the seafloor, which slows the movement of the deep water relative to the surface. Inside each wave, water moves in an orbital way with particles at the surface moving in a circle of diameter equal to the wave height. At a depth of half the wavelength, no orbital motion is present in the water mass. As waves approach the shore and the depth decreases to less than half the wavelength,

July Temperature
and Ocean Currents
(Northern Hemisphere –
Summer)

ACTUAL
SURFACE
TEMPERATURE
°C
30
20
10
0
-10

Ocean Currents
Cold Warm Speed (knots)
Less than 0.5
0.5 – 1.0
Over 1.0

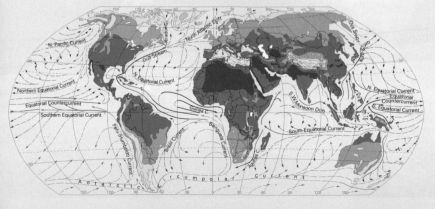

the particle movements become more elliptical until they can no longer maintain their orbit and the wave breaks. Breakers on a gently sloping shore may either surge up the beach or break gradually as water spills down the wave front. Where the shore steepens abruptly, the wave overturns as a plunging breaker.

Waves cause the most damage when they strike the shore. The interaction of a wave with the shoreline is controlled by the speed of the wave, its direction of approach, and the nature and shape of the onshore topography. As a wave approaches the shore, its speed decreases due to shallowing. Although the wavelength is compressed, there is no reduction in the wave energy, which is proportional to the square of its height times its wavelength. Since energy always remains constant in a column of water, wavelength compression results in an increase in the wave's height. This is why waves can turn into hazardous monsters when they crash onto land. Wave refraction, or the bending of waves in shallow water, is controlled by the topographic shape of the coastline. Headlands and promontories are particularly vulnerable to wave damage because of focusing of waves as they approach such topographic extensions. Similarly, when a breakwater is erected offshore to protect a harbour from the full force of ocean waves, only a part of each wave strikes the barrier; the remaining wave motion leaking around the harbour-opening and focusing wave energy on the very area the barrier was meant to shelter.

▼ *Sea-spray off breakers as waves hit the shore. When waves enter shallow water, their crests pile closer together and topple over, causing the water to race forwards. The stack in the background of the picture is the result of erosion caused by waves on the headland. Cracks in the rock are easily eroded, forming a cave. This in turn erodes to form an arch, which finally collapses leaving behind a finger of rock.*

Storm waves

High waves occur most frequently when storm waves drive up against a continental shelf. As waves move away from the storm centre they change shape, becoming less ragged and take the form of long, smooth swells. During storms, waves receive so much energy that they are whipped into waves of different periods, lengths and directions, and the resulting chaotic pattern is known as a 'wind sea'. At the heart of intense storms, waves may swell to heights of between 12 and 15 metres (39–49 feet), although the largest recorded wave was 35 metres (115 feet) high.

Coastal breezes

The surface waters of the oceans are intimately linked with atmospheric conditions. This is perhaps nowhere more obvious than in short-term weather events such as the daily pattern of onshore and offshore breezes that occur in many coastal areas all over the world. Because the land is heated more rapidly than the sea during the day, the air above the land rises and is replaced by air flowing from the sea to the land. Cool, onshore breezes thus help to moderate the heat of the day. At night, however, the direction of the wind reverses. As the land cools down to a temperature below that of the adjacent sea, gentle offshore breezes spring up. In addition to the transfer of heat from ocean to atmosphere, water vapour also enters the atmosphere from the sea surface. Where wind flows over a warm ocean, it picks up moisture and if it subsequently encounters colder ocean water, dense ocean fog forms as water droplets condense in the atmosphere. During the summer months in the north-west Pacific, for example, southerly winds flow over the warm Kuroshio Current and as they pass over the cold Oyashio Current, they give rise to areas of dense ocean fog.

Waves and the weather

Tides are ultimately the result of the relative positions of the Earth, Moon, and Sun. While a detailed understanding of how they are generated remains incomplete, sufficient is known to allow reasonably accurate tidal predictions. One complicating factor arises, however, because atmospheric and climatic conditions can have strong positive or negative effects. Fierce winds or extremes of atmospheric pressure may alter a tidal height by up to 3 metres (10 feet). The wind may actually blow water toward or away from the shore, and whereas high atmospheric pressure weighs the water down and prevents it from rising, low pressure allows water to rise up more than it otherwise would. A change of just 1 millibar (up or down) in atmospheric pressure can make a difference of about 1 centimetre (0.4 inches) in the height of the sea, while the maximum tidal surge produced by atmospheric fluctuation is of the order of 50 cm (20 inches).

Storm Surges

Winds generated by large storms or tropical cyclones can be severely damaging, but it is often the associated storm-surge that results in most devastation. As the low-pressure 'eye' of a storm approaches a shoreline, the mean water-level rises because of the decrease in atmospheric pressure. When the storm passes, the water level returns to normal, producing a landward wall of water – the storm surge – that sweeps inland. Storm surges are responsible for the great majority of hurricane fatalities, with numbers of deaths being highest when a surge strikes the coast at high tide. In 1900, this resulted in the most lethal natural disaster in US history when a hurricane struck Galveston, southern Texas. The waters of the Gulf of Mexico at the Galveston Island shoreline rose over 1 metre (3.3 feet) in just 4 seconds, overwhelming much of the city and resulting in the loss of an estimated 6,000 lives.

Vulnerable locations: Bangladesh

Offshore or barrier islands like Galveston and low-lying coastal areas like those of Bangladesh are most vulnerable to storm surges. Much of Bangladesh's coast is less than 2 metres (6.6 feet) above mean sea-level. When the 15 metre (49 feet) -high storm-surge of November 13, 1970, was added to normal high tide, the result was one of the worst natural disasters of modern times, with estimates of the

▲ *A Bengali mother carries her infant across muddy flood waters from a makeshift field hospital, Bangladesh, 1971. Those people who did not drown in the original 1970 storm surge in Bangladesh faced death from malnutrition and lack of clean drinking water. In 1971, it is estimated that 30,000 refugees crossed into India from Bangladesh every day.*

death toll ranging from 300,000 to 500,000 people. In 1991 another hurricane struck the country, claiming at least 138,000 lives. Bangladesh's geographic 'bad luck' is compounded by poverty and overpopulation, and Bengalis have spread into the hazardous low-lying areas because the land there is fertile and ideally suited to the cultivation of rice. The majority of the population live in fragile houses of straw and bamboo that are easily destroyed in strong storms, let alone major hurricanes. Furthermore, the country, like most poor nations, does not have the infrastructure to establish effective evacuation procedures.

The formation of a storm surge

Several factors contribute towards the formation of a storm surge. First, the speed, duration and direction of the wind are important, and a strong, persistent wind that agitates coastal waters is an important precursor. Second, the reduced atmospheric pressure associated with approaching storms or hurricanes is a critical factor. This fall in atmospheric pressure temporarily raises the local water-level before the storm arrives. When the storm finally descends, it adds to the already high water-level and drives rolling waters toward the shoreline. Once the storm moves on, the slope of the seafloor controls the height of the surge, with shallow seafloors producing the highest waves. The final factor is timing, with storm-surges striking at high tide always being the most destructive.

Storm-surge prediction and mitigation

Since most of the flooding and fatalities arising from hurricanes and other storms come not from the associated strong winds and intensive rains, but from the storm surge that succeeds them, it would be very useful if we could predict when and where surges will happen. Two of the observable parameters of storm surges are their height and frequency of occurrence. In some parts of the world, data on these features are regularly collected and have been for some time. The data that has been collected allows us to estimate the average recurrence time and size of 'big' surge events,

▼ The effect of a storm surge on coastal communities. A storm surge is water that is pushed toward the shore by the force of storm winds. This advancing surge combines with the normal tides to create the hurricane storm tide, which can increase the mean water-level by 4.5 m (15 feet) or more. In addition, wind-driven waves are superimposed on the storm tide. This rise in water level can cause severe flooding in coastal areas, particularly when the storm tide coincides with normal high tides.

5.2 m (17 ft) Storm tide

4.5 m (15 ft) Surge

0.6 m (2 ft) Normal high tide

Normal sea level

but not their timing. For any natural hazard, a large, rare event occurring today does not preclude, statistically speaking, a similarly disastrous event happening tomorrow. The long-term average may not change, but there are sporadic or cyclical clusters of events over smaller intervals of time that are both intriguing and perplexing. Unfortunately, it is human nature to assume after one rare and devastating storm surge that another of such magnitude is not due for a long time. This is a very dangerous assumption.

Short-term forecasts of hurricanes and other massive storms that have a strong probability of generating a storm surge are reasonably accurate, but such warnings only limit loss of life if they are heeded and acted upon. In 1970 the government of Pakistan, which then controlled Bangladesh, did not issue an evacuation order to vulnerable populations until the evening the hurricane struck, although it had received strong warnings about the approaching hurricane. Hundreds of thousands of people perished without a chance of survival. The warning system is not flawless, and false alarms are sometimes issued that can make people cynical and less likely to respond to future alerts, but there is little doubt that the monitoring of storms and timely warnings of possible storm surges have saved many lives in recent years.

Can we build defences against storm surges?

It is possible to plan defences in advance of a storm surge. For some countries, flood defences are an essential form of

▼ *Flooded village of Stellendam, on the island of Goeree Overflakkee, south-east Netherlands, 1953. In 1953, a storm surge struck the coasts of the Netherlands and eastern England causing extensive damage and killing thousands of people. The disaster prompted the Dutch government to develop one of the world's largest flood defence systems.*

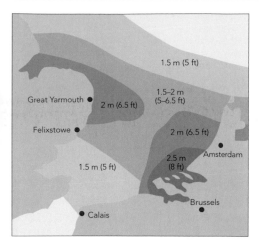

1.5 m (5 ft)

1.5–2 m
(5–6.5 ft)

Great Yarmouth ●   2 m (6.5 ft)

Felixstowe ●

2 m (6.5 ft)

2.5 m
(8 ft)   ● Amsterdam

1.5 m (5 ft)

Brussels
●

● Calais

▲ *Map showing open-sea surge heights for the 1953 storm surge. The surge resulted in sea levels rising to nearly three metres (10 feet) above normal high-water marks and coastal defences in Britain and the Netherlands were both damaged and breached by huge waves. The 1953 flood has been described as the worst national peacetime disaster to hit the United Kingdom. Exceptional weather conditions, coupled with poor communications, meant that communities were given insufficient warning of the advancing threat.*

government spending. Forty percent of the Netherlands lies below mean sea-level making it extremely vulnerable to flooding. On February 1, 1953, a strong storm-surge struck the coast of the Netherlands, drowning 1,800 people, flooding 324,000 hectares (800,000 acres), and collapsing many dykes. Following the disaster, the Netherlands constructed the world's largest flood barrier in Zeeland, south-east Netherlands. Known as the Eastern Scheldt Storm-Surge Barrier, it forms part of the Delta Project – a huge engineering operation that built a chain of flood defences to protect the Netherlands from a repetition of the 1953 catastrophe.

The surge was powerful enough to reach the eastern coast of England and was responsible for one of Britain's worst peacetime disasters. In total, 307 people were killed and nearly 100,000 hectares (247,000 acres) of eastern England was flooded. An enquiry into the lack of warning and protection during the surge prompted the government to implement a major coastal-defence reform programme. A flood warning organization was also proposed. The British Meterological Office helped to establish the 'Storm Tide Forecasting Service', a system that continues to provide 24-hour forecasts of tidal surge and wave activity.

After the 1900 catastrophic storm surge in Galveston, southern Texas, a 6 metre (20 foot) -high storm wall was built. While this provides some protection, many believe it can be breached in the future by a surge associated with a powerful hurricane. In the meantime, other coastal areas in the world are far less protected, mainly due to poverty or lack of political will. The coast of Bangladesh, for example, remains in as much jeopardy as ever and the annual monsoon rains increase its vulnerability. In 1998 the monsoon floods killed about 1,500 people and left 23 million people homeless. Furthermore, Bangladesh's precarious situation may be exacerbated by global warming.

Coastal Erosion

Erosion involves the modification of landforms by the wearing away of rock and soil and the removal of the resulting products (as opposed to weathering, which involves *in situ* modification). The agents of wind, water, ice, and living organisms are responsible for erosion. In chemical erosion, minerals in the rock react to other substances, such as weak acids found in rainwater, and are broken down. Physical erosion, on the other hand, invokes powerful forces such as rivers and glaciers to first abrade or break up rock and then transport it elsewhere. Erosion can have disastrous economic consequences, including the removal of topsoil, the gradual destruction of buildings, and the detrimental modification of river systems. In coastal regions most erosion is the result of wave-action, while inland the most dramatic erosion arises from the action of rivers.

Shaping the coasts

Over hours or days, atmospheric movements may result in considerable changes in the surface waters of the oceans. When strong winds combine with high tides, the water-level at the coast may rise much higher than normal, sometimes resulting in coastal flooding and the penetration of salt waters into estuaries. Most coastal erosion occurs, however, over much longer periods of time as a consequence of battering by storm waves generated during a particular season of the year by strong atmospheric disturbances. In many areas, beaches change their shape from season to season, reflecting differences in the predominant wind direction and consequent changes in the sites of deposition and erosion along the shore. Winds that are at a slight angle to the shoreline result in the lateral movement of the water mass (along the shorelines), which in turn causes the drift of sediment in the direction of the current.

Eroding shorelines

Shorelines are highly varied in their form since they are shaped by the action of both wind and waves. The movement of material by currents in near-shore waters may result in the deposition of sands, gravel or larger material, such as boulders, depending on the power of the waves. In other areas, where sedimentary material is scarce and the waves move material away from the shoreline, erosion dominates the coast. Eroding shorelines tend to occur in areas of high wave energy, while depositional shorelines are characteristic of sheltered coasts.

▼ *Rivers (1) erode their channels through the flow of water and the abrasion of the load they are carrying against the banks and riverbed. Erosion is most forceful at the outside of bends (2), where the banks are undercut (3), often creating cliffs or bluffs (4) down which material moves. Flood-surges magnify the erosive force. On a smaller scale, rainwater will move material down a hillside (5). Soil is thrown down a slope by the impact of raindrops or by rivulets, which carry particles of soil. Vegetation reduces such erosion by binding the soil together.*

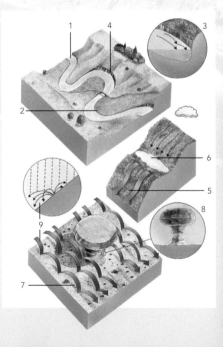

Where vegetation is removed, as on tracks (6), erosion is accentuated. In arid conditions, wind erosion can carve distinctive features. Sand and stones blown by the wind (7) have the same effect as shot-blasting, and mushroom-shaped formations or pedestals (8) are often the result. These are caused because there is a maximum height at which the erosive sand is carried by the wind (9), and above that height the rock is untouched.

▼ *The erosive power of the sea exploits areas of weakness in a hard rock deposit (1). Waves will then cut away any softer rock behind (2), eroding back until they reach another strata of harder rock (3). When bays join (4), islands of hard rock can be left across the mouth (5).*

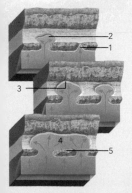

An upland area sloping gently into the sea is not a stable configuration, and waves soon attack the slope and erode it at the base. The first-formed feature of coastal erosion is usually a notch in the slope, forming a small cliff at high-tide level. This is then worn back by the action of waves cutting into the base, forming an overhang that eventually collapses. A wave-cut platform is left as the cliff is worn back and an offshore terrace is built of eroded material.

Cliffs and other dramatic rocky features, such as the Giant's Causeway on the coast of north-west Ireland, characterize eroding shorelines. Although the height of cliffs facing the sea is largely determined by the height of the land behind them, their form depends on a wide variety of factors, including the properties of their constituent rocks and sediments, the local topography, and the geological structure. Great variations are possible but features such as promontories, blowholes, arches and sea stacks are frequently formed in well-jointed rocks, giving rise to some of the most distinctive coastal scenery.

The effect on different rock faces

In general the nature of eroding shorelines reflects the ability of the rock to resist the erosive forces of the waves and the suspended materials contained therein. It is not the water itself that erodes the land, but the sand, pebbles and gravel that are hurled against the cliff-face by the force of the waves. Most erosion takes place along weaknesses in the rock such as faults, joints, bedding planes and layers of softer material interspersed between harder bands. Erosion occurs in a relatively narrow band centred on mean sea-level; the width of the band being narrow in areas with a small tidal range and wider where the range is greater. The restricted width of the zone of active erosion means that the main removal of material occurs at the foot of the cliff and results in the slumping or collapse of materials as they are undercut by wave action. Where cliffs are made up of soft rock, the rate of erosion may be limited only by the rate at which longshore currents remove the slumped material from the base of the cliff where it forms a protective beach. In the case of hard rock formations, the undercutting may result in only infrequent collapse of the cliff-face above, and shallow sea-caves or overhangs may develop. A vertical cleft subjected to constant erosion will eventually enlarge to form a cave, due to the air therein being repeatedly compressed by wave action, and the resulting pressure forcing a hole in the roof. Continued deepening of caves on opposite sides of a headland causes them to meet, forming a rock arch. A natural arch will continue to widen until its lintel collapses, leaving an isolated sea-stack. In rocks such as sandstone, which have bedding planes, erosion occurs along the planes, wearing away softer strata more rapidly, leaving a ragged profile to the cliff face. In fine-grained rock, such as chalk, where bedding planes are poorly defined or non-existent, smooth, sheer cliff faces develop; while in basalt, erosion occurs along cooling joints giving the appearance that the rock is built of individual blocks.

COASTAL EROSION

Beaches at eroding shorelines

Along any eroding shoreline a beach of eroded material will be formed as the cliff-face collapses into the sea. These erosional products, removed by currents, may be deposited as an off-shore terrace or a wave-cut platform beneath the eroding face of the cliff or deposited further away from their source. The barrier-island coastline of eastern North America between New Jersey and South Carolina has been eroding from storms and hurricanes at varying rates since the 1930s. The amount of coastal erosion and accretion along the Atlantic coastline is spatially variable, ranging from +10 to −30 metres per year, but the effects are most severe when over-washing of the barrier islands occurs. Particularly dramatic erosion on the Atlantic seaboard was produced during the Ash Wednesday storm of 1962. On a global scale 70 percent of the world's sandy beaches are eroding at a rate of 0.5 to 1 metre (1.9–3.3 feet) per year. This appears to be partly the result of more frequent storms, perhaps related to climate change, but it can also be attributed in part to the construction of groynes and offshore breakwaters that inhibit the shoreward movement of sediment. Beachgoers also play a role in beach erosion.

Coastline evolution

When a wave approaches the shore, it slows down in shallow areas and on meeting an irregular coastline turns along the shore. Most of the wave's energy dissipates against project-ing headlands and as a result these erode more rapidly than bays or beaches where sand and gravel accumulate. Eventu-ally a headland may be completely eroded and a straight shoreline will evolve. A headland or cliff erodes first along joints or bedding planes, which enlarge to form deep clefts.

The beaches found at the foot of cliffs are transitory, often modifying their form with the season as changing wind and

▼ *Pacific Ocean eroding the beach under sea-front houses, at Pacifica, California, USA. The demand for ocean-view housing has encouraged development on fragile coastlines. The action of waves and weather on the world's coasts means that they are constantly changing shape. Houses on the coast risk destruction from crumbling foundations and assist in the destabilization of the very land on which they are built.*

wave patterns alter the rate of removal of the material. In general, the finer materials move more rapidly so that pebbles, cobbles and even boulders tend to dominate such beaches. Most of the erosional material that form these beaches are removed offshore to deeper waters, or moved along the coastline to more sheltered areas where depositional coastal formations occur. Along some coastlines, such as those of the eastern Mediterranean, pocket beaches are found at the heads of small inlets. High cliffs generally surround such beaches, which are highly susceptible to changes in sea level or wave patterns that can result in the sediments being lost offshore. On many Mediterranean islands that have been formed by uplift along fault lines, cliffs descend vertically into the sea and erosion rates may be quite slow since the tidal range is small. In contrast, along low-lying coastlines where relative sea-level is rising and the materials are soft and unconsolidated, erosion rates may be extremely high, as much as several metres a year. Often erosion occurs in short periods associated with storms, resulting in the development of a protective scree slope that is only gradually removed.

Urban coastlines

Currently, around 60 percent of the world's population lives within 60 km (40 miles) of the coast, and in many countries the proportion is much higher. In addition, the populations of coastal areas in many tropical countries are growing at twice national rates, due largely to migration from inland areas to the coast. This problem is not confined solely to developing countries. Historically, large-population centres tended to develop in coastal locations, deriving much of their economic viability from international trade and commerce. Today, more than two-thirds of the world's cities with populations greater than one million people are located on the coast. These centres often develop in highly productive estuarine areas where the productivity of both the coastal land and inshore waters are lost as a consequence of the urbanization of the land surface and pollution of the coastal waters through urban and industrial discharges.

Coastal development

As a consequence of these trends, problems of conflict between different uses of coastal space and inshore waters have escalated considerably in recent years, and demand for highly priced coastal land near major ports and harbours has resulted in expensive reclamation schemes. In some situations, where land is limited, such as on islands, the need for living space has necessitated the creation of new land on the surface of neighbouring coral reefs or in shallow water areas. This is exemplified by Male, capital of the Maldives, which occupies the entire surface of an island 1,700 metres (5,600 feet) long and 700 metres (2,300 feet) wide, on which 56,000 people live. Around half the island has been artificially constructed by pumping lagoon sand onto the coral reef flat to create new land. As a result, the island occupies virtually the entire surface of the coral-reef platform on which it stands, and the southern edge of the island is only some 30 metres (100 feet) from the edge of the reef platform. To protect the island, a sea wall was constructed around the entire perimeter to a height of about 2 metres (6.6 feet) above sea level. This wall proved to be an inadequate protection against long-distance swells from a severe storm in the Indian Ocean in 1987, which resulted in extensive flooding of Male. A breakwater, costing US$12,000 per metre (US$39,000 per foot), has now been built on the southern side of the island in an attempt to prevent a recurrence of the event. Land reclamation and the subsequent need to protect the investment inevitably results in further investment in protection. A good example is the Thames Flood Barrier (see page 102) in London, England, which will have to be upgraded within the next 30 years if it is to remain an effective protection.

Coastal investment and protection

As the investment in coastal areas soars, so does the need to protect that investment against flooding, storm surges, tsunami and the general erosive action of winds and waves. Shorelines are armoured, sea walls constructed, groynes extended seawards, and beaches replenished with sand to cater for the increasing influx of tourist visitors to coastal areas. Shorelines change under natural conditions, with sediment moved onshore and offshore according to the relative influence of different wind and wave patterns. In many areas, sediment is moved along a coastline (longshore drift) and the construction of hard structures at right angles to the shore interrupts this flow of sediment, resulting in accretion on the up-current side of the groyne and enhanced erosion on the down-current side.

The dynamic nature of natural shorelines is an inconvenience to many human activities, and authorities expend considerable effort trying to hold the shoreline in a constant position. A retreating coast, which threatens structures such as

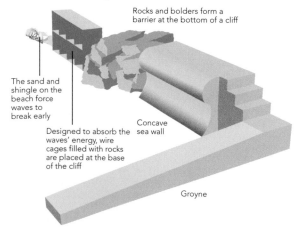

Rocks and bolders form a barrier at the bottom of a cliff

The sand and shingle on the beach force waves to break early

Designed to absorb the waves' energy, wire cages filled with rocks are placed at the base of the cliff

Concave sea wall

Groyne

◀ Groynes are one of a number of common sea defences designed to stop the erosion of the shoreline. The aim of the defences is to absorb the force of larger waves and to resist gradual erosion by smaller waves and currents. A low barrier of concrete or wood is built out into the sea from a seawall or promenade. It slows down the movement of longshore drift, and

hotels or roads, may be armoured. Although this may protect the individual site, it frequently results in increased erosion elsewhere along the coast as these structures alter the pattern of waves and local currents. In many seaside tourist resorts, hotels are constructed close to the shore, often without proper regard to the dynamic changes that might be expected as a consequence. When erosion commences, sea walls may be built to protect a hotel, and groynes constructed in an attempt to trap sand on the beach area in front. Loss of sand may result in expensive beach replenishment schemes, so sand is pumped from deeper waters offshore onto the beach to maintain the beach's form. Like dredging of harbours and estuaries, this activity is an on-going expense.

The nature of many coastlines around the world are being dramatically altered. In many places, such as the Netherlands, the entire coastline is artificial and what was once a dynamic boundary between land and sea, subject to erosion and/or accretion, has been fixed in space. Much of the Netherlands is actually below sea level, having been reclaimed through the construction of dykes and the pumping out of water from the resulting enclosed polder. Land reclamation inevitably requires protection, and maintaining this dry land requires constant and continuous pumping of water into the sea from behind the protective dykes that line the coast. Many of these dykes are based on old sand dune systems, but unlike the dunes, which would have changed position over time, the dykes must be constantly maintained if the sea is not to encroach on what has become intensive farmland and densely populated areas. Maintaining artificial coastlines will become increasingly expensive as global warming causes an acceleration in sea-level rise.

Changing levels of the sea

Anyone who has lived near the sea or spent time on the seashore is aware of the daily rhythm of the tides. The tides can change the meeting point of sea and land by as much as 15 metres (50 feet) vertically and several kilometres horizontally. In addition to the daily variation in sea-level resulting from the tidal cycle, the position of high and low water varies between spring and neap tides depending on the phase of the lunar cycle. Unusually high water-levels may occur when onshore winds occur at the same time as high tides. During such events, seawater may penetrate far inland along freshwater courses and inundate coastal land that is normally above sea level.

The more subtle and gradual changes in sea level are less obvious. Some of these changes represent long-term trends, such as the observed rise in global sea level of around 1.5 mm (0.06 inches) per year that has occurred over the last century. In contrast, other changes represent shorter-term responses to major shifts in ocean currents, such as the lowering of sea level in the western Pacific by as much as 14 cm (5.5 inches) during El Niño years. Far greater changes in sea level have occurred in the recent geological past, with the glacial and interglacial periods being marked by changes in sea level of up to 120 m (394 feet).

also protects the seawall from the direct battering of the waves. The length and number of groynes depend on the angle at which the prevailing waves come in to shore. Many coastal towns erect groynes in order to protect the coastline and save money on sea defences, since groynes are more cheaply and easily repaired and replaced than buildings or roads.

Ice Hazards

On April 15, 1912, the *Titanic*, the largest ship afloat at the time, left on her maiden voyage across the North Atlantic. The ensuing catastrophe is well known: the liner collided with an iceberg and about 1,500 people out of a total of 2,200 passengers and crew lost their lives. After the tragedy, an International Ice Patrol was established to track the movement of icebergs and warn ships of their location.

Icebergs

Huge glaciers, which are very slowly moving masses of freshwater ice, cover Greenland and Antarctica. At their edges, over bays and other sheltered waters, a permanent ice-shelf forms that seasonally seeds the ocean with floating chunks of ice, or icebergs, that eventually find their way to the open seas. Close to their source, these hazards to shipping can rise 60 metres (200 feet) above the ocean's surface and extend several times that below the surface at their point of origin. They typically wear away to maybe one-tenth that size by the time they reach warmer latitudes. Icebergs rarely move further south than 40°N latitude or farther north than 40°S latitude – one exception being a berg reported, in 1894, close to the Tropic of Capricorn, at 23.5°S latitude. The year the *Titanic* sank there was an extraordinary number of icebergs in the North Atlantic, but even in ordinary years icebergs on the open sea constitute significant menaces to shipping, fishing, and offshore oil-drilling.

Sea ice

Icebergs are formed from freshwater land ice, although sea ice can also prove to be an oceanographic hazard. There is a permanent cover of sea ice 3 to 4 metres (10 to 13 feet) thick over 70 percent of the Arctic Ocean and encircling the Antarctic continent. For much of the year, solid and floating sea ice is also found around Greenland, Iceland, the many northern islands of Canada and Russia, and the oil-drilling areas off Norway and Scotland. Icebreakers, ships that are equipped to cut a channel

▼ *Pack ice in the Antarctic Peninsula, Antarctica. Pack ice breaks off from icebergs and glaciers and floats away. It is generally found in more enclosed waters and can create blockages in shipping routes. Fast-moving pack ice can be a danger to shipping and oil platforms.*

through icebound waters for other boats to follow, make passage possible during part of the year through such icy waters as the Barents Sea, Norwegian Sea, and Arctic Ocean. When ocean currents and winds form hummocks or pressure ridges on the sea ice, ice can form a barrier that even the breakers cannot penetrate. Pack ice is another problem, forming from chunks of floating sea ice driven together into a single mass. It occurs in the more enclosed bodies of water in the higher latitudes, such as the Bering and Baltic Seas, the seas of Japan and Okhotsk, and the Gulf of St Lawrence. When pack ice drives toward the shore, it can block harbours, and, like icebergs, drifting pack ice can also threaten offshore oil-drilling platforms.

▶ Icebergs form in several ways. When a glacier reaches the sea, it floats away from the bed. The movement of waves and tides exerts pressures on this floating ice, causing lumps to break away (A). If the glacier is moving rapidly when it reaches the sea, a projecting shelf of ice forms under the water. The buoyancy of this shelf exerts an upward pressure causing pieces to break off (B). The snout of the glacier may be above the level of the sea, and lumps may break off under the force of gravity and fall into the water (C). The forming of new icebergs is known as 'calving'. Illustrations D to I show typical shapes of icebergs. Northern icebergs come from the Greenland ice-sheet, but the largest bergs (J) originate in Antarctica. The largest iceberg ever reported was 336 km (208 miles) long and 97 km (60 miles) wide.

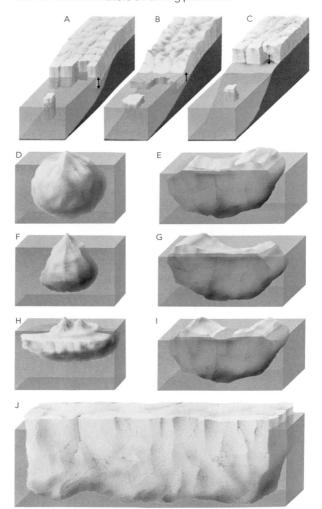

Flooding

Floods are the result of a multitude of naturally occurring and human-induced factors, either acting singly or in concert, but they can all be simply defined as the accumulation of too much water in too little time in a specific area. Floods can be classified as river floods and coastal floods. The former is usually atmospherically driven and arises from excessive precipitation, but can also be caused by landslides into a river, by dam or levee failures or by ice-jams. Coastal floods typically result from storm surges associated with tropical cyclones and mid-latitude windstorms, but can also be produced by tectonically - initiated tsunami. Sudden flooding events, often triggered by extreme precipitation in mountainous regions are termed flash floods.

Regional floods

Very large-scale flooding, sufficient to affect an entire geographical region, often occurs seasonally when winter or spring rains, coupled with melting snow, fill river basins with too much water too quickly. As in the case of the central European floods of 2002, regional floods may also occur as a result of sustained, extreme precipitation over a few days at any time of the year. In the case of winter and spring floods, the ground may be frozen, reducing infiltration into the soil and thereby increasing runoff. Such was the case for the New England, USA, flood of March 1936, in which more than 200 lives were lost and property damage totalled US$300 million. Extended wet periods during any part of the year can produce saturated soil conditions, after which any additional rain runs off into streams and rivers, until river capacities are exceeded. Regional floods are often associated with meteorological conditions that involve slow moving, low-pressure or frontal storm systems including decaying

▼ ► Map and table detailing 20 of the worst floods since 1900. China has the worst history of flooding. South America and Bangladesh also suffered from 'killer' floods. In China, the majority of flooding disasters take place along the densely populated banks of the Yangtze and Huange He (Yellow) rivers. The Yangtze River basin has a population of 80 million, most of whom work in agriculture and rely on the river. In 2003, China closed the sluice gates of the huge Three Gorges dam, a project designed to ease the burden on the Yangtze river and generate electricity. The project, which will create a lake 600 km (375 miles) long, is steeped in controversy and has already displaced 600,000 people.

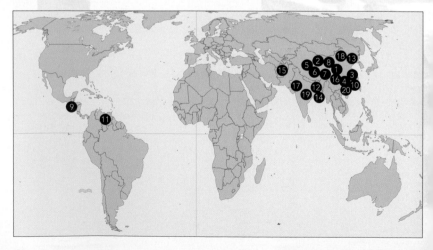

		MAJOR FLOODS SINCE 1900		
	Location	Date	Killed	Total Affected
1	China	July 1931	3,700,000	28,500,000
2	northern China	July 1959	2,000,000	
3	Henan, China	July 1938	500,000	
4	Henan, China	July 1939	500,000	
5	China	1935	142,000	10,030,000
6	China	1908	100,000	
7	China	1911	100,000	
8	China	July 1949	57,000	
9	eastern Guatemala	October 1949	40,000	
10	Wuhan, Hubei, China	August 1954	30,000	
11	Venezuela	December 19, 1999	30,000	483,635
12	Bangladesh	1960	28,700	38,000,000
13	China	1933	18,000	3,600,000
14	Bangladesh	1960	10,000	
15	Afghanistan	June 1988	6,345	166,831
16	China	June 1980	6,200	67,000
17	India	July 1968	4,892	7,500,000
18	Manchuria, China	August 28, 1951	4,800	
19	north and north-east India	July 1978	3,800	32,000,000
20	China	August 6, 1998	3,656	238,973,000

hurricanes or tropical storms, and deep depressions at higher latitudes. Persistent wet meteorological patterns are usually responsible for very large regional floods such as the 1993 Mississippi River Basin flood in the Midwest of the United States, in which damage costs approached US$12 billion.

The Mississippi flood, USA, 1993

In the summer of 1993, the Mississippi and its tributaries overwhelmed levees, erased towns, knocked out bridges and airports, and rearranged the landscape of much of the US Midwest. US citizens watched as week after week television cameras captured the spectacle of inexorably rising waters, people's desperate efforts to barricade their homes and towns by heaping sandbags, concrete, dirt and rock upon the levees, and their desperation as the river repeatedly undid their work. By the end of the summer, the flood had spread across 354 counties in nine states, causing 45 fatalities, displacing at least 50,000 people, and inundating 13.5 million acres (5.46 million hectares).

In April 1993 the great flood started in Iowa, when the usual spring rains refused to let up. All spring and early summer and into August, parts of the Midwest received as much as 10 times the normal amount of rainfall, which swelled the

Mississippi and its 50 tributaries, including the Missouri and Ohio rivers. The Mississippi is the largest river in the United States, draining 3.25 million square km (1.25 million square miles). Ordinarily when its waters rise, there is a backflow into its tributaries. These waters then rise higher than normal and overflow their banks and levees in local floods of small or medium magnitude. What made the 1993 flood such an unprecedented catastrophe was that the unceasing rains resulted in most of the tributaries being in full spate simultaneously – the first time this had happened in history. With nowhere for the waters to back up, they flowed down in a slow, inexorable tide, overtopping embankments and reclaiming floodplains. Where farms and towns had once flourished, now there were huge lakes. Rescue boats cruised among the rooftops, picking up stranded people.

The Mississippi River had flooded badly before, and in the course of the previous centuries a grand scheme of 28 locks and dams and more than 9,000 km (5,600 miles) of levees had been built to keep the river and its tributaries manageable and navigable. The locks and dams held up well, as did almost all of the levees built by the federal government. But 70 percent of the levees on the Mississippi floodplain, mostly built by the municipalities or the private sector, failed.

The central European floods, 2002
One of the most devastating regional floods occurred in central Europe in August 2002, when sustained and torrential rainfall from two depressions approached the Czech Republic, Austria and Germany from the south in quick succession. These meteorological conditions were similar to those that had triggered similar widespread flooding in the region in 1997. As the first of the two low-pressure systems

▼ *Evacuation of residents following the flooding of the Mississippi River, USA, July 11, 1993. Heavy rains simultaneously overwhelmed each of the river's tributaries, causing unprecedented flooding. The floods caused US$12 billion worth of damage, the most expensive US flood and the fifth most costly flood of the 20th century.*

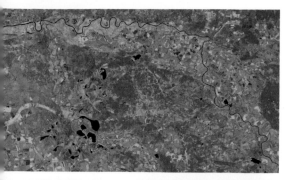

▲ *In 2002, heavy rains in central and eastern Europe led to the worst flooding the region had witnessed in more than a century. The false-colour image of the River Elbe and its tributaries (bottom) was taken on August 20, 2002, 14 days after the flooding began. On the right-hand side of the image, the Elbe resembles a lake just south of the town of Wittenberg, east-central Germany. Earlier in the week, the floodwaters inundated Dresden to the south. In Dresden, the water reached levels not seen since 1845. Normally, the river would resemble a thin line (top image, August 14, 2000).*

swung north from the Mediterranean Sea, they caused flash floods in Italy and Austria, saturating the ground and swelling the rivers. The second system followed, dumping more than 40 cm (16 inches) of rain over the Elbe and Vltava catchments in just three days. Widespread flooding started on August 6, and continued until the end of the month, with peak discharges on the Vltava, the Danube and the Elbe exceeding any volumes recorded in more than a century. The great floods resulted in more than 320,000 people being evacuated in Germany and the Czech Republic alone. In Germany, Dresden bore the brunt of the flooding but severe damage to buildings and infrastructure occurred all along the Elbe as far as Hamburg. The Czech capital, Prague, was also severely affected, with many historic buildings badly damaged and the underground railway system inundated. Tens of thousands of homes were affected in Upper and Lower Austria, Salzburg, the Tyrol, and along the Danube in Slovakia. Transportation was seriously disrupted for months and extensive power cuts resulted from damaged electrical installations. Economic losses were estimated at US$18.5 billion, and the event proved to be the largest insured loss of the year.

Flash floods

Flash floods occur with little or no warning on time scales ranging from several seconds to several hours. They can be deadly because they result in rapid rises in water levels and have devastating flow-velocities. Several factors contribute to flash flooding. Among these are rainfall intensity and duration, surface conditions, and topography – especially the slope of the receiving basin. Urban areas are particularly susceptible to flash floods because drainage channels are often fixed (as culverts, storm drains, or canalized rivers and streams) and a high percentage of the surface area is covered by impervious concrete and tarmac and building roofs from which runoff occurs very rapidly. Mountainous areas are also highly susceptible to flash floods, as steep topography may funnel runoff into narrow valleys or canyons. The most important factor in flash floods is not the size of the water channel, but the peak discharge of the floodwaters compared to mean annual discharge. Damaging floods are those that produce discharges many times higher than the mean discharge. Small streams have a high flash-flood potential if they are in an area of steep slope, thin soil cover, and intense local rainfall.

Floodwaters accelerated by steep stream slopes can cause the flood wave to move downstream too fast to allow escape, either on foot or in vehicles, and can increase the death toll. Flood waves in excess of 10 metres (33 feet) have been reported many kilometres from the intense rainfall that may have sourced the flood, catching people unaware. Dry stream courses (arroyos) in desert areas are also commonly utilized by flash floods, often as a consequence of thunderstorms that might be quite remote but which can still produce rapid rises in water levels in the otherwise dry channels. Early-warning gauges upstream in these and similar environments can save lives by providing advanced notice of potential deadly flood waves.

A thunderstorm in the wrong terrain can produce a sudden violent flood capable of devastating a sizable area. When heavy rains fall over an area that drains into steep trenches, these quickly choke, forming torrential streams that can travel many kilometres with astonishing speed. The climate and topography of the south-west of America make it particularly vulnerable to these flash floods. Central Texas, although dry for most of the year, is seasonally subjected to harsh storms coming in from the Gulf of Mexico, when its steep drainage slopes make it prone to flash floods. Colorado, Utah, Arizona, and southern California are other areas whose terrains make them susceptible to flash floods during sudden brief storms. It is not just the water that provides flash floods with their destructive power. As the torrent pours through gullies and small valleys, it picks up masses of earth, rock, and other debris. In these circumstances, the flood can turn into a dense, viscous mudflow that slows and spreads out, pushing boulders, trees, cars, and even houses before it.

In areas with good vegetation cover and deep soil, most water

▼ *Watersheds and major rivers. Most major floods occur when heavy rains causes a river to burst its banks. The worst floods of the past century were caused by the world's largest rivers. These included the Huang He (Yellow) and Yangtze Rivers in China, the Ganges in Bangladesh, the Indus in Pakistan, the Rhine in Germany, the Paraná in South America, and the Mississippi in USA.*

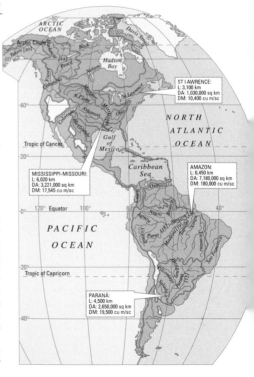

[1] = Rivers ranked by length
L = Length
DA = Drainage area
DM = Discharge of river at mouth in cubic metres per second

Caribbean Sea-Gulf of Mexico

Mediterranean Sea

Arctic Ocean

Atlantic Ocean

Pacific Ocean

Indian Ocean

Inland basins, ice caps and deserts

generated by storms can be absorbed. In arid lands with only a thin covering of soil, the surface layers become saturated much more quickly and water flow over the surface begins sooner. If the intensity of the rain exceeds the rate at which the soil can absorb the water, runoff rapidly courses down hills and fills channels to cause flash floods. Heavy storms, while not very common, can devastate areas with steep slopes and thin soil. In 1935, for example, a flood of some 12 million cubic metres (424 million cubic feet) of water passed through the city of Colorado Springs in the central United States in just two hours, causing immense damage. The stream bed, dry for most of the year, could have accommodated this amount of water if it had taken 20 hours or longer to fall, but the speed and intensity of the flood, rather than the total amount of water, created severe problems.

In arid areas, flooding of permanently flowing rivers can also cause problems. For example, in 1988 the River Nile breached its banks, causing much destruction in Sudan. In 1990, it was reported from Mogadishu that tens of thousands of people had been evacuated in southern Somalia when their villages, which are built in normally arid areas,

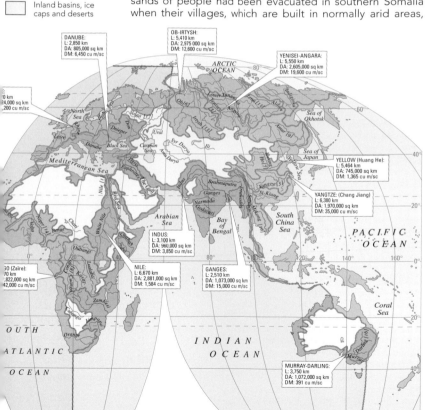

DANUBE:
L: 2,850 km
DA: 805,000 sq km
DM: 6,450 cu m/sc

OB-IRTYSH:
L: 5,410 km
DA: 2,975,000 sq km
DM: 12,600 cu m/sc

YENISEI-ANGARA:
L: 5,550 km
DA: 2,605,000 sq km
DM: 19,600 cu m/sc

YELLOW (Huang He):
L: 5,464 km
DA: 745,000 sq km
DM: 1,365 cu m/sc

YANGTZE: (Chang Jiang)
L: 6,380 km
DA: 1,970,000 sq km
DM: 35,000 cu m/sc

INDUS:
L: 3,100 km
DA: 960,000 sq km
DM: 3,850 cu m/sc

NILE:
L: 6,670 km
DA: 2,881,000 sq km
DM: 1,584 cu m/sc

GANGES:
L: 2,510 km
DA: 1,073,000 sq km
DM: 15,000 cu m/sc

MURRAY-DARLING:
L: 3,750 km
DA: 1,072,000 sq km
DM: 391 cu m/sc

were submerged under the floodwaters of the River Juba. Such events are difficult to monitor and predict, and the water does not benefit anyone because much of it runs off into oceans and is lost.

Flash floods are common across the world, affecting developed and developing countries alike. Most recently, in October 2000, torrential rains triggered flash floods and mudslides in Italy and Switzerland, taking 28 lives. Again, in 2002, western Europe was hit badly when flash floods struck south-east France, claiming 24 lives and resulting in the evacuation of more than 1,000 people due to rapid flooding of the River Rhône. Vineyards producing Châteauneuf-du-Pape red wine were badly affected and in the town of Gard more than 80 percent of vineyards were destroyed and more than a dozen wine-producing centres badly damaged. Up to 67 cm (26 inches) of rain fell in some places, more than three times the annual rainfall for Paris. Around the city of Nîmes, floodwater was up to 3 metres (10 feet) deep.

▲ *A car drives down a flooded street in Mogadishu, capital of Somalia, in December 7, 1992. The River Juba (Giuba) in southern Somalia is prone to flash flooding.*

Ice-jam floods

Ice-jam floods occur on rivers that are totally or partially frozen when a rise in water level breaks up the frozen channel to form ice flows that pile up against bridges and other potential obstructions. The jammed ice effectively creates a dam, upstream of which water levels rise rapidly and overflow the channel banks. Flooding moves downstream when the dam fails, and the water stored behind it is released. At this time, the flood takes on the characteristics of a flash flood, with the added danger of ice flows that, when driven by the energy of the flood wave, can cause serious damage to structures. Anyone unlucky enough to be caught up in an ice-jam flood

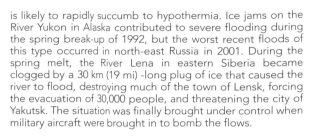

▼ *In the first image, taken on May 22, 2001, the mostly frozen River Lena in Siberia appears as a white ribbon. In the second image, taken only eight days later, large sections of the Lena and the River Vilyuy seem to have almost completely thawed. Explosives were detonated to dislodge huge blocks of ice that blocked rivers and caused serious flooding.*

is likely to rapidly succumb to hypothermia. Ice jams on the River Yukon in Alaska contributed to severe flooding during the spring break-up of 1992, but the worst recent floods of this type occurred in north-east Russia in 2001. During the spring melt, the River Lena in eastern Siberia became clogged by a 30 km (19 mi) -long plug of ice that caused the river to flood, destroying much of the town of Lensk, forcing the evacuation of 30,000 people, and threatening the city of Yakutsk. The situation was finally brought under control when military aircraft were brought in to bomb the flows.

Storm-surge floods

Storm-surge flooding involves the inundation of coastal margins by the sea due to severe onshore winds, often accompanied by low atmospheric pressure and sometimes by high tides. Friction between the water and the moving air creates drag that, depending upon the distance over which this occurs (fetch) and the velocity of the wind, can pile up water to depths greater than 7 metres (23 feet). Intense, low-pressure systems and hurricanes are the main instigators of storm-surge flooding, as pounding waves create very hazardous flood currents. Nine out of ten hurricane fatalities are caused by the storm surge, which is at its most dangerous when coincident with high tide. Storm surges may also trigger river flooding inland through impeding the entry of river water into the sea.

In September 1900, a hurricane and storm surge at Galveston, southern Texas, killed more than 6,000 people, making it the worst natural disaster in the history of the United States. More recently, in February 1953, a strong storm surge struck the coasts of the Netherlands and eastern England, breaking through coastal defences and taking more than 2,000 lives. Much of the Netherlands, in particular, is below sea-level and protected from the sea by an extensive system of dykes. The 1953 storm surge collapsed many of the dykes, drowning 1,800 people and flooding 324,000 hectares (800,000 acres). This storm surge, with a probability of occurring once every 400 years, had a height of 2.7 metres (9 feet). The Dutch subsequently raised their dykes to withstand a 5 metre (16.4 foot) -high storm surge. *See also* **Storm surge**, pages 78–81

Dam- and levee-failure floods

Dams and levees are built for flood protection and are usually engineered to withstand a flood with a computed risk of occurrence. For example, a dam or levee may be designed to contain a flood at a location on a stream that has a certain probability of occurring in any one year – one in

250 years say. If a larger flood occurs, then that structure will be overtopped, and if – during the overtopping – the dam or levee fails or is washed out, the water behind it is released to become a flash flood. Failed dams or levees can create floods that are catastrophic to life and property because of the tremendous energy involved in the sudden, catastrophic release of water.

Dam and levee failure remains a relatively common event, which does not provide a good advert for their engineering and construction. On June 9, 1972, in the Black Hills of South Dakota, USA, more than 1 metre (3.3 feet) of rain fell in six hours, with pressure of accumulated water causing a dam to break. A wall of water engulfed Rapid City, South Dakota, killing 237 people and leaving thousands injured. Property damage, including 1,500 destroyed cars, is estimated to have cost US$1.2 billion. Dam failures are commonly caused by inadequate maintenance. Other causes include poor design and inadvertent location on an unstable geological feature. On June 4, 1976, almost exactly four years after the Black Hills' event, the Teton Dam in south-east Idaho collapsed. Forewarning reduced the death toll to 11 people.

The Johnstown Dam disaster, USA, 1889

On May 31, 1889, one of the worst dam disasters in United States' history occurred in Johnstown, eastern Pennsylvania. Johnstown was a steel-producing city of 10,000 inhabitants and a 40-year old earthen dam that impounded Lake Cone-maugh, perched at a height of 150 metres (490 feet) and 17 km (11 miles) from the city. The dam, completed in 1852, was 90 metres (295 feet) wide at the base, 7 metres (23 feet) wide at the top, and 27 metres (89 feet) high. Five cast-iron pipes, about 70 cm (27.5 inches), in diameter were set into stone culverts at the base to allow for drainage. Famous industrial-

▼ *Debris from the Vaiont Dam tragedy covers a bridge, October 10, 1963, Longarone, north-east Italy. Floodwaters unleashed by the dam roared through this Alpine valley region, killing more than 2,000 people and shattering half a dozen villages.*

▲ Flooding of the Conemaugh River in July 1977, Johnstown, eastern Pennsylvania, USA. Johnstown was the site of one of the worst natural disasters in the history of the United States. On May 31, 1889, after torrential rain, the South Fork Dam collapsed, sending 20 million tonnes of water from its reservoir down the valley of the Little Conemaugh River, carrying away people, livestock, and houses.

ists, among them Henry Clay Frick, Benjamin Ruff, Andrew Carnegie and Andrew Mellon, either ignorant or unaware that the cast-iron pipes had been ripped out by the previous owner and sold for scrap in 1875, developed an elaborate recreational preserve, the South Fork Fishing and Hunting Club that surrounded the lake above the dam. Attempts were made to strengthen the dam with rock and other debris, but members of the club had little understanding of the drainage requirements needed for a dam, such as discharge canals and culverts. In May 1885, a road was built across the spillway for the convenience of the industrialists, which had the unfortunate effect of lowering the crest of the dam by nearly 2 metres (6.6 feet).

Earthen dams are vulnerable to collapse from excessive rainfall that erodes the face of the dam, leading eventually to failure of the entire structure. On May 31, 1889, after torrential rains, the Johnstown Dam broke, discharging a wall of water 20–30 metres (66–100 feet) high. The entire lake behind the dam emptied in about 36 minutes, destroying Johnstown and seven other towns in the valley. A stone-arch railroad bridge withstood the strain but acted as a collection point for flood-driven debris such as houses, trees, telegraph poles, and locomotives. The debris pile caught fire from an overturned railway carriage, and about 100 people clinging to the debris pile burned to death. In total, 2,209 people lost their lives in the Johnstown flood, one of the worst disasters to strike the United States in the post-Civil War period. There is no doubt that the dam was of faulty construction, lacking discharge pipes or conduits at its base and that the surrounding land had been stripped of its protective timber, thereby promoting rapid run-off. The heavy, unprecedented rains brought on the disaster, but repairs and maintenance of the dam were lacking, apparently due to indifference or ignorance on the part of the club members.

The Vaiont Dam disaster, Italy, 1963

In 1963, Europe was struck by a devastating flood resulting from the construction of a dam across a tributary of the River Paive river in the Alps of north-eastern Italy. At 262 metres (860 feet) the dam – one of the tallest in the world – blocked a narrow defile where the tributary entered the main Piave valley. The dam was completed in 1961, and the filling of the reservoir behind it began soon after. Two years later, it became apparent that the rising water levels were destabilising Mount

Toc, causing the entire mountain to slide towards the growing lake. Engineers attempted to control the landslide by lowering water levels, but to no avail. Following torrential rain, the mountain slid into the lake on the night of October 9, generating a gigantic wave that overtopped the dam and swept down the Piave valley. Within minutes, the flood had killed more than 2,000 people, obliterating the town of Longarone and neighbouring settlements. The dam still stands, largely undamaged, as testimony to this terrible man-made flood.

Natural dam-failures may also result in catastrophic floods. These include the bursting of ice-dammed lakes (floods known by the Icelandic term *jokulhaups*), failure of the walls of volcanic crater-lakes, and the overtopping of landslides that have dammed river valleys.

Debris flows

Debris flows are mixtures of water, mud and debris of various consistencies ranging from muddy water to a thick, viscous sludge. They can form in a number of ways, but all are characterized by the combination of debris and a large mass of water. Torrential rains falling on exposed ground can rapidly trigger debris flows as happened at Sarno, Campani, southwest Italy in 1998, where devastating flows killed more than a hundred people and left thousands homeless. Volcanic mudflows (known as lahars) are also common, and were generated by the eruptions of Mount St Helens, Washington State, USA, in 1980, and at Mount Pinatubo, Philippines, in 1991. Lahars were also responsible for one of the worst volcanic disasters of the last century, when pyroclastic flows melted the ice-and-snow cap of the Nevado del Ruiz volcano in west-central Colombia. Billions of litres of water poured down the valleys that drained the volcano, mixing with debris to form thick, muddy flows that killed nearly 23,000 people in Armero and neighbouring towns.

▼ Map of Bangladesh showing the areas affected by the great floods in 1998. The areas worst affected were around the Ganges, Brahmaputra, and Padma rivers.

Affected areas

Severely affected areas

Bangladesh floods, 1998

Bangladesh is an extremely low-lying country, which is prone to annual flooding, but between July and October 1998, it was devastated by prolonged floods that, at their height, affected almost two-thirds of the country and lasted for more than two- and-a-half months. The last major monsoon-related floods had been a decade earlier, but a cyclone in 1991 had killed 1,500 people and left a further 5 million people homeless. There is increasing evidence that the consequences of human activ-

ity exacerbated the effects of a particularly unfortunate group of environmental coincidences. Following an El Niño event in 1997, a La Niña event in 1998 led to greatly increased rainfall during the monsoon season both in Bangladesh and in the catchment areas of the Ganges and Brahmaputra rivers in Nepal and India. At this stage, the Bangladeshi government realized that the floods would be worse than usual, and instituted emergency measures. However, the true scale of the disaster had yet to emerge. Deforestation in Nepal caused greatly increased soil erosion there and silting up of the rivers farther downstream. As there was less soil to absorb the rain in Nepal, a greater volume of water flowed downstream more quickly, where the silted-up deltas did not have the capacity to absorb it. This problem was exacerbated by unregulated construction work, including roads, bridges, and homes that seriously interfered with normal drainage patterns and further increased surface runoff.

Finally, a combination of factors led to particularly high sea levels in the Bay of Bengal, which further hampered the flow of water from the rivers. La Niña caused sea-levels to rise slightly in the Indian Ocean, and added to this were high tides in mid-August and mid-September and a series of small surges caued by earthquakes in the Bay of Bengal. By mid-August, when the floodwaters would usually be expected to be receding, they were still rising and the government of Bangladesh decided to appeal for international aid. Original estimates showed that some US$2 billion would be needed to cover immediate food needs and the cost of reconstruction. By the time the floods peaked on September 14, more than 1,500 people had died and 23 million people were homeless. More than 100,000 square kilometres (38,500 square miles) of the country was affected: 575,000 hectares (1,420,856 acres) of farmland were underwater and more than 26,000 cattle had died. The damage to the country's infrastructure was huge: 16,000 km (10,000 miles) of roads, 4,500 km (2,800 miles) of embankments, 900,000 homes, and 6,900 bridges and culverts were damaged or destroyed. Once the floodwaters began to subside, the Bangladeshi government instituted a programme of dredging the rivers to remove excess silt in order to reduce this aspect of the problem, but many of the factors that led to the floods are beyond its control. Of particular concern is the possibility that raised sea-levels caused by global warming will cause permanent loss of land, and it is forecast that 16 percent of the country will be submerged by 2050.

Flood monitoring and forecasting

Effective flood-forecasting strongly depends on monitoring water flow in flood-prone areas. This data can be used to construct useful working models that are able to predict the conditions under which future flooding might occur. The United States Geological Survey (USGS) maintains such a monitoring network, comprising more than 7,000 stream-monitoring stations throughout the United States, Puerto Rico, and the Virgin Islands, which providing stream-flow data to federal, state, and local agencies as well as the general public. Some of these stream-gauging stations have been in operation since before 1900, providing more than a century of flow-data for the country. In addition to providing critical information on flood heights and discharges, these stations provide data used in the effective management of water supply and water quality, protection of aquatic habitat, recreation, and water-resources research. The basic building block for a stream-flow data network is the stage-discharge relation that is developed at each monitoring station. Measurements of the flow (discharge) are related graphically to the respective water depths (stage), which then enables the discharge to be determined from stage data. Discharge measurements can either be direct, using a current meter, or indirect, determined using mathematical flow equations. Both methods require that an elevation of the floodwater surface is determined by a water-depth gauge or by a detailed survey of high-water marks. If time allows and conditions are safe, a direct measurement by flood engineers is preferred. During major floods, direct measurements are often impossible or extremely dangerous, and indirect methods

▼ The Thames Barrier, London, England. If a high surge coincides with a high 'spring' tide (spring tides occur twice a month), there could be a real danger of flooding along most of the tidal Thames. The barrier is a series of ten separate movable gates positioned end-to-end across the river (1). Each gate is pivoted and supported between concrete piers that house the operating equipment (2). Closing the barrier seals off part of the upper Thames from the sea.

▼ *When not in use, the six rising gates of the Thames Barrier rest in curved recessed concrete cills on the riverbed, allowing free passage of river traffic though the openings between the piers (**A**). If a dangerously high tidal surge threatens, the rising sector gates are moved up though about 90° from their riverbed position and the four radial gates are bought down into the closed, defence position. The gates thus form a continuous steel wall facing down river ready to stem the tide (**B**).*

A Gate in open position (Flush with riverbed)

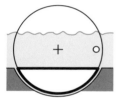

Gate rising

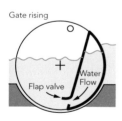

B Gate in flood-control position

must be used. Accurate identification and measurement of high-water marks from floods are very important in the accurate mapping of inundated areas as well as in the analysis of water-surface profiles for indirect discharge measurements. These elevations, in combination with flood frequency analysis using many years of annual flood maximums, are used by the US Federal Emergency Management Agency (FEMA) to determine flood-insurance rates.

Flood prevention and mitigation

River flooding has always been a hazard of global extent because large numbers of people have congregated on floodplains for their fertile soil and to benefit from the commercial advantages offered by a navigable river. What has changed in modern times is the degree to which the valleys of rivers and streams that drain away normal flood waters have become crowded, both in terms of population and industry. Floodplains have been modified to suit our needs to an unprecedented extent, and by paving over increasing amounts of the Earth's surface, we are minimizing natural drainage and increasing the risk of catastrophic floods. Where once a flood of great magnitude could flow with little consequence except, perhaps, to agriculture, today it can wreck the infrastructure of a nation.

At least, flood hazard is now recognized as a serious issue, and that is an important first step in mitigating the problem. Succeeding steps include accurate risk assessment, reliable forecasting, improved warning and emergency response systems, and sound flood-control programmes. In addition, much greater attention needs to be paid to controlling land-use in flood-prone areas.

Risk assessment for river floods involves an evaluation of the likelihood that a region will be inundated to a certain depth. The depth of a one-in-20-year flood is estimated and plans are made accordingly. This does not mean that a flood of the specified depth will definitely occur once every 20 years but that, on average, one such flood is to be expected every two decades. Prudent planning allows for this average recurrence interval. Damaging floods are costly and repeatedly demonstrate that the biggest flood hazard is not El Niño, failing levees, un-dammed rivers or melting ice, but rather the construction of new housing on the floodplains. In California, millions of people play the state lottery where the chance of winning is tens of millions to one, but the same people buy homes on floodplains never conceiving that there is a one-in-four chance that they will be flooded before their 30-year mortgage is paid off. In England, 11 percent of new homes (27 percent by value) built in recent years are located in the flood plain, an extraordinary statistic in a country where some five million people are already at risk from flooding.

Flood forecasting and warning systems are essential for minimizing loss of life and property damage, and most developed countries now have dedicated centres or agencies to monitor dangerous river conditions and warn people of coming floods. Developing countries, however, still have little in the way of a forecasting infrastructure, and effective flood warnings are rare. This is a major problem as the chance of saving lives rises in proportion to the length of the warning time.

Emergency response to flooding remains problematical in both developed and developing countries. The response of the US Federal Emergency Management Agency (FEMA) to the 1993 floods in the Midwest United States was creditable. Given a flood of this magnitude, it is vital to have in place a 'nerve centre' that can coordinate actions by federal, state, and local governments to avoid duplication in one area and inaction in another and, by and large, FEMA managed this very well. US local and state emergency-response systems in flood-prone areas have, however, ranged from excellent to inept in recent years. It is crucial that emergency personnel have a clear understanding of what kind of flood might happen, where it is likely to take place, and how quickly it will develop. They must also have well-trained workers, adequate supplies, and workable delivery systems. The same issues arise elsewhere in the world, and in 2002 were tested to the limit in Germany and the Czech Republic in the 2002 floods in central Europe.

Flood control systems
Flood control has been practiced by advanced civilizations for several millennia, although total control remains an ideal. One effective measure is to plant trees and deep-rooted grasses on natural drainage slopes in order to absorb more water. Another solution that has been implemented in many parts of the world, often in tandem with the first, is the con-

◀ *US Coast Guard personnel patrol the flooded streets of East Grand Forks, north-west Minnesota, April 1997. Water remained in this neighbourhood for more than a week after the river peaked.*

▲ A flooded residential area in the Midwest, United States, 1994. Homes, businesses, and personal property were all destroyed by the high flood levels. A total of 534 counties in nine states were declared for federal disaster aid. As a result of the floods, 168,340 people registered for federal assistance.

struction of flood-control reservoirs. If a second flood arrives soon after the first, it may not be possible to draw down the filled reservoirs in time to accept the new onslaught of flood waters, and in fact this is exactly what happened in the 2002 floods in central Europe. Sedimentation (or siltation) is also a problem in many rivers. This shallows the river and ensures that even a small volume of excess water will make the river overflow. Dredging to deepen the river channel is an expensive but not impossible solution.

The most elaborate systems of flood-control use dams, locks, dykes, diversion channels, and levees in an attempt to bend rivers to our will. These protective systems have permitted expansion of agricultural land, improved transportation, and enabled the building of communities, often on land unsuitable for housing. The 1993 flood in the US Midwest played an important role in transforming thinking about flood control in the US, where relentless development of the floodplains has been cancelling out flood-control programmes. More than anything else, the 1993 floods demonstrated how the most ingenious schemes for impeding the natural flow of a river in full flood can exacerbate the situation. Every containing dam, every levee to prevent overflow of the riverbanks, every obstruction that is put in the river's way, raises the level of the waters behind the obstruction, and increases the potential flood level. Removing some of these human-made obstructions would increase the discharge capacity of many river channels, and make serious flooding less likely.

Given the great demand for housing and industrial development, land-use controls are controversial the world over. But it is time to acknowledge that we cannot do without them. Ideally, housing and industrial construction should not be permitted in areas that are estimated to be susceptible to a one-in-10-year severe flood. It may indeed be cheaper to maintain farmland as a natural floodplain than to build, or rebuild levees. These areas could become nature reserves with perhaps limited hunting and fishing allowed. Environmental laws need to be enforced against the dumping of mining refuse in rivers, mill sluice-gates, excessive fish-traps, weirs, and over-expansive bridge piers, all of which obstruct the flow of water and raise the likelihood of flooding. Flood prevention and mitigation requires that we spend both on flood control and on slowing or stopping the development of river floodplains, and this applies equally well to China and Bangladesh as it does to the United States, Germany, or the United Kingdom.

Winds

Dust devils and other small-scale wind phenomena

Dust devils are small whirlwinds of dust and sand commonly found in arid and semi-arid regions of the world. A dust devil can turn into a disturbingly strong vortex, leaving an individual completely disoriented if the sun is directly overhead. Warm air from extreme surface heating during the summer is the main contributor to the formation of these phenomena. Their vortices are too small to be governed by the Coriolis effect that controls the rotation direction of tropical cyclones – so dust devils can rotate either counter-clockwise or clockwise. They are typically only a few metres across with heights of about 100 metres (330 feet), but wind speeds can reach 100 kilometres per hour (60 mph). Dust devils are short-lived phenomena, usually lasting up to several minutes, and it is very rare for them to persist for an hour or more. A dust devil is not a fatal hazard but, when it appears to track you across the open plain or desert, it can be a terrifying experience.

Strong updrafts of air, resembling dust devils but modified by variations in topography, are found in mountainous regions bordering plains. One notable site for tornado-like vortices generated by strong winds blowing over the surface is Boulder, Colorado, a community bordering the eastern front of the Rocky Mountains. Strong, winter winds roaring down the mountainside create a horizontal vortex that can split in two and turn upright when encountering an obstacle, producing a small tornado-like feature called a mountainado.

▼ *General circulation is the movement of the atmosphere that gives rise to particular pressure systems and winds. Hot air rises at the equator, at the intertropical convergence zone (ITCZ), causing an area of low pressure. The air cools and falls, creating the Hadley cells (1) of circulating air. The Hadley cells drive the Ferrel cells (2) and polar cells (3), which are also affected by temperature differences between places nearer to and further from the north and south poles. Air circulation has a major influence on rainfall.*

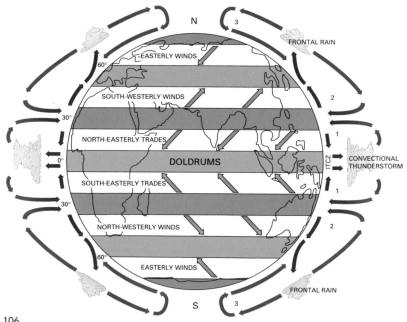

Clouds of dust billow around a street during a dust storm in Patagonia, Argentina.

Dust storms are windstorms without accompanying rainfall. They are known across the world, from the pampas of Argentina or southern Australia to the Sahara and Sahel of Africa, and from the Middle East and Central and southern Asia, to the North American plains. A combination of low precipitation, poor land use, and improper irrigation can produce dust storms that devastate agriculture. The frequency of dust storms is greatest in those regions where the annual rainfall lies between 100 and 200 mm (4–8 inches). Areas of even lower rainfall do not permit the substantial production of clay and silt particles that is needed to supply sufficient dust to feed the dust storms.

Winds do not have to rotate in order to be dangerous. Straight-line winds can be as damaging as a small tornado. Such powerful winds, found associated with thunderstorms, are called 'derechos'. Bursts of straight-line winds up to 100 kilometres per hour (60 mph) with durations of 10–15 seconds can take place. On July 15, 1995, a system of thunderstorms moved rapidly southward into the State of New York before losing strength in New York City. Wind speeds up to 170 kilometres per hour (106 mph) were recorded, millions of trees were blown down, and there were five fatalities.

BEAUFORT SCALE			
Scale	Number	Description (km/h)	Wind Speed (mph)
0	Calm	0	0
1	Light air	1–5	1–3
2	Light breeze	6–11	4–7
3	Gentle breeze	12–19	8–12
4	Moderate breeze	20–28	13–18
5	Fresh breeze	29–38	19–24
6	Strong breeze	39–49	25–31
7	Near gale	50–61	32–38
8	Gale	62–74	39–46
9	Strong gale	75–88	47–54
10	Storm	89–102	55–63
11	Violent storm	103–117	64–72
12	Hurricane	118+	73+

Hurricanes

The intense winds called 'hurricanes' in the Atlantic and eastern Pacific Oceans, are known by many different names. The term comes from the Spanish *huracan* and the Portuguese *huracao*, which in turn are believed to originate from the Carib word *urican*, meaning 'big wind'. In the western Pacific, they are known as 'typhoons', a term believed to originate from a Chinese dialect phrase *tai feng*, again meaning 'big wind'. Around the Philippines, they are called *baguios*; in Japan, *reppus*; along the Arabian coast, *asifats*; while in the Indian Ocean, they are simply 'cyclones'. Only when the wind speed in a tropical storm exceeds 33 metres per second/108 feet per second (120 km/h or 75 mph) should it be called any of these names.

How hurricanes are formed

Hurricanes are the most lethal and destructive storms on Earth. For instance, the hurricane that struck Bangladesh in 1970 killed 500,000 people. The busiest time for hurricanes in the northern hemisphere is between July and October, with a peak during August and September when sea-surface temperatures are at their height, feeding more water vapour into the weather systems through evaporation. Similarly, in the southern hemisphere, the peak season occurs when the sea is warmest, in January and February. More than one-third of these extremely hazardous weather systems occur across the low latitudes of the north-west Pacific and its 'downstream' land areas. In contrast, the north-east Pacific averages just 17 percent and the North Atlantic typically sees 12 percent of

▼ *Satellite image of Hurricane Floyd on September 14, 1999. Floyd was a large and intense Cape Verdean hurricane that pounded the central and northern islands of the Bahamas, seriously threatened Florida, struck the coast of North Carolina, and then moved up the east coast of the United States into New England. It neared the threshold of Category 5 intensity on the Saffir-Simpson Hurricane Scale as it approached the Bahamas, and produced a flood disaster of immense proportions in the eastern United States, particularly in North Carolina, where it killed 52 people.*

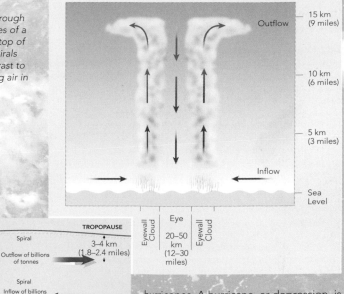

▶ Vertical slice through the central features of a hurricane. At the top of a hurricane, air spirals out in direct contrast to the inward swirling air in the lowest few kilometres of the troposphere.

▲ If the mass of air ejected from a hurricane is greater than the rate at which it is being supplied in the lowest kilometre, surface pressure will fall and the wind speed will probably increase.

hurricanes. A hurricane, or depression, is a system of atmospheric low pressure that occurs when a cold air mass moving south from the Arctic meets a warm air mass moving north from the tropics to create a circulating air mass (or vice versa in the southern hemisphere). Along the warm front (the boundary on the ground between the warm and cold air), warm air flows upward over cold air, producing a sequence of clouds that help forecasters to predict a depression's advance. Along the cold front, the advancing cold air forces warm air to rise steeply, causing towering cumulonimbus clouds to form in the rising air. When the cold front overtakes the warm front, warm air is pushed above ground level to form an occluded front. Cloud and rain persist along occlusions until temperatures equalize, the air mixes, and the depression dies out. A hurricane is characterized by relatively low pressure at the centre and by counterclockwise wind movement in the northern hemisphere or clockwise motion in the southern hemisphere.

Two types of hurricane are recognized: the normally relatively benign type associated with temperate latitudes, and the tropical hurricane, which is much more violent and usually affects a smaller area. A tropical hurricane is typically 500 to 800 km (300–500 miles) across with an average wind speed of 64 knots. A tropical storm is less intense and characterized by winds between 34 and 64 knots. Both storms and hurricanes are given a name or a number depending on the ocean basin over which it originated. Although many names are recycled, names allocated to storms or hurricanes that caused serious damage and loss of life are never used again. Among others, this was the case for David and Frederick (1979), Allen (1980), Alicia (1983), Elena and Gloria (1985), Gilbert and Joan (1988), Hugo (1989), Bob (1991), Andrew (1992), and Mitch (1998).

Hurricane characteristics

Hurricanes are characterized by average wind speeds of force 12 or greater on the Beaufort Scale. They develop over ocean water that is at or above a temperature of 27°C (80°F). A hurricane is composed of bands of thunderstorms and cumulus clouds that spiral around the storm centre – the calm, cloud-free eye – which is typically 30 to 40 km (20–25 miles) across. In the cloud-wall around the eye exceptional wind speeds occur: generally speaking, the smaller the eye, the higher the wind speeds. Very high winds occur around the edge of the eye where the horizontal pressure-gradient is steepest. Within the eye itself, there is hardly any change of pressure across the surface, and this zone is characterized by deeply subsiding air and generally cloud-free skies. Surrounding it, however, is the eye-wall cloud, which is like an upright cylinder and composed of extremely deep and vigorous cumulonimbus clouds. It is across this zone that the strongest winds and most torrential rain occur. Extremely strong winds and heavy precipitation are also encountered elsewhere within the circulation of a hurricane, particularly in the spiral rain bands that are also composed of very deep cumulonimbus clouds.

At the top of a hurricane, the air spirals out in direct contrast to the inward swirling air in the lowest few kilometres of the troposphere. The strength and depth of this outflow plays a crucial role in determining whether the system will weaken or persist and become more vigorous. If the mass of air being thrown out in the highest reaches of a hurricane is greater than the rate at which it is being supplied in the lowest kilometre above the sea's surface, the surface pressure will fall and the winds will probably increase. Although the

▼ *Cut-out view of the central features of a hurricane. A hurricane is typically 500 to 800 km (300–500 miles) across and 15 km (9 miles) deep.*

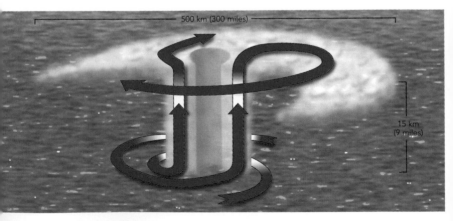

500 km (300 miles)

15 km (9 miles)

SAFFIR-SIMPSON SCALE

Category 1 (weak hurricane)
65–82 knot winds; surge 1.2–1.5 m (4–5 feet) above normal water levels.

Category 2 (moderate hurricane)
83–95 knot winds; surge 1.6–2.4 m (6–8 feet) above normal water levels.

Category 3 (strong hurricane)
96–113 knot winds; surge 2.5–3.7 m (9–12 feet) above normal water levels.

Category 4 (very strong hurricane)
114–135 knot winds; surge 3.8–5.5 m (13–18 feet) above normal water levels.

Category 5 (devastating hurricane)
More than 135 knot winds; surge more than 5.5 m (18 feet) above normal water levels.

traditional definition of a hurricane is Beaufort Force 12 winds (defined as 'air filled with foam, sea completely white with driving spray, visibility greatly reduced'), nowadays the Saffir-Simpson scale is used, especially along the east and Gulf coasts of the United States. This scale classifies hurricanes according to their 'damage potential' on a five-point scale, ranging from minimal (1) to catastrophic (5). Such measurement is based on air pressure in a storm's eye, because the lower the pressure, the greater the wind speeds. A hurricane that measures five on the scale is characterized by air pressure below 920 millibars, resulting in wind speeds of more than 250 km/h (155 mph), and a storm surge in the sea of more than 5.5 metres (18 feet) above normal. Fortunately, less than one percent of all hurricanes fall within this category.

Category 5 hurricanes

The damage associated with rare Category 5 hurricanes is tremendously costly, in both economic and social terms. It is defined as follows:

Most trees and signs blown down. Very severe and extensive roof, window, and door damage. Complete failure of roof structures on most homes and many industrial buildings. Some large buildings suffer complete structural failure, while some smaller ones are overturned and may be blown away. Complete destruction of mobile homes.

Surge creates major damage to lower floors of all structures less than 5.5 metres (18 feet) above mean-sea-level and within 450 metres (1,500 feet) of the shore. Low-lying escape routes are cut by rising water three to five hours before the storm centre arrives. Massive evacuation of residential areas situated on low ground within 8–16 km (5–10 miles) of the shore may be required.

Hurricane speed and direction

Most hurricanes in the northern hemisphere are normally westward and poleward, although some storms make baffling changes of directions, even doubling back on themselves. As the hurricane moves north from the equator, the Coriolis effect, due to the Earth's rotation, enhances the angular momentum of the winds circling the eye, feeding the storm as it moves. The lateral rate of movement of the eye ranges from 24 to 80 km/h (15–50 mph) and a hurricane can travel many thousands of kilometres in the open ocean before dissipating. Once a hurricane travels outside the zone of hot, tropical seas, it weakens, either because it strikes land where there is dry air or because it

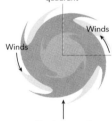

Forward right quadrant

Winds

Winds

Hurricane motion

▲ *In the northern hemisphere, the force of a hurricane is greatest in the forward right quadrant. In the southern hemisphere, the wind force is greatest in the forward left quadrant.*

HURRICANES

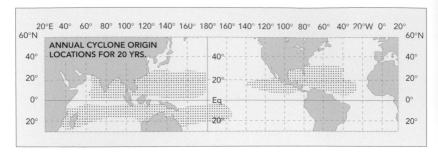

ANNUAL CYCLONE ORIGIN
LOCATIONS FOR 20 YRS.

approaches cooler ocean surface waters that rob it of its supply of warm moist air. Even in its weakened state, hurricane winds can cause great damage, but it is the storm-surge generated by a hurricane that is most devastating. This is caused by the sea's surface becoming 'up-domed' beneath the intense low-pressure system (in contrast, the sea surface is 'squashed' down by high pressure). This response of the sea's surface is called the 'inverse barometer effect', and for a 1 millibar change in air pressure, the sea level will rise or fall by roughly 1 centimetre (0.5 inches). Consequently, a travelling region of elevated sea surface will mirror a very intense hurricane. To compound the impact of the storm surge, the hurricane's direction of motion adds to its height, as does the force of the wind on its forward right quadrant. The same applies on the forward left quadrant of such systems in the southern hemisphere.

▲ Hurricane origins during a 20-year period. About 30% of all hurricanes originate in the north-west Pacific region.

Hurricane Gilbert, North America, 1988

Hurricane Gilbert was a huge, Category 5 storm, 1,500 km (930 miles) across, that swept through the Gulf of Mexico in September 1988. The amount of energy generated by the storm was enormous: as Gilbert passed over Jamaica, it is estimated that it generated as much energy as the country would need – at current rates of consumption – for the next 1,000 years. Although Gilbert travelled along its track at a sluggish 18–25 km/h (11–16 mph), the wind around the eye at the centre, where air pressure was a record low of 885 millibars, reached speeds in excess of 320 km/h (200 mph). A tidal surge of 6 metres (20 feet), flash floods from torrential rainfall (up to 380 mm/15 inches in a few hours), and the spawning of 24 tornadoes wreaked devastation as the storm struck land. The storm claimed 338 lives, 100,000 people were evacuated from the Mexican coast, and 500,000 people were rendered homeless in Jamaica. The hurricane raged through the resorts of Cozumel and Cancún on the Yucatán Peninsula of south-east Mexico with wind speeds of 280 km/h (175 mph), before turning to strike the north-east coast of Mexico, south of Brownsville, Texas.

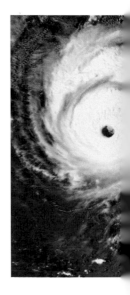

Hurricane Andrew, United States, 1992

Hurricane Andrew was the costliest natural disaster ever to strike the United States. Andrew crossed the Bahamas as a

Category 4 storm before moving on to southern Florida, where it left a trail of damage from August 23 to August 27, 1992. Its eye moved onshore at Dade County, south-east Florida, narrowly missing downtown Miami to the north where damage would have been far greater. At landfall, the central surface pressure of 922 millibars was the third-lowest this century, and the maximum sustained wind speed (averaging more than one minute at a height of 10 metres/33 feet) was some 220 km/h (140 mph) gusting to 265 km/h (165 mph) at landfall. Andrew took 15 lives in Dade County and left about 250,000 people homeless. Andrew took four hours to cross the Florida peninsula during which time it weakened to a Category 1 storm. Once free to move across the warm waters of the Gulf of Mexico, it regained most of its vigour and had a second, less devastating, landfall near Morgan City, south-west Louisiana. It then proceeded north and inland, rapidly losing its power, and weakening to tropical storm strength within 10 hours.

1998 – the year of the hurricane

The 1998 Atlantic hurricane season was a particularly busy one. The year started quietly: not until mid-August did the first of a string of storms begin to form and head towards the Caribbean and the United States. Hurricane Bonnie was the first of significance – running into the Bahamas before slowing and idling off the south-eastern shores of the US. Bonnie finally moved slowly into South Carolina and North Carolina, then headed north-eastwards to skirt the coast for many hundreds of kilometres. Bonnie was followed by tropical storm Charley, which crossed the southern Texas coast near Corpus Christi to bring much-needed rainfall to drought-ridden

▼ *Time-lapse satellite images of Hurricane Andrew, August 1992. Andrew is one of only three Category 5 hurricanes known to have struck the United States. Category 5 storms have winds in excess of 250 km/h (155 mph) and storm surges generally more than 5.5 metres (18 feet) above normal sea level. On August 24, Andrew cut a destructive swathe through southern Florida and entered the Gulf of Mexico. On August 26, it made landfall, 160 km (100 miles) south-west of New Orleans, south-east Louisiana. The next day, it was downgraded to a tropical depression, north-east of Jackson, west-central Mississippi.*

areas in central and southern parts of Texas. Some lives were lost to drowning, particularly in and around Del Rio on the Rio Grande, where some 500 mm (200 inches) of rain fell in the course of a couple of days. The summer of 1998 was the first since 1892 that the North Atlantic experienced four hurricanes simultaneously. The 1998 hurricanes were Georges, Ivan, Jeanne, and Karl. Luckily, the last three roamed across the ocean without making landfall, although they did pose a threat to shipping and the remnants of Karl produced some wet and windy weather across parts of western Europe in late September. It is not uncommon for the remnants of hurricanes to rove that far, especially in late summer and early autumn. Of all the year's storms, Georges proved to be the most lethal as it rampaged across the Caribbean taking more than 600 lives. The Dominican Republic suffered particularly badly, losing virtually all of its crops. Georges also struck north towards the Mississippi Delta region, provoking the evacuation of some 1.5 million inhabitants from New Orleans and adjacent coastal areas. New Orleans is about 2 metres (6.6 feet) below sea level and is protected by huge levees and drainage channels built to withstand a Category 3 hurricane. Georges moved sluggishly towards the coast at about 9 km/h (6 mph), while the winds roared around its centre at approximately 160 km/h (100 mph). It dumped some 200 mm (8 inches) of rain at Pensacola in north-west Florida, while other areas were predicted to receive over four times that amount. The eye made landfall near Biloxi, southern Mississippi, with 165 km/h (102 mph) winds.

Hurricane Mitch, 1998

The 1998 season reached its tragic climax with the appearance of Hurricane Mitch in October, a real sting in the tail of an already painful hurricane season. Mitch was the strongest hurricane on record to form so late in the year, developing on October 21, about 600 km (370 miles) south of Jamaica. By the morning of October 24, Mitch had attained hurricane intensity. It then deepened rapidly to reach a minimum surface pressure estimated to be 905 millibars on October 26. Maximum sustained surface winds are thought to have approached almost 285 km/h (175 mph) close to Honduras, where Mitch made landfall on the morning of October 29. The hurricane then moved south across Honduras and Guatemala over the next two days, producing prolonged and extremely

▼ Rescue-workers provide first aid to the victims of Hurricane Mitch, Posoltega, north-west Nicaragua, November 2, 1998. The resulting floods and mudslides killed more than 3,100 people in Nicaragua and devastated the local infrastructure. More than 18,500 lives were lost across Central America as a result of the hurricane.

WORST HURRICANES IN THE YEARS 1975–2001					
Location	Country	Date	Name	People killed*	People affected
Southern districts	Bangladesh	March 30, 1991	Brendan	138,866	15,000,000
Central America	–	October 26, 1998	Mitch	18,599	3,240,200
Tamil Nadu, Andhra Pradesh, Kerala	India	November 12, 1977	–	14,204	9,037,400
Islands and southern districts	Bangladesh	May 25, 1985	–	10,000	1,300,000
Orissa	India	October 29, 1999	05B	9,843	12,625,000
Negros and Leyte	Philippines	November 5, 1991	Thelma (Uring)	5,956	598,454
Binh Dinh provinces	Vietnam	November 2, 1997	Linda	3,682	697,225
Gujarat, Rajasthan, Maharasthra	India	June 9, 1998	–	2,871	4,600,000
Caribbean	–	August 1979	David and Frederick	1,440	1,270,000
South-east Asia	–	September 1984	Ike	1,412	1,237,224

People killed directly by hurricane

intense downpours as it did so. Devastating floods and mudslides resulted that killed more than 11,000 people and wrecked the Honduran and Guatemalan economies. It is estimated that not since 1780 have so many people died in a hurricane disaster in the Caribbean/Gulf region.

Hurricane Hugo, Caribbean, 1989

One of the worst hurricanes of recent times was Hugo, which swept across the Caribbean in 1989, reaching the island of Guadeloupe on the night of September 16. At one point, average surface winds reached 210 km/h (130 mph), destroying homes and cutting off all electrical power. On September 18, Hugo tracked northwestwards towards Puerto Rico dumping 125 mm (5 inches) of rain at Arecibo on the north coast and 344 mm (13.5 inches) at Lower Rio Blanco in the north-eastern mountains. Staff at the San Juan Weather Service Forecast Office in Puerto Rico ran the risk of shocks from electrical equipment as heavy rain drove through the building's hurricane shutters. Hugo killed 49 people and caused damages of US$7,000 million.

The East Pakistan (Bangladesh) Hurricane, 1970

The worst hurricane in history and one of the worst natural disasters of the 20th century began at 9 am on November 10, as a low-pressure area developed in the Bay of Bengal. As this area moved north-west, it became a cyclonic storm with winds reaching 250 km/h (155 mph). The overpopulated islands in its path suffered the full brunt of the hurricane's force. Waves 7.5 m (25 feet) high swept over the Ganges delta, destroying everything in their path, taking houses, crops, animals, and people. Whole harvests of rice and grain were carried off into the sea, the loss of which would provide further devastation to the suffering population once the hurricane departed. Estimates put the loss of human life anywhere between 350,000 and one million. One million livestock animals drowned. The calm after the storm revealed the extent of the devastation. Houses had been crushed beyond recognition or simply carried away by the storm. The landscape had been levelled, all livestock and crops destroyed. Human and animal corpses hung from trees. The land was littered with hundreds of beached fishing boats and ships. Entire villages had been wiped out on some of the islands. The resulting homelessness, disease and mass starvation claimed many more lives than the hurricane itself. The entire infrastructure of the south coast was wiped out and refugees poured into neighbouring India.

The central goverment's poor response to the tragedy exacerbated political tensions between West Pakistan and East Pakistan. Indeed shortly after the hurricane hit East Pakistan its citizens declared independence. In 1971, the rebels emerged victorious from a short and bloody civil war, and the nation of Bangladesh was born. The disaster and war severely damaged the economy of the newly independent nation and, as a consequence, many of the hazard-alleviation programmes proposed after 1970 remained unimplemented. The full implications of this neglect became apparent in 1991, when another storm hit the region killing an estimated 100,000 people. The vast majority of these casualties could have been avoided through the adoption of storm-prediction systems and the use of proper communication channels.

Forecasting a hurricane

Forecasting the power and track of a hurricane remains problematical. Weather satellites often give adequate warning of their approach, but this does little to prevent the often severe damage and loss of life caused by the high winds and extreme rainfall, particularly in the West Indies and along the south-eastern and eastern coasts of the United States. Deaths due to hurricanes in the US have declined in recent decades because of improved forecasting and higher levels of disaster preparedness. However, increasing coastal development from Texas to Maine ensures that there is a constant rise in the number of people who are vulnerable to the winds, torrential rain and coastal inundation from the surge that accompanies a hurricane. Florida's population, for example, has more than doubled since 1970 to 15.9 million. Although the number of fatalities has reduced this century, the cost of hurricane damage has increased significantly. The US National Weather Service issues 'watches' and 'warnings' as a matter of routine, to alert the public to the risk of an impending serious weather hazard. A 'hurricane watch' means that a specific region faces the threat of hurricane conditions within 24–36 hours. This does not require evacuation but it does constitute notice that the population should be prepared for evacuation if a 'warning' is issued. A hurricane warning is issued when severe weather has been reported or is imminent; at which stage everyone should take the necessary precautions. While the

MOST EXPENSIVE HURRICANES BETWEEN 1975 AND 2001					
Location	Country	Date	Name	Peple killed	Cost in US$ (thousands)
Florida, Louisiana, Bahamas	United States	August 24, 1992	Andrew	48	30,250,000
south-west, west, and central France	France	May 16, 1992	–	88	11,060,000
North Korea and South Korea	–	August 31, 2000	Prapiroon (Typhoon 12)	71	6,155,576
Hiroshima, Kure districts (Kyushu island)	Japan	September 27, 1991	Mireille (Typhoon 19)	66	5,200,000
Kauai, Nihau, Oahu, Hawaii	United States	September 11, 1992	Iniki	4	5,000,000
southern and eastern USA	United States	June 8, 2001	Allison	50	4,000,000
Japan and South Korea	–	September 22, 1999	Bart	29	3,304,268
Gujarat, Rajasthan, and Maharasthra	India	June 9, 1998	–	2,871	3,010,000
Mexico and southern USA	North America	October 6, 1995	Opal	38	3,000,000

United States can organize mass evacuation very effectively, this is not the case for many Caribbean States, where the infrastructure and means of communication are often less well developed.

Hurricane warnings are not always accurate or reliable. In 1999, an evacuation warning was issued in response to the threat of Hurricane Floyd, leading to 300,000 residents leaving the coastal areas of the south-eastern state of Georgia. The evacuation cost was estimated to have been US$1million per mile evacuated and resulted in traffic chaos and gridlock. In the event, Hurricane Floyd never struck the Georgia coast.

Taming a hurricane

When a hurricane travels across the ocean and finally reaches the coast, it begins to die as its supply of energy from the warmer ocean is cut off and as the increased surface friction upsets the storm's circulation and reduces the wind speeds. Even the ferocious Hurricane Gilbert was eventually tamed. If a hurricane's energy could somehow be reduced while the storm is over the ocean, then its destructive power on landfall could be dramatically reduced. An attempt to weaken a hurricane was attempted under the auspices of Project Stormfury, with silver iodide or dry ice used to seed the storm some distance outside the eye-wall clouds. The intention was to produce rainfall, so releasing latent heat that would otherwise have sustained the high wind speeds in the eye-wall. It was hoped that a fall in wind speeds would cause the hurricane simply to fizzle out. Instead, a new eye-wall was created farther out, with lower wind speeds. Research into tackling hurricanes continues, and further experiments can be expected.

Tornadoes

A tornado or 'twister' is a funnel-shaped, violently rotating vortex extending downwards from the cumulonimbus cloud in which it forms. Tornadoes are always linked to a parent cumulonimbus cloud, and are therefore intimately associated with violent thunderstorms. Strictly speaking, to be classed as a tornado, the vortex of rapidly spinning air must be in contact with the ground. If the vortex does not make contact with the surface it is referred to as a 'funnel cloud'. Sometimes flying debris may be visible even if there is no obvious funnel cloud, indicating that a tornado is present. The centre of a tornado is characterized by extreme low pressure, which sucks up dust to form a dark-grey funnel rising into the sky. Around this funnel of rising air are very strong winds capable of destroying crops and buildings. Tornadoes occur in deep, low-pressure areas, associated with fronts or other instabilities.

Tornado-prone areas

Tornadoes are most common in the interior of the United States, particularly east of the Rocky Mountains in Texas, Oklahoma, Kansas, and Missouri. In fact, this portion of the central United States is known as 'Tornado Alley.' Tornadoes commonly rake this region in afternoons or evenings in the months of April, May, and June, when they are spawned by violent thunderstorms along the boundary between cold air

◀ A tornado strikes a farm in the Midwest, United States. Tornadoes are most common in the continental heartland of the United States. They can last from several seconds to more than an hour. Two-thirds of tornadoes last less than three minutes.

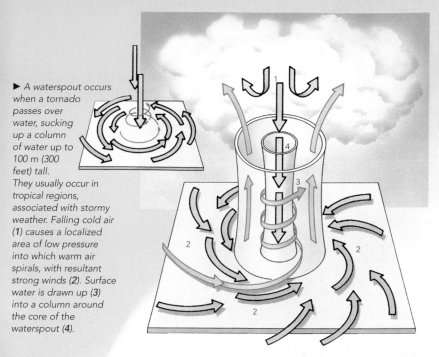

► *A waterspout occurs when a tornado passes over water, sucking up a column of water up to 100 m (300 feet) tall.*
They usually occur in tropical regions, associated with stormy weather. Falling cold air (1) causes a localized area of low pressure into which warm air spirals, with resultant strong winds (2). Surface water is drawn up (3) into a column around the core of the waterspout (4).

from the north and warm, moist air from the south. They are also triggered by intense heating in the continental heartland in late summer, when temperatures are at their hottest.

Although 80 percent of all tornadoes occur in the United States, other regions of the world are not immune. Mini-tornadoes (known as 'willy-willys' or 'cockeye bobs') form during winter and spring in the south-eastern coastal areas of Australia, although these are not as destructive as their US counterparts because their wind speeds are lower. Occasionally tornadoes strike in Europe, Africa, and on the Indian subcontinent, and the violent storms that occur at the start of the rainy season in western Africa are also called tornadoes. They bring strong winds and torrential rain, which is caused by mild air coming in from the sea and meeting dry air from the Sahara Desert. When tornadoes cross over water they become waterspouts, sucking up water instead of dust and soil to build the funnel clouds.

Tornado shape and movement

A tornado vortex is a swirling or spinning mass of air descending from a storm cloud and taking the form of a long, tapering long funnel that ends at the surface. The inward-and-upward whirl of the winds explains why tornadoes are popularly known as 'twisters' in the United States. The lateral movement of a tornado is faster than that of a tropical cyclone, with wind speeds typically ranging from 50 to 200 km/h (30–125 mph), and internally sometimes achieving velocities as high as 500 km/h (310 mph) – about double the maximum wind speed of the most powerful hurricanes. For all their violence, two-thirds of the world's tornadoes last less than three minutes and their destructive paths on the surface rarely exceeds 10 km (6 miles). Their tracks are very narrow and can be discontinuous, reflecting periodic breaking of contact with the surface. Although sometimes confused with hurricanes, tornadoes are very much smaller, usually about a hundredth the size, and a typical tornado 'footprint' is around 100 m (330 feet). Less than two percent are true 'killer torna-does', which create swathes of destruction hundreds of metres wide and more than 150 km (93 miles) long. The most frequently observed size of a tornado's damage path is about 50 metres (100 feet) wide with a track of 2–4 km (1–2 miles). However, the largest damage swathe can exceed 2 km (1 mile) in width, and the narrowest, about 10 m (33 feet).

◀ Tornadoes are mainly formed at the mid-latitudes. They are produced by thunderstorms, such as the cyclones of Asia and Japan. The USA suffers many tornadoes, especially at its centre, where humid air streaming north from the Gulf of Mexico meets cold, dry air moving westwards from the Rocky Mountains. The thermal (1) does not begin to spin at ground level, but within the cloud. Rotation gradually extends to the surface as a funnel (2) stretching from the base of the parent cloud. The flat top of a tornado's parent cloud (A) is at the so-called equilibrium level (3), where the temperature within the cloud matches that of the environment, but the updraft of the tornado is so strong that rising

The barometric pressure within the heart of a tornado can suddenly fall as low as 20 percent below normal ambient pressure, generating a pressure differential that can lift automobiles and roofs skyward and cause a closed building to explode.

Why do tornadoes form?

Broadly-speaking, three conditions need to be satisfied for a thunderstorm to spawn a tornado in the United States. First, there must be a flow to the north of warm, humid tropical air from the Gulf of Mexico. Second, a cold mass of dry air moving southward from Canada or eastward from the Rocky Mountains at speeds of around 80 km/h (50 mph). Third, high altitude winds (the jet stream) coming from the north-west at speeds of 250 km/h (150mph). When these three masses of air meet, shearing conditions are set up that impart a spin to a thundercloud. As the warm air rises, it is sheared and spun one way at mid-levels and then rotated in another direction at higher levels by the fast moving north-westerly flow of the jet stream. The resulting cyclonic vortex is enhanced by warm air rising on the leading edge of the thunderstorm and cool air descending on the trailing side.

The United States seems to have the perfect geography for hatching tornadoes. Every spring, cold air moves down from the Arctic, condensing into rain clouds over the western Coast Ranges. By the time this cold air mass has crossed the Rockies into the Great Plains, it is wrung dry. The humid Gulf Coast, meanwhile, produces torrential rains along the Texas' coast. The meeting of these two air masses in tornado alley has given rise to some memorable tornadoes. In April 1974, such an encounter generated 148 twisters in less than 24 hours, which whipped across 4,000 km (2,500 miles) and 13 states, killing more than 300 people. In the south-eastern United States, multiple tornadoes can also form in the southeast quadrant of a slowly moving hurricane. This kind of tornado formation occurs during the hurricane season in late summer and autumn, generating twisters that typically track in an easterly-northeasterly direction.

It is a little known fact that tornadoes have also been triggered by technological accident, namely the 1986 Chernobyl nuclear disaster in Ukraine. Here, large thermal plumes rose up

air overshoots this level (4) before falling back into the cloud. The shelf cloud (5) forms where a cool downdraft caused by rain (6) undercuts warm air ahead of the path (7) of the storm. The highest wind speeds in a tornado occur in a tight spiral at its centre. Powerful tornadoes, however, can generate miniature airspirals around the edge of the main 'twister', with even greater wind speeds. These minivortices account for some freak damage, such as the destruction of one side of a house while the other half is left intact. Waterspouts are weaker tornadoes that form over seas or lakes from cumulonimbus or towering cumulus clouds. The strongest are characterized by wind speeds of up to 160 km/h (100 mph).

WIND RATING		
Category	Average wind speed (km/h)	Damage description
F0	< 115	light
F1	116–179	moderate
F2	180–251	considerable
F3	252–330	severe
F4	331–416	devastating
F5	> 417	incredible

into the atmosphere from the wrecked reactor, where their tremendous energy was sufficient to form tornado-like vortices through interaction with only light to moderate winds.

Classifying tornadoes

Tornadoes are classified using a scale devised by Japanese-American meteorologist Tetsuya (Theodore) Fujita (1920–98) in the late 1960s (*see* table, page 121). This allocates a tornado to one of five categories (F0–F5), according to average wind speeds. Tornado winds cannot be measured directly, so a rating on the Fujita scale is determined by an assessment of the worst storm damage. The damage signature of an F4 tornado, for example, is the levelling of well-constructed houses, structures with weak foundations blown some distance, and cars thrown into the air to accompany other large airborne 'missiles'. An F5 level tornado will lift strong frame houses from their foundations, break them up and carry them considerable distances. Automobiles will be picked up and carried through the air for distances in excess of 100 m (330 feet). Studies are underway that demonstrate that measurable seismic energy is generated by a tornado at its touchdown point, with an F5 tornado rotating at maximum wind-speed providing an energy yield comparable to a moderate earthquake.

The damage legacy of tornadoes

Because its path is typically short and narrow, the average tornado is not responsible for a high number of deaths. For the same reason, property damage also tends to be limited. Severe tornadoes or tornado-clusters like the April 1974 event, however, have killed hundreds of people and destroyed entire towns. Like a giant vacuum-cleaner in the sky, a large tornado

▲ *On August 11, 1999, a tornado hit Salt Lake City, Utah, USA. Winds up to 250 km/h (150 mph) swept through the capital of Utah, causing US$1.5 million worth of damage and killing one person.*

can lift heavy trains, trees, iron bridges, and concrete piers and hurl them back to Earth sometimes kilometres away.

The tri-State tornado, USA, 1925

The most lethal tornado swarm in the United States was the tri-State outbreak of March 18, 1925, when 689 people across Missouri, Illinois, and Indiana lost their lives. On the morning of March 18, the residents of Annapolis, south-east Missouri, were awakened by the roar of a tornado moving toward their community. This unusually wide tornado was following a north-easterly path at a lateral speed of about 75 km/h (45 mph). It proceeded to flatten the town, cutting a swathe of destruction at least 1.2 km (0.75 miles) across. The tornado continued on the same path into southern Illinois, devastating the town of Murphysboro where wrecked buildings caught fire, the water-supply system was destroyed, and 210 residents were killed. The tri-State tornado is the largest known: its track covered a distance of 350 km (220 miles), along which 23 small communities were destroyed. It should be noted none of the top 25 'killer tornadoes' in the United States have occurred since 1953. This is a function of improvements in forecasting the severe convection with which torndaoes are associated, and adoption of more effective ways of communicating tornado watches and warnings to the general public.

Despite the relative decrease in tornado-related deaths over the past 55 years, the cost of damage highlights the power of recent tornadoes. Three very costly 'twisters' were those of May 16, 1995 (US$10 billion in south-eastern USA), 16 May 1998 (US$3 billion in north-eastern USA) and May 3, 1999 (US$1 billion in Oklahoma and Kansas).

The Oklahoma tornado outbreak, USA, 1999

The worst tornado outbreak ever to hit Oklahoma occurred on May 3, 1999. Tornadoes are well known in the state, but this event was of extreme severity and one that unfortunately affected heavily populated areas. More than 50 'twisters' ran across central Oklahoma in a single day, taking 40 lives in and around Oklahoma City. There were also outbreaks on the same day in parts of north Texas, eastern Oklahoma, and south-central Kansas, where five people died in Wichita. One tornado in particular became the major killer, spawned by a massive so-called 'super-cell thunderstorm' that had already produced a crop of up to F3 twisters. It touched down close to

▼ *Wrecked cars litter the streets following the 1999 tornado in Oklahoma, USA. The tornado wrought incredible devastation to homes, businesses, and personal property. Forty tornadoes are thought to have hit the state, claiming 49 lives.*

the small town of Chickasha, central Oklahoma, as an F1, then sped north-east towards the metropolitan region, gearing up to an F4 then declining to an F3 on the way. Over the community of Bridge Creek, the tornado re-intensified to an F5, destroying 680 homes. A second, more destructive, 1.5 km (1 mile) -wide tornado grew near to the Canadian River during the evening. It quickly attained F5 status and devastated Moore, a suburb of Oklahoma City. The destruction here was severe, with 1,225 houses and 274 apartments obliterated along with 50 businesses, two schools and churches, and up to 4,500 homes damaged. The estimated total cost was close to US$1 billion. Timely warnings were issued for all the affected areas and played a role in minimizing deaths and injuries. Such was the intensity of the twisters, however, that even the most solidly constructed properties could not withstand their ferocity.

The Petersburg tornado, USA, 1993

Twisters are relatively rare in the Atlantic states, with Virginia, for example, averaging only eight per year, but they do cause damage and loss of life. On August 7, 1993, a sudden tornado struck the historic Civil War town of Petersburg, located just south of the capital city of Richmond. The tornado descended without warning from a heavy thunderstorm tearing apart houses that had withstood the Civil War, flipping tractor-trailers and scattering cars. Because of the antiquated radar operating in the mid-Atlantic states at the time, the National Weather Service did not issue a tornado warning until almost five minutes after the twister had touched down. Conventional radar measures the reflection of radar waves from rain droplets and hail, while radar operational in tornado-prone states can measure the rotation of winds inside a thunderstorm.

Tornado casualties

The largest number of tornado deaths per capita in the United States occur in the states of Mississippi, Arkansas, Kansas and Oklahoma. The highest fatality rates in tornadoes occur among the elderly, residents of mobile or trailer homes and those unaware of tornado alerts. Traditional protection involves evacuation to a cellar or basement. Unfortunately, more and more homes in the rural United States are being built without cellars, so some residents of tornado-prone states are constructing interior safe rooms with thick concrete walls, a steel door and a concrete roof, similar to a

▼ In May 2003, neighbourhoods in Gladstone, eastern Missouri, were badly damaged by tornadoes. In the first week of May, 298 tornadoes were reported in the United States – the most in one week since records began. Forty-four people were killed in Missouri, Tennessee, Kansas, Georgia, and Illinois. In Oklahoma, more than 130 people were injured and 300 homes destroyed – causing an estimated US$100 million worth of damage.

THE WORST TORNADOES SINCE 1975				
Location	Country	Date	Killed	Affected
Manikganj, Dhaka, Tangail districts	Bangladesh	April 26, 1989	800	102,000
Colorado	USA	June 13, 1984	600	–
Orissa	India	April 16, 1978	500	1400
North-east Moscow	Soviet Union	June 1984	400	–
West Bengal, Orissa	India	March 24, 1998	250	450,500
Casamance	Senegal	August 21, 1999	165	–
Ghorasal, Tungi, Sirajganj	Bangladesh	May 7, 1991	121	300
Orissa	India	April 17, 1981	120	10,000
Pennsylvania, Ohio, Missouri	USA	May 31, 1985	104	500
West Bengal	India	April 16, 1978	100	100

bank vault. These proved particularly effective during the May 1999 tornado in Oklahoma City, Oklahoma, where some residents emerged unscathed from their safe-rooms to find their home destroyed.

Predicting and monitoring tornadoes

It may never be possible to predict the precise location and timing of a tornado, even just 24 hours into the future. Currently, forecasters are well-aware of the risk of severe convection one-day ahead, and based on this knowledge, they issue warnings for areas that may encompass a few US states, or regions within states. The situation is monitored by routine surface-observing stations, although these are not able to provide the fine detail of precipitation. Radars map the extent and intensity of rainfall, and indicate the location and movement of severe storms. However, such storms only register on this type of precipitation radar once they have started up. Doppler radar, on the other hand, is able to map regions of convergence in the lower atmosphere – high-risk areas that are often precursors of deep convection. Once severe storms develop, changes in movement and intensity can be monitored virtually continuously from the ground. Rapid scans (up to an image a minute) from US geosynchronous weather satellites are also studied when conditions indicate a high risk of severe convection. This relates to troposphere-deep cumulus (10 km/6 miles and above) cloud that produces dangerous weather such as lightning, hail, extreme gustiness and tornadoes. Investigators from the National Severe Storms Laboratory in Norman, central Oklahoma, are discovering that some tornadoes form much more rapidly than previously thought, emerging in just five to 10 minutes rather than 20 to 30. This drastically reduces the warning time, making accurate prediction even more problematical. It is also now appreciated that tornadoes can form around thunderstorms that are too small to be detected between weather stations, placing yet another obstacle in the path of useful and effective prediction.

Storms

During late autumn, winter, and early spring, very strong low-pressure systems develop off the east coast of North America. The meeting of such a system with a large dome of high-pressure cold air riding along the west-to-east moving jet stream generates strong northeasterly winds over the eastern United States as the low-pressure systems move north along the Atlantic Coast. These storms, locally known as nor'easters, often bring rain, snow, sleet, freezing rain, and coastal flooding to the east coast of the United States. Because of the deflection of the jet stream to the south, forming a trough over the Gulf Coast states, cold air moves south over the east coast where it meets air warmed by the Atlantic. Hurricane-force winds can be generated as a result, associated with storms that are often, in fact, mistakenly identified as hurricanes. Historically, nor'easters have brought the heaviest snowfalls to the east coast of North America. In addition, these sudden, violent storms have sunk many ships attempting to cross the northwestern Atlantic Ocean, and a particularly intense nor'easter formed the story-line for the Hollywood movie *The Perfect Storm* (2000).

The most severe nor'easters are called 'bomb cyclones', and occur when the area of low pressure has a drop in barometric pressure of at least 24 millibars in 24 hours. Some bomb cyclones even develop an eye similar to that found at the centre of a hurricane. It is important to stress, however, that bomb cyclones have four characteristics that are not typical of hurricanes. First, they contain cold air and possess cold fronts, so whereas hurricanes feed on warm tropical air, bomb cyclones utilize cold air. Second, the development of bomb cyclones requires the interaction of strong high-altitude winds that would destroy a hurricane, being brought in by the jet stream. Third, whereas hurricanes typically form between late spring and early autumn, bomb cyclones are formed from late autumn to early spring. Finally, whereas hurricanes form in tropical

▶ *Surface weather map shows the Burns' Day Storm as it strikes the United Kingdom on January 25, 1990. The Burns' Day Storm was only one component of this dramatic winter, but was well predicted before its arrival. The storm claimed the lives of 47 people and destroyed more than 3 million trees in the United Kingdom.*

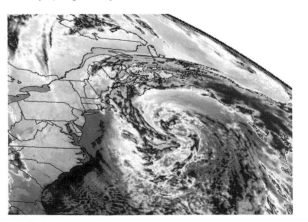

◀ *The colour-enhanced infra-red image of 1200 UTC October 30, 1991, depicts a monster storm off the eastern seaboard of the United States, which was described by the US National Weather Service as the 'perfect storm'. In this image, the storm was at its peak intensity. The storm became subtropical 30 hours later, just before the inner core of the storm developed into a tropical storm and later an unnamed hurricane.*

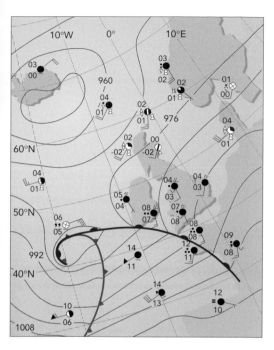

Plotting convention for wind observations in knots

○	0
	1–2
	3–7
	8–12
	13–17
⁝	etc
	48–52

Cloud cover

○	0		6
	1		7
	2		8
	3	⊗	9
	4	⊖	/
	5		

waters between 15° and 20° north and south of the equator, bomb cyclones are encountered only at higher latitudes. These severe storms are not confined solely to the east coast of North America, and also form over the north-western Atlantic and Pacific Oceans, and occasionally in other parts of the world. The worst storm ever recorded on the east coast of the United States was the Ash Wednesday storm of March 7, 1962. The storm never reached shore but it paralleled the coast in its four-day passage northward causing extensive damage to the summer homes located on the barrier islands along the coast. Since then the concept of the coastal set-back line has been developed; to the seaward side of which it is not possible to buy property insurance.

Disastrous cold-core storms also strike the United Kingdom and north-west Europe. On February 1, 1953, a deep depression formed north of Scotland before sweeping south-east across the North Sea making landfall in the Netherlands. A 4 metre (13 feet) -high storm surge was created, which flooded much of the coastline of eastern England and breached the dykes fronting the Zuider Zee in the eastern Netherlands. In England, 307 people lost their lives, evacuations were needed and 24,000 homes were damaged. Coastal flooding in the Netherlands was catastrophic, leading to 1,800 fatalities. Severe autumn and winter storms continue to batter the UK and Europe every few years, most notably the inaccurately termed 'hurricane' of autumn 1987, which caused severe damage to buildings and toppled millions of trees across southern England. Hurricanes are never experienced in the UK. Winds may reach hurricane force on the Beaufort scale, but they are produced by frontal depressions, not the systems that consist of an eye and spiral rainbands. Since the October storm of 1987, the most damaging frontal system to hit Britain and Ireland has been the so-called Burns' Day Storm that rushed through on January 25, 1990. The British winter of December 1989 to February 1990 was the wettest and warmest since 1914–15. The storm swept across the British Isles during the night of January 25, bringing torrential rain and causing extensive wind damage. Groundwater levels for the UK in February 1990 had no modern precedent; run-off rates were enormous and caused widespread flooding.

Rain and Hail

Heavy rains from thunderstorms are particularly hazardous in the south-western United States. Central Texas holds many records for the amounts of rain that is dumped within a 24-hour period. In 1935 the community of D'Hanis, located 60 km (40 miles) west of San Antonio, south-west Texas, received 56 cm (22 inches) rain in less than three hours, while 70 cm (28 inches) of rain fell in the vicinity of Austin, Texas, in 1921 in about 12 hours. The torrential rain in 1921 produced flash flooding in seven counties of Texas, killing 224 people, and causing US$19 million in damages. Warm, moist air from the Gulf of Mexico is a ready supplier of rain as it moves inland. Topography is a key factor in the formation of thunderclouds over Texas. As the warm, moist air flows landward from the Gulf of Mexico over the gently sloping coastal plain, it is deflected upward by the north-east trending Balcones Escarpment, an eroded fault scarp that still has sufficient elevation to cause the warm air to ascend and condense into towering thunderclouds.

Torrential, short-duration rainfall is associated with one or more thunderstorms, while large amounts of rain falling over several days are usually associated with tropical cyclones. Continuous rainfall over weeks to months is found in those regions subjected to seasonal monsoons. In some years in India, monsoon winds sweeping in from the Bay of Bengal to the Himalayas have produced as much as 2,000 cm (800 inches) of rain in a year. However, heavy monsoonal rains are not as damaging to the environment as intense short-term bursts of torrential rain. Areas that receive perennial heavy rains have developed dense vegetation to absorb rain and have established natural drainage patterns to disperse the expected runoff. Problems arise when humans alter the configuration of normal drainage channels, leading to an increased threat of flooding, particularly during torrential cloudbursts.

Hailstorms

Large crystals of ice that form within, and fall from, a cumulonimbus cloud and strike the ground are known as hail. Strong up-draughts and down-draughts characterize such deep

▼ *Shallow clouds and those in the tropics do not reach freezing level, so ice-crystals do not form (A). Instead, a larger-than-average cloud droplet may coalesce with several million other cloud droplets to reach raindrop size. Most rainfall in the mid-latitudes is the result of snowflakes melting as they fall (B). It takes many millions of moisture droplets and ice crystals to make a single raindrop or snowflake heavy enough to fall from the cloud. Yet a snowflake can be*

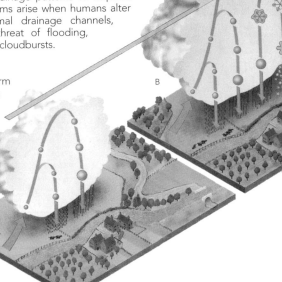

grown from ice crystals in only 20 minutes. Large hailstones need strong upcurrents of air in order to form (C). A 30 mm (1.2 inch) diameter hailstone probably needs an updraught of 100 km/h (60 mph). The turbulent air currents in a thunderstorm turn a frozen water droplet into an embryonic hailstone. There can be as many as 25 layers in a hailstone.

convective clouds, moving growing ice granules up and down, and allowing them to increase in size. Hailstones grow from graupel (large ice granules), which act as a nucleus, becoming larger due to the accretion of super-cooled water droplets as they are borne upwards on rapidly ascending air. It is not uncommon for golf ball-size hail to occur in the United States, Australia, South Africa, China and other countries prone to powerful summer thunderstorms. Such large hailstones are likely to have been carried up and down through the same cloud a number of times, over the course of 10 minutes or so, before they acquire sufficient layers of ice to be heavy enough to fall out of the cloud and on to the surface.

How damaging is hail?

It seems paradoxical that the largest hailstones are observed during late spring and early summer. Although surface heating is intense, this is also the season when cold air at upper levels can lead to deep overturning motions within the troposphere, expressed by deep convection. Furthermore, water-vapour concentrations are also high at this time due to enhanced evaporation. Such conditions reach their height across the North American high plains, stretching from Texas to Alberta. Hail conditions are also achieved in other parts of the world characterized by hot summers. In recent years, major, destructive hailstorms struck Australia and China, causing extensive damage and loss of life.

The number of hailstorms reported in the United States peaks in May and June, although April and July are also busy months. Damage to property ensues when hailstones reach some 25 mm (1 inch) in diameter, not an uncommon experience when an average May and June will each experience more than 2,000 storms producing hailstones in excess of 50 mm (2 inches) across. The largest authenticated hailstone to fall in the United States was at Coffeyville, south-east Kansas, in September 1970. It weighed 757 grammes (26.7 ounces) and had a diameter of some 14 cm (5.5 inches). Every year, hail causes about US$100 million worth of damage to property and crops in the United States. On July 11, 1990, the costliest hailstorm on record struck Denver, north-central Colorado, resulting in damage totalling US$625 million.

Australia also suffers from major hailstorms. On April 14, 1999, a a 45-minute storm generated hailstones as large as grapefruits at Sydney, New South Wales. Across an area of 2,500 sq km (1,000 sq miles), more than 30,000 roofs were damaged or destroyed and more than 40,000 vehicles damaged, resulting in total losses in excess of US$667 million.

Lightning

The power of lightning

Lightning is the visible flash of light that accompanies a massive electrical discharge and which neutralizes the charges that accumulate in a thundercloud. A typical discharge consists of several lightning strokes, which are initiated by leaders that follow an irregular path of least resistance known as the lightning channel. Intense heating by the discharge expands the channel rapidly up to a diameter of 10–25 cm (5–10 inches), creating the sound waves that are heard as thunder.

The power of a lightning strike is truly awesome: 10,000–100,000 amperes of current surge to Earth down a narrow air channel that reaches temperatures of 30,000°C (54,000°F) – more than five times the temperature at the surface of the Sun. But lightning doesn't just strike downwards. A lightning flash consists of alternating upward and downward strokes, each of which may be more than 30 km (20 miles) long.

Lightning that reaches the ground develops within the cloud, where electrons move rapidly down towards the base of the cloud in a stepped fashion. Every discharge runs for about 100 metres (330 feet), then halts for about 50 millionths of a second before continuing downwards. This process is continued as an invisible stepped leader until, near the ground, the potential gradient is so large that an upward positive current leaves the surface from tall objects such as trees

▲ *Lightning storm over Boston c. 1967. Tall buildings, television aerials and trees are struck most frequently by lightning, but people outdoors also face a serious risk, and the danger is increased if they are holding a metal object such as a golf club or umbrella.*

and buildings. Once these two currents meet, electrons flow down to establish a channel that is used by a larger return stroke. This massive, brilliant up-current is what we see, and it lasts typically for just one ten-thousandths of a second.

When lightning strikes, it travels along an air channel 1 to 5 cm (0.5 to 2 inches) across. If lightning strikes a moist surface such as a tree, road or wall, the heating effect is so great that the moisture boils explosively, sometimes blowing the object to pieces. If lightning strikes a vehicle it can travel across the metal surface before jumping to the ground through the air or across a wet tyre, which it sometimes blows out.

Thunder and lightning

Only about one in five lightning strokes are from cloud to ground. Each instantly heats the channel of air through which it flows to about 30,000°C (54,000°F). This means that the air expands incredibly quickly and very dramatically to produce a shock wave that travels away from the lightning stroke at the speed of sound. The flash from lightning effectively reaches our eyes instantaneously, whereas the sound of thunder travels at approximately 330 metres per second (730 mph). This forms the basis of a rule that we can use to estimate our distance from the ground stroke. Count the seconds between the flash and the thunder – every second indicates a distance of about 330 metres (1,000 feet). Therefore, a pause of three seconds means that the lightning hit about 1 kilometre (0.6 miles) away. This rule holds good for distances of up to 5 kilometres (3 miles); beyond which we only rarely hear the accompanying thunder, because the sound is absorbed and refracted by the air.

The dangers of lightning

Lightning strikes occur in the vicinity of thunderstorms. It generally kills people singly or in small groups, mostly during late spring and summer when tall, unstable clouds are produced. In the 21-year period from 1959–80, there were 2,286

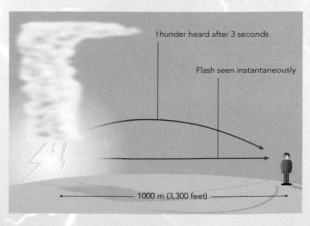

▶ Delay between seeing lightning and hearing thunder. This is because lightning travels at the speed of light – c. 300,000 km/sec (186,000 miles per second) – while thunder travels at the speed of sound – c. 330 metres/sec (730 mph).

Thunder heard after 3 seconds

Flash seen instantaneously

1000 m (3,300 feet)

fatalities in the United States from lightning strikes, mostly in Florida and Texas; an average of about 100 fatalities per year.

The downward flowing pathway of electrons, or stepped leader, of lightning always seeks out the best conducting route to the ground. Tall buildings, television aerials and trees are struck most frequently, but people in the open also face a significant risk, and the danger is increased if they are holding a metal object such as a golf club or umbrella. Taking shelter beneath a tall, isolated tree is a big mistake: the lightning is initially attracted to the tree because of its height, but may side-flash through or over the body of anyone underneath because the human body offers a better path to the surface. About a quarter of all lightning victims are struck while misguidedly sheltering under a tree.

Several basic rules should be followed to avoid being a fatality during a lightning storm. Stay inside and do not touch anything conductive: people have been killed talking on the telephone. If inside a vehicle do not touch anything: if outside avoid tall structures and do not lie down since lightning can flow through the earth.

In many parts of the world, lightning strikes are the main cause of wildfires. During a recent ten-year period in the United States, for example, more than 15,000 such fires occurred. These resulted in damage amounting to several hundred million dollars and the destruction of some 800,000 hectares (2 million acres) of forest. One curious electrical phenomenon observed at times during thunderstorms is known as 'St Elmo's Fire'. This is a luminescent electrical discharge observed on radio masts, church spires, or airplane wings. Although described as a 'fire' it does not burn, and it always remains attached to the object.

▲ *An electrical storm lights up the night sky over the prairies of the central United States.*

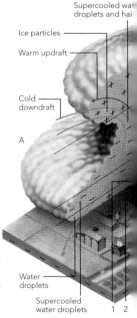

Supercooled water droplets and hail

Ice particles

Warm updraft

Cold downdraft

A

Water droplets

Supercooled water droplets

1   2

▼ Once an electrical potential of 1 million volts per metre (3.3 million volts per foot) has been created in a cloud, the lightning process begins (**A**). A stream of electrons flows down, colliding with air molecules and freeing more electrons, and in the process giving the air molecules a positive charge. This intermittent low-current discharge forms a branched pathway, known as a 'stepped leader' (**1**). As the leading negative branches of the stepped leader near the ground they induce short upward streamers of positive electrical charges from good conducting points (**2**). When a branch of the stepped leader

contacts an upward positive streamer, a complete channel of ionized air has been created. This allows a huge positive current, called the 'return stroke', to flow upward into the cloud in the form of a lightning stroke (**3**). The return stroke causes the first of the shock waves we hear as thunder (**B**). A fraction of a millisecond after the return stroke (**3**), a negatively charged dart leader passes

down the ionized channel (**4**) and triggers another upward stroke. The process is repeated several times within fractions of a second, until the charge is neutralized. Lightning conductors (**5**) generate a strong positive

-70°C ┬ 11 km
-60°C ┼ 10
        ┼ 9
+50°C ┼ 8
-40°C ┼ 7
-30°C ┼ 6
-20°C ┼ 5
-10°C ┼ 4
        ┼ 3
0°C ┼ 2
10°C ┼ 1

5   4

streamer that encourages electrical contact. Potential lightning strikes within 50 to 100 m (160–320 feet) of a building are attracted to its conductor. Thunder (**B**) is caused by the narrow lightning stroke heating the column of air (**6**) surrounding it to around 30,000°C (54,000°F) and expanding it explosively (**7**) at supersonic speeds under a force 10–100 times normal atmospheric pressure. The immense shock wave becomes a sound wave within about 1 metre (3.3 feet), producing the sound of thunder.

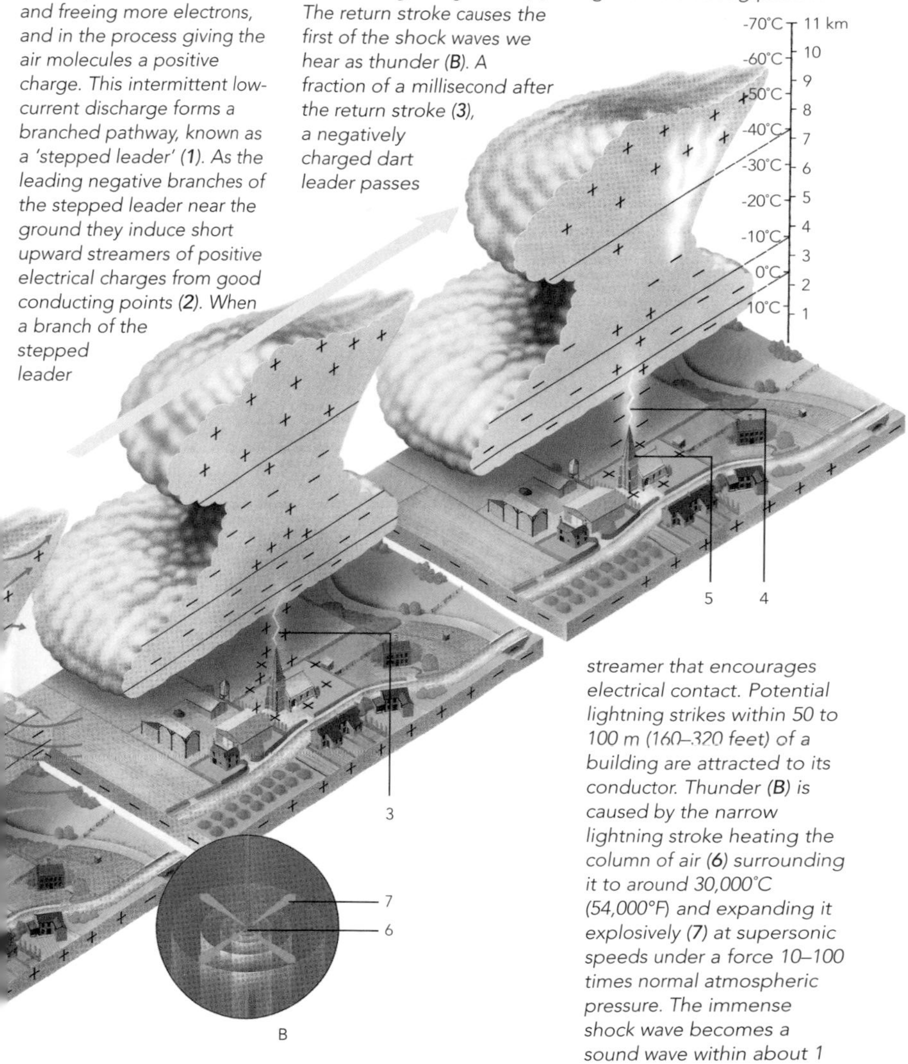

3

7
6

B

Snow and Ice

Winds in the atmosphere result from differences in barometric pressure. The current of air that flows from west to east over mid-latitudes at a height of about 12 km (7.5 feet) is known as the jet stream, and its position is related to seasonal variations between masses of expanded, warm, tropical and denser, cold, polar air. Differences in temperature are needed to create the jet stream, but the jet stream itself also exerts a very important influence on the movement of warm and cold air masses that are formed over the oceans and continents. The boundaries between such air masses are marked by weather fronts that can be either 'cold' or 'warm'. In the northern hemisphere, cold fronts in the winter bring thunderstorms and ultimately snow, ice, or rain. Blizzards are formed when winds reach speeds of 60 km/h (40 mph), together with temperatures of less than −6°C (21°F) and accompanying snow. The area of greatest snowfall is usually located about 200 km (125 miles) north of the associated low-pressure centre, where moist air from the south moves cyclonically around the centre. Progressing southward from the area of heaviest snowfall, sleet and freezing rain are found, followed even further south by rain.

How snow is formed

Since it must first be in liquid form, freezing rain can only form when the air temperature in the cloud cover is below freezing. With surface temperatures below freezing, the liquid rain freezes as it strikes the cold ground surface. Sleet is the result of an upper-atmosphere temperature inversion. Liquid raindrops form above a colder freezing layer and

▼ *A satellite view of the east coast of the United States after the snow storm of January 25, 2000. The winter storm affected much of the east coast of the US on January 24–25, 2000. Snowfall totals of 100 cm (4 inches) or more were recorded in every eastern seaboard state from South Carolina to New Hampshire, and included 61 cm (24 inches) in Montgomery County, North Carolina, and 51.6 cm (20.3 inches) at Raleigh, North Carolina (a record accumulation for any single event or any single month). The storm also brought strong winds – wind gusts of 54–74 knots were recorded off the North Carolina coast – which caused blowing and drifting snow.*

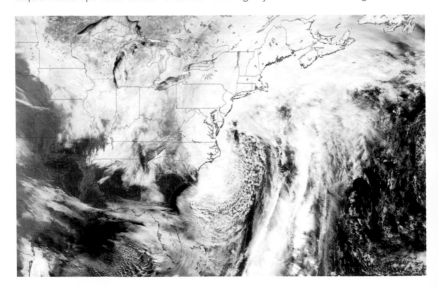

▲ *Snow-covered cars outside the 96 Street subway station in Manhattan, New York, USA. The blizzard of 1996 dropped more than 55 centimetres (22 inches) of snow.*

become frozen as they fall through the freezing layer, forming sleet at the surface. Snow requires a temperature below freezing for formation. Heavy snow warnings are issued when the expected accumulation is 10 cm (4 inches) within 24 hours. Blizzard warnings are issued when the wind speeds and minimum temperatures are appreciable.

Snowstorms

One of the coldest US winters on record took place during January–February 1977. Snow reached the second storey of some buildings in the state of New York, and thousands of people were unemployed because industries had to be closed due to shortages of fuel. The following year, a severe blizzard killed almost 100 people in the eastern United States. Blizzards can be particularly deadly when they are followed by a sudden burst of warm weather that can trigger flooding. In January 1996, a very strong blizzard from Canada blew into the north-eastern United States, killing more than 154 people and resulting in record levels of snowfalls in the states of Ohio, Pennsylvania, West Virginia, and New Jersey. The blizzard was followed by unusually warm weather with rain rapidly melting the snow cover and creating severe flooding. The severe seesawing in temperatures resulted in an additional 200 deaths due to flooding and US$3 billion in property damage.

In the United Kingdom, two of the most severe winters occurred in 1947 and 1962. In 1947, snow fell everyday somewhere in the UK from January 22 to March 17, and with temperatures rarely struggling above freezing, snow progressively accumulated. The winter of 1962–63 was even colder – in fact the coldest for more than 220 years – with mean maximum temperatures during January more than 5° C below average across much of Wales and England. In southern England, deep snow lay on the ground from December 26 until early March.

Icestorms

In 1998, as much as 100 mm (4 inches) of freezing rain created one of the most expensive natural disasters in Canadian history. From January 4–10, 80 hours of freezing rain produced Can$3 billion (US$2.2 billion) of damages in the provinces of Ontario, Quebec, and Newfoundland. The main power system, transmission towers, wooden utility poles and power lines collapsed under the sheer weight of clinging ice. More than 700,000 people were left without power for as long as a month, and damage was so severe that repairs were impossible and the entire network had to be rebuilt. The modern economy's dependence on electrical power made the impact of the icestorm much greater than it would have been a century ago.

Avalanches

The word avalanche is derived from the French dialect word *avalance*, meaning descent. An avalanche is a mass of snow, sometimes mixed with ice, soil, pebbles, and boulders, that hurtles down the side of a mountain destroying everything in its path. Avalanches often produce an accompanying strong wind that uproots trees along the margins of its downward course. Above the snow line, where the supply of snow exceeds loss by evaporation or melting, surplus snow, often compacted to ice, slowly descends to lower altitudes in the form of glaciers or more rapidly as an ice-fall or avalanche. The rate of descent is most rapid and the consequences for people and property is most severe on the steepest slopes. The loosening effect on the basal foundation of a mass of snow, either due to spring rains or the warm, dry föhn winds common in mountainous areas, can result in the wholesale break-away and sliding of snow and ice accumulations on a mountainside or peak. Once primed in such a way, a single skier, thunder, or even a loud shout can set an overloaded or unstable mass of snow on its downward descent.

Types of avalanche

Snow avalanches occur most frequently on slopes of between 25 and 40°, although they have also been recorded on slopes as low as 15° and as high as 60°. Below and above these limits, they cannot occur. This is because at the lower angles, the role of gravity is too small to help promote failure on the snowpack, while the higher angles do not allow the snow to accumulate to unstable thicknesses. Avalanches, as we generally use the term, consist primarily of snow and ice,

▼ *A powder avalanche crashes through the Savoia Pass on the north-west side of K2, Karakoram Range, Himalayas, Pakistan.*

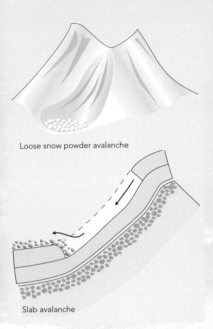

Loose snow powder avalanche

Slab avalanche

perhaps with some contained rock, soil and other debris, loosened by freeze-thaw action. The three main types of snow avalanche are: powder avalanches, slab avalanches, and wet-shot avalanches.

Powder avalanches

Powder avalanches usually start from a single point and accumulate snow as they move down the slope forming a snowball effect. This type of avalanche is most common following heavy snowfall of 2 cm/h (1 inch per hour) or more, often on a smooth surface after rain or frost. The new snow is very light and mixes with the air forming a powder. The snow starts to move as a soft slab and gathers speed and more snow. The snow will ride up on a cushion of air and become an airborne powder avalanche travelling at 100 to 300 km/h (62 to 186 mph). In front of the avalanche will be a blast wave that can have devastating effect on contact with obstacles. Inhalation of snow and suffocation is often a major cause of death with this type of avalanche.

▲ *Loose-snow powder avalanches form in snow with little internal cohesion among individual snow crystals. They originate at a point and grow wider as they sweep up more snow in their descent. Slab avalanches begin with the fracture of snow slopes. Cracks multiply quickly and follow complex paths that rely on slope geometry for anchorage. In contrast to loose-snow powder avalanches, slab avalanches depend on the propagation of fractures by stored energy in a relatively cohesive layer.*

Slab avalanches

This is the most common type of winter avalanche and it is associated with the build-up of fresh snow on leeward slopes. A slab is a compact snow surface layer that can detach from the rest of the snow cover slipping forward onto ground or further snow creating an avalanche. The snow requires wind speeds of 16–50 km/h (10–30 mph) in order to maintain movement. After a heavy snowfall, it could occur on any degree of slope. The slab moves as a single unit but breaks up as it flows over the ground. If there is enough fresh snow and the slope is steep enough, then a slab avalanche may become a powder avalanche.

The hard slab avalanche represents one of the greatest snow dangers because it appears as a solid mass despite its instability. It is most often triggered by a combination of strong winds (more than 50 km/h or 30 mph) and particularly cold temperatures. An extensive cold spell increases the possibility of these avalanches. Hard slab avalanches release in one unit like a soft slab, but break up into chunks of snow and ice that have enormous destructive power. Hard slabs can be identified by local subsidence and by cracking or dull booming noises emanating from the snow surface.

Wet avalanches

Wet avalanches occur after a warm spell or during the spring thaw. The snow becomes heavy as it begins to turn to water, changing density from about 350 to 500 kg/cu m (22–31 lbs/

AVALANCHES

cu feet). Wet avalanches frequently occur and are generally small and unimportant. These are the easiest to predict due to the weather conditions for their formation. Cracks in the snow and the appearance of large balls of snow rolling down are visible clues.

Debris avalanches
Debris avalanches take the form of disaggregated landslides, consisting entirely of rock fragments. The most massive avalanches are preceded by air blasts and turbulent air currents that can travel at twice the speed of the avalanche itself and which can be lethal and destructive in their own right. Like other rapidly moving gravity flows – such as pyroclastic flows – avalanches often carry sufficient momentum to climb up valley sides and to overtop ridges and other topographic barriers. Two principal types are recognized: **channeled**, where they are limited within valleys, chutes or gullies; and **unconfined**, where they occur on open mountainsides. Some unconfined avalanches composed of dry snow give the appearance of a mass of powder whirling in the air. This type is called an airborne powder-avalanche.

Avalanche size and scale
Avalanches mixed with rock and debris can have relatively high densities, for example 400 kg/cubic metre (25 lbs/cubic feet), whereas airborne suspensions dominated by dry snow may have densities lower than 10 kg/cubic metre (0.5 lbs/cubic foot). Knowing the downward velocity and density it is possible to calculate the impact pressure of an avalanche. Small powder avalanches have impact pressures, ranging from 0.1 to one tonne per square metre (0.01–0.1 ton/square foot), sufficient to bury or suffocate an individual. The larger pressures generated by faster and more dense avalanches are capable of knocking a train off

	THE WORST AVALANCHES OF THE 20TH CENTURY*			
	Location	Country	Date	Killed
1	Sirnak, Siirt, Elazig, Batman, Bingol, Diyarbakir, Hakkari, Tunceli provinces	Turkey	February 1, 1992	261
2	Jammu and Kashmir, Ladakh,	India	March 15, 1988	250
3	Kashmir province	India	January 17, 1995	250
4	Caucasus Mountain	Russia	January 28, 1993	239
5	Blons, Langen Valley	Austria	January 12, 1954	200
6	Ozengeli	Turkey	January 18, 1993	135
7	Near Karmadon (North Ossetia-Alania)	Russia	September 20, 2002	111
8	Salang region	Afghanistan	March 1993	100
9	Mazar-E-Sharif	Afghanistan	March 27, 1997	100
10	Phuban (Astor Valley)	Pakistan	March 11, 1983	95
11	Manag, Panchathar districts	Nepal	November 11, 1995	95

* does not include fatalities where the cause was a combination of avalanche and earthquake

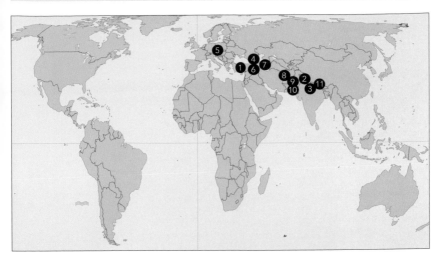

▲ Map of the worst avalanches of the 20th century. Locations are marked by circles. Most countries now operate an avalanche warning system based on weather conditions. Unfortunately, however, not all avalanches are predictable.

its tracks (2–2.5 tonnes/square metre, 0.2–0.25 tons/square foot) and moving or dislodging concrete structures (100 tonnes/square metre, 10 tons/square foot). There is no international standard for avalanche size, but the Japanese have devised an avalanche magnitude scale. This ranges from one to seven, with the magnitude of an event defined as the logarithm to base 10 of the mass of the snow involved in tonnes.

Analogous to a landslide, the downward velocity of an avalanche will depend on the slope angle, the density of the snow mass, the shearing resistance at the base of the slide, and the total length of its downward path. Rates of movement can range from very slow to a record 370 km/h (230 mph), but typical velocities are on the order of 40–60 km/h (25–40 mph). Wet, loose, snow avalanches have velocities in the 15 to 65 km/h (10–40 mph) range, while movements of dry, loose snow travel at speeds of 65 to 100 km/h (40–60 mph), and dry, airborne avalanches at velocities as high as 330 to 370 km/h (200–230 mph). In 1962 the avalanche on Mount Huascarán in the Andes of north-west Peru achieved speeds of 100 km/h (60 mph) and maintained an average of 60 km/h (40 mph) as it sped down the valley. The avalanche consisted of about 13 million cubic metres (460 million cubic feet) of material, of which only 25 percent was ice and snow. In March 1982, a large snow avalanche struck Alpine Meadows, a ski resort at Lake Tahoe, Sierra Nevada, north-east California. The avalanche achieved speeds of 130 km/h (80 mph) before slamming into the ski lift and adjoining structures killing seven people.

Avalanche fatalities

Death by avalanche may occur in any one of a number of very different ways, including impact, suffocation, snow inhalation, hypothermia, exhaustion, or shock. Every year, avalanches affect a small percentage of the many millions who enjoy winter sports, and casualties are usually skiers, snowboarders, climbers, and walkers. Sometimes, large avalanches also impact upon towns and villages in mountainous areas, where population increases are leading to more construction in areas of higher avalanche risk. Inter-annual variation in fatalities is significant but numbers are broadly increasing. Compared to other natural hazards, they remain small, annually averaging 35 in Austria, 30 each in France and Japan, 25 each in Switzerland and Italy, and 14 in the United States.

Mitigating the avalanche threat

Some countries and communities have introduced avalanche zoning, and in France communities under potential threat are classified into red (high hazard) and blue (moderate hazard) areas. Construction is forbidden in the red zone, and special building-construction codes must be followed in the blue zone. These include the use of heavily reinforced concrete and the absence of windows and roof overhangs on those parts of buildings that face upslope. A similar zonation has also ben adopted in the ski resort of Vail, north-central Colorado. Here, an avalanche-influence zone divides into a red area, where impact pressures are expected to exceed 2.9 tonnes per square metre (31 tons per square feet) and all residential construction is banned, and a blue area, where construction is permitted but must be engineered to withstand specific impact-velocity thresholds.

Both structural and non-structural means are utilized to mitigate avalanches hazard. Structural methods involve the modification or protection of avalanche-prone terrain, and

AVALANCHE DANGER SCALE

US and European avalanche danger-scales rate avalanche hazard similarly, but use different colours for some of the levels. The differences are noted below.

Danger level	Colour	Likelihood of avalanche	Travel safety
LOW	Green	Snowpack is generally stable. Only isolated areas of instability Natural or human-triggered avalanches unlikely	Back-country travel is fairly safe
MODERATE	Yellow	Some areas of instability. Natural avalanches unlikely; human-triggered avalanches possible	Back-country travel possible with caution
CONSIDERABLE	Orange in America, Ochre in Europe	Unstable areas probable. Natural avalanches possible; human-triggered avalanches probable	Back-country travel possible with extreme caution
HIGH	Red in America, Orange in Europe	Unstable areas highly likely on various slopes and aspects. Natural and human-triggered avalanches highly likely	Back-country travellers should avoid steep slopes and wind-loaded slopes
EXTREME	Black in America, Red in Europe	Extremely unstable layers in snowpack. Natural and human-triggered avalanches are certain. Large, destructive avalanches probable	Back-country travellers should avoid any steeply angled terrain

▲ *Avalanche defences above the town of Wengen, south-central Switzerland. The fences are designed to slow down, or arrest the advance of an avalanche.*

include placing wind baffles on the windward side of the avalanche area to help prevent snow build up. Snow fences can also be built to prevent snow drifting and encourage accumulation in areas where avalanches are not expected to occur. Tree planting along known avalanche tracks or paths also has a role to play in reducing the hazard, although many avalanches start above the tree line. In this regard, it is worth pointing out that deforestation has contributed to a large increase in the number of avalanches over the past 200 years, particularly in Austria.

Non-structural methods are directed towards modifying the volume of the accumulated snowpack. This involves artificially triggering avalanches before the snow accumulates to dangerous levels and before the tourist season begins. Avalanches are intentionally triggered by means of strategically placed explosive charges, or by the firing of specially designed artillery shells. At times, artillery pieces have been pre-positioned in avalanche-prone zones to be fired blind at susceptible areas during blizzards.

Landslides

Landslides happen in almost every region of the world, constituting a hazard that is both ubiquitous and potentially deadly. Landslides include fast-moving debris flows, slow-moving slumps, and a variety of flows and slides triggered by earthquakes, volcanoes, and excessive rainfall. Each year, these hazards cost billions of dollars and cause numerous fatalities and injuries. Awareness and education about these hazards is a first step toward reducing their damaging effects.

Landslides and other forms of mass movement by themselves can do enormous damage to property, destroying roads, homes, bridges, dams, port facilities, airports, and recreational areas, and at times cause injury and loss of life. No building, regardless of its structural configuration, can withstand the effects of downslope land movement, which is a particular problem as much landslide damage occurs in hillside housing developments where the land has been improperly graded. In a common land-grading procedure called 'cut and fill', material is cut from the upper slope and graded to construct a horizontal surface for grounding a building. The rock debris brought downslope to produce this level surface is called fill. If the cut is too steep, the upper mass of soil can move downslope, pushing a building off its foundation. If the fill is not properly compacted, it too can move downslope, destabilizing a building's foundation.

Slope instability
Imagine a beautiful natural landscape with hills and valleys. Why does a portion of the land change and migrate down

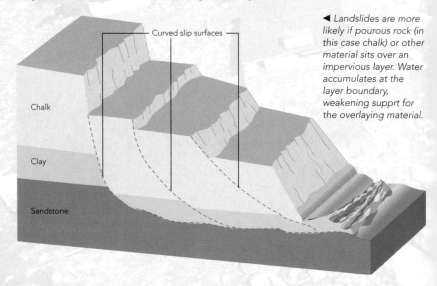

Chalk

Clay

Sandstone

Curved slip surfaces

◄ Landslides are more likely if pourous rock (in this case chalk) or other material sits over an impervious layer. Water accumulates at the layer boundary, weakening supprt for the overlaying material.

THE WORST LANDSLIDES OF THE 20TH CENTURY			
Location	Country	Date	Killed
Yungay	Peru	June 13, 1970	18,000
Khait	Tajikistan	1949	12,000
	Europe	December 13, 1916	10,000
Huaraz	Peru	December 1941	5,000
Colima	Honduras	September 20, 1973	2,800
Ranrahirca	Peru	January 10, 1962	2,000
Longarone	Italy	October 9, 1963	1,189
Bihar, Bengal	India	October 1, 1968	1,000
Villatina, Medellín	Colombia	September 27, 1987	640
Chungar	Peru	March 18, 1971	600
Guangzhou	China	March 23, 1934	500
Assam	India	September 18, 1948	500

slope? What force governs downslope movement of rock and soil? The answer is gravity. Not the vertical component of gravity, but the component that is tangential to the potential or active slip surface. When this component exceeds the shearing resistance of the rock or soil, either because its driving force has been increased by a steepening of the slope or because the shearing resistance of the rock or soil has been reduced, there will be downslope movement. Both types of slope instability can be generated by natural or human agents.

Slope stability is influenced by three principal factors: (i) the slope's exposure to transient agents, such as climatic changes or earthquakes; (ii) the nature or make-up of the slope, its history of downward movement, and the level of human interference – for example, the slope may have been steepened by the removal of material at its base or the addition of material at its top; and (iii) the inherent shearing resistance of the rock or soil. The slope's material make-up is very important in determining the ease of downslope motion. A number of factors, therefore, are important in determining the intrinsic strength or cohesion of the slope material. These stability factors are offset by changes in the fluid pore pressure and the slope angle. Some hillsides are intrinsically weak due to pre-existing geological conditions, such as the presence of ancient slip surfaces, rock layers dipping at different angles from the natural slope, or contacts between different rock types.

Types of landslide
Landslides can involve a broad range of material, including rock, soil, landfill, ice, and snow. Velocity is the most important criteria for characterizing all types of mass movement. Rates of downslope movement are said to be rapid, moderate, or slow with various subdivisions. Rockfalls have extremely rapid velocities ranging from 3 to 100 metres (10 to 330 feet) per second. Rapid velocities are characterized by

speeds of about 1.5 metres (4.9 feet) per day, slow velocities typically 1.5 metres (4.9 feet) per year, and very slow velocities by about 0.3 metres (1 foot) every 5 years. It is important to emphasize that a single landslide type can display a wide range of downslope velocities. Debris avalanches range from 100 metres (330 feet) per second to 0.3 metres (1 foot) per minute, rockslides from 100 metres (330 feet) per second to as slow as 6 cm (2.36 inches) per year, and mud and debris flows typically from 3 metres (9.8 feet) per second to a very slow 6 cm (2.36 inches) per year. The latter rate of movement is termed creep and such a flow is called a 'creep slide'.

Rock falls

Rock falls can happen without warning and have devastating consequences. The province of Alberta, western Canada, has been subjected for millennia to erosion by glaciers that have produced a steep topography susceptible to rock-falling and landsliding. In 1903, a massive rock fall sent about 82 million tonnes (30 million metres^3) of limestone plunging into the town of Frank, south-west Alberta, at speeds approaching 100 metres (330 feet) per second. In two minutes, the town was obliterated.

Avalanches

An avalanche is a mixture of snow, ice, soil, rock, and boulder that moves downslope at terrifying speed, annihilating everything in its path. It can generate a strong accompanying wind that tears trees from their roots. On a steep slope, the underlying material supporting the massive snow cover can give way because it has been soaked by spring rains or destabilized by alternating periods of precipitation and warm, dry winds (föhn or foehn) flowing down the leeward side of a slope. Sometimes a slope is so unstable that thunder or even a loud shout is sufficient to trigger sliding of the overloaded snow (which is why skiers are asked to observe complete silence when crossing potentially unstable areas). An avalanche can travel at speeds ranging from 40 to 300 km/h (25 to 190 mph), depending on the angle of the slope, the density of the snow mixture, and the length of its path.

▼ *Debris avalanches and debris flows, or 'mudslides', are shallow landslides that travel rapidly downslope as wet slurries. The avalanche carries rocks, bushes, and other debris as it pours down the slopes. Debris slides are most likely to occur on steep slopes where loose layers of rocky colluvium overlie. Debris flow and mudslide tracks are characterized by long stretches of bare, generally unstable channel banks that have been eroded by the rapid movement of debris.*

Scar area of initial failure

Track (may or may not be eroded)

Zone of deposition (fan)

Bedrock

Soil or colluvium

► *The Slumgullion landslide, Hinsdale County, south-west Colorado. The Slumgullion landslide probably dammed Lake Fork between 800 and 900 years ago. It appears to be the only landslide in the area with continuously moving material.*

Debris flows

Debris flows start on slopes steep enough to make walking difficult. Once started, however, debris flows can even travel over gently sloping ground. The most hazardous areas are canyon bottoms, stream channels, areas near the outlets of canyons, and slopes excavated for buildings and roads. Debris flows (also referred to as mudslides or mudflows) typically occur during or following intense rainfall on water-saturated soil. They usually start on steep hillsides as soil slumps or slides that liquefy and accelerate to high speeds. Multiple debris flows that start high in canyons commonly funnel into channels. There, they merge, gain volume, and travel long distances from their source. Debris flows commonly begin in swales (depressions at the top of small gullies) on steep slopes, making areas down slope from swales particularly hazardous. Road-cuts and other altered or excavated areas of slopes are particularly susceptible to debris flows. These and other landslides onto roadways are common during rainstorms, and often occur during milder rainfall conditions than those needed for debris flows on natural slopes. Areas where surface runoff is channelled, such as along roadways and below culverts, are common sites for the formation of debris flows and other landslides.

Not surprisingly, water plays a major role in mudflow and debris flow formation and transport. These flows occur on slopes where heavily water-saturated soils lubricate incipient basal failure planes, decreasing their shear resistance to movement and facilitating downward flow. The rate of downslope movement can be as rapid as 3 metres (10 feet) per second or as slow as 6 cm (2.36 inches) per year and the material can move in surges. Mud and debris flows are common in many parts of the world, including the Czech Republic, Slovakia, Switzerland, France, Italy, Indonesia, the Philippines, and the United States. Even when they are not sudden catastrophes with very fast velocities, they can result in substantial surface deformation and damage. The marked, substantial decline of a mass of land along a coast or road cut is called a slump. Slumping is a perennial problem where coastal cliffs are interleaved with thin layers of clay that are easily lubricated during the rainy season, decreasing their frictional resistance to downslope sliding. This is the case in the coastal regions near Santa Monica, south-west California, where the rainy season is typically followed by slow-moving landslides or slumping. This type of movement is also common around parts of the British coast, particularly in Dorset and the Isle of Wight. Movement is initially slow and usually can be recognized before the slump is too far advanced.

▼ *Aerial view of Los Corales sector of Caraballeda, western Venezuela, 1999. Debris flows and sediment-laden flash floods caused by torrential rain destroyed or damaged most structures on this alluvial fan.*

Mass movement on volcanoes

Several types of mass movement are volcano-driven or are initiated as a consequence of the volcano's existence. Fast-moving avalanches of hot ash, rock fragments, and gas can move down the sides of a volcano during explosive eruptions or when the steep side of a growing lava dome collapses and breaks apart. These pyroclastic flows can be as hot as 600–800°C (1,100–1,500°F) and typically move at velocities 160 km/h (100 mph) or more.

Volcanic debris flows

Debris avalanches, which involve rapid downhill movement of rock – sometimes accompanied by other debris, snow or ice, can also form on the slopes of volcanoes, where they range in size from small movements of loose debris at the surface to large-scale collapse of the entire summit or flanks. Steep volcanoes are susceptible to landslides because they are built partly of layers of loose volcanic rock fragments, some of which may have been altered to soft, slippery clay minerals by circulating hot, acidic ground water. Landslides on volcano slopes are triggered when eruptions, heavy rainfall, or large earthquakes cause these materials to break free and move downhill. At least five large debris avalanches have swept down the slopes of Mount Rainier, Washington, USA, during the past 6,000 years. The largest volcano debris in recent years occurred at the start of the eruption of Mount St Helens on May 18, 1980, but it is estimated that such events occur perhaps four or five times every century.

Lahars

Mudflows or debris flows composed mostly of volcanic materials on the flanks of a volcano are called lahars. These flows of mud, rock, and water can rush down valleys and stream channels at speeds in excess of 60 km/h (40 mph), and can travel distances of more than 100 km (60 miles). Some lahars contain so much rock debris (up to 90 percent by weight) that they look like fast-moving rivers of wet concrete. Close to their source, these flows are powerful enough to rip up and carry trees, houses, and huge boulders kilometres downstream. Farther downstream, they entomb everything in their path in mud. Historically, lahars have been one of the deadliest volcano hazards, and they can occur both during an eruption and when a volcano is quiet. The water that creates lahars can come from melting snow and ice (especially water from a glacier melted by a pyroclastic flow or surge), intense rainfall, or the breakout of a summit crater lake.

Seismogenic landslides

Nevados Huascarán is the highest peak in the Peruvian Andes. On January 10, 1962, without any known triggering event, a huge mass of rock and glacial ice fell from the west face of the peak initiating a debris flow. The flow moved rapidly down slope along river valleys, discharging as a 10–15 metre (33–50 foot) -high wall of debris into the town of

Ranrahirca, killing 2,000 people. A scar with a 1 km (0.6 mile) -high overhanging cliff was left on the top of the mountain. On May 31, 1970, an earthquake measuring 7.9 on the Richter scale, occurred in a subduction zone beneath the Pacific Ocean, about 135 km (85 miles) away from Huascarán. The ground shook for 45 seconds and a portion of the same west-facing slope failed with an explosive sound. One hundred million cubic metres (3,500 million feet^3) of the mountain fell away and hurtled downslope at speeds of between 280 and 335 km/h (175–210 mph). The flow dropped 4 km (2.5 miles) in just three or four minutes and buried the town of Yungay. Eighteen thousand people were lost beneath 30 metres (100 feet) of rock. The remaining glacier face above the 1962 and 1970 scars remains unstable indicating that the downslope areas, which are now repopulated, are still highly vulnerable.

Large deposits of the wind-deposited silt and dust known as loess, cover large parts of China near the northern border with Mongolia. Loess is strong enough to form vertical slopes when deposited, but it loses its strength instantly once the ground starts to shake. On December 16, 1920, an earthquake, measuring 8.6 on the Richter scale, produced about 30 seconds of ground shaking that affected more than 50,000 square kilometres (19,000 square miles) of Gansu province, in north-west China. Hills of dry loess moved laterally creating an airborne suspension of material that flowed down valleys burying villages in its path and taking the lives of an estimated 180,000 people.

Precipitation-triggered landslides

Much of southern California's coastline is underlain by a thick sequence of sedimentary rocks that are prone to mass movement. The phenomenal rate of post-World War II growth in southern California provided tremendous pressure to develop the region's extensive coastal canyon-lands, despite the canyons being characterized by ancient landslides and inter-bedded clay deposits. Grading operations completed in the late 1960s, which involved massive amounts of earth moving and major topographic re-contouring, greatly exacerbated the potential for landslides. The heavy rains of 1977–78 caught southern California by surprise. Homeowners covered their yards with sheets of plastic to prevent additional flow into the already saturated hill slopes. In the early morning of October 2, 1978, the Bluebird Canyon, near Laguna Beach, suffered a catastrophic landslide that destroyed or damaged 40 homes and forced the evacuation of 260 people. Residents heard the popping sounds of downed electrical lines and the cracking of wood-framed houses. Over a three-hour interval, residents watched as a continuous movement of earth split and smashed their homes, causing damage totalling US$10 million. A headwall scarp 800 metres (2,600 feet) long and 10 metres (33 feet) -high was created. The Laguna landslide was the result of the reactivation of an ancient slide surface. The walls of the canyon and the bedding planes of the sedimentary rocks are both inclined at an angle of 25°. Sliding was promoted due to the reduction in shearing resistance by the slow percolation of rainwater into a clay seam located about 20 metres (65 feet) below the surface and by the fact that the ground surface was parallel to the dip of the underlying rock strata.

Monsoon landslides, Nepal, 2002

Nepal's close proximity to one of the youngest mountain ranges in the world means that it is a frequent victim of natural disasters. The Himalayas experience some of the highest rates of erosion in the world, made more acute by the adverse geology, topography, and land use in the region, and worsened by the humid sub-tropical temperatures. The extreme temperatures and annual monsoon season means that rapid rock weathering and heavy rainfall are predominant features of this area and are responsible for inducing major landslides and erosion.

In addition, deforestation is rapidly destroying Nepal's delicate mountain environment, which increases its vulnerability to landslides and flooding. Although soil erosion is a natural process in the unstable Himalayas, deforestation doubles the normally expected soil loss, and livestock grazing on the cleared fields exacerbates the problem. In 2002, a particulary heavy monsoon season caused severe flooding throughout south-east Asia and landslides throughout Nepal, killing close to 500 people in 47 of Nepal's 75 districts.

The destruction caused by the landslides in Nepal was exacerbated by the proximity of villages to potentially hazardous hills and mountains and the poor quality of the housing itself. About 92 percent of the population lives in

▼ *Landslide of chalk cliff near St Margaret's Bay, Dover, south-east England, 2000. The white cliffs recede about 2.5 cm (1 inch) each year through erosion. The landslide in 2000 was blamed on periods of heavy rain followed by cold temperatures. Rain is absorbed into the cliff-face, freezes, then expands when temperatures rise again, causing cracks within the chalk.*

the hills and lowland areas underneath the mountains. These districts regularly experience mild to violent seismic activity that often sets off devastating landslides that, due to the traditional construction of houses and their positioning on slopes, cause a high loss of life, livestock, and property. Limited accessibility often cuts off such areas for days or weeks from the outside world and, in the case of the 2002 disaster, cuts off aid and rescue teams. Despite the severity of the monsoon rains in 2002, landslides are common throughout the region and could be prevented through careful planning. The small rural communities generally affected by the landslides, however, rely on their proximity to the mountains.

Landslide mitigation

The best form of landslide prevention is simply to avoid building in landslide-prone areas. If this is not feasible, lives can be saved by official warnings to evacuate homes when the danger of landslide is imminent. Are there ways, however, to mitigate or rectify potential problems so that these kinds of stark personal decisions do not have to be made? Landslides are often the result of human activities, like the excessive cut-and-fill constructions discussed earlier, the denudation of hillside vegetation (which facilitates downslope loss of soils), and the alteration of the pattern of natural drainage systems. One measure to limit landslide risk, therefore, is to introduce and enforce restrictions.

▼ There are various constructions that can help mitigate against damage caused by rock falls and avalanches. Retaining walls, barricades, grating cribs, netting, and the planting of trees can all help to slow down and arrest slides of rock or snow.

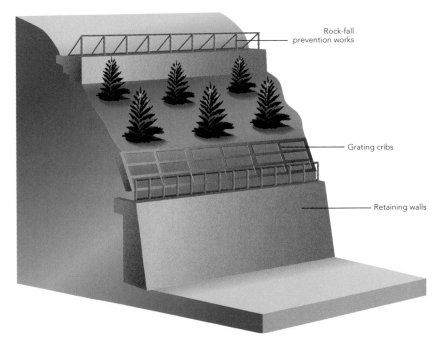

Rock-fall prevention works

Grating cribs

Retaining walls

Suppose, however, that social considerations like the need to expand habitable areas because of overcrowding make it undesirable to enact such bans in areas vulnerable to debris flows, landslides, rock-falls, and avalanches. If we cannot feasibly bar construction in these hazard-prone areas, then at least we can enforce engineering countermeasures that will make them a lot safer. Properly engineered construction can slow, deflect, or trap moving mud and debris flows. The key here is proper groundwater drainage and the diversion of surface water away from gully areas, which tend to focus downslope drainage. For this purpose, rock-fall chutes and debris run-out areas can be constructed in some areas. Mechanical stabilization of hillsides to prevent landslides is also possible. Revetments or barricades such as wickerwork fences and retaining walls of stone or concrete can be constructed to stabilize downslope movements. Anchors can be inserted into firm bedrock to minimize damage from movements of more mobile overlying rock and soil material. Treatment of steep-angled slopes with gunite (a mixture of cement, sand, and water sprayed onto a mould) is helpful, particularly if it is reinforced with wire mesh. In California, as at many sites in developed countries, prosperity has allowed homebuyers to build large, elaborate houses in marginal areas in the expectation that engineering will keep them safe. But there are no guarantees that engineering measures will withstand the worst-case landslides. Engineering can clearly minimize landslide risks but it is impossible to guarantee against disaster.

Desertification

Desertification is the process by which a desert gradually spreads into neighbouring areas of semi-desert, transforming them into true desert. The change may result from a natural event, such as the destruction of vegetation by fire or a small climatic change, but it occurs most frequently as a result of human activity. In many semi-arid areas and dry grasslands, the vegetation becomes overgrazed by domestic animals, so that the land is left bare. Wind and rain then erode the soil, removing any residual fertility, so that no new vegetation can survive. Once the vegetation and soil have disappeared, the land becomes desert.

In 2001, seven years after the founding of the United Nations' Convention to Combat Desertification, the UN Secretary-General Kofi Annan warned, "drought and desertification threaten the livelihood of over one billion people in more than 110 countries around the world". Desertification is the degradation of the arable drylands on the margins of deserts; arid but arable lands are those regions of the world

▶ Villagers clearing wind-blown Saharan sand from a house in Mauritania, West Africa. Moving dunes are most problematic around desert margins. In these regions, overgrazing, wood cutting, and intensive agriculture can remove the scant natural vegetation that helps to contain the drifting sand.

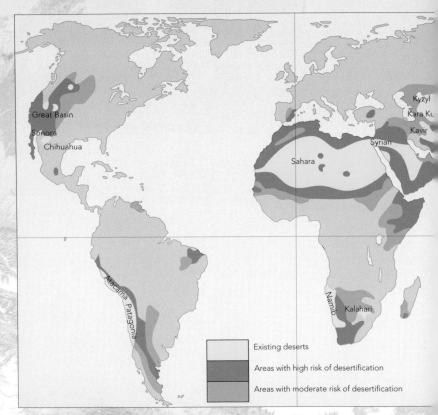

Great Basin
Sonora
Chihuahua
Sahara
Kyzyl
Kara Ku
Kavir
Syrian
Atacama
Patagonia
Namib
Kalahari

Existing deserts

Areas with high risk of desertification

Areas with moderate risk of desertification

Gobi
Takla Makan

ar

Great Sandy
Gibson   Simpson
Great Victoria

that receive an annual rainfall of 25–200 mm (1–8 inches). Desertification is a major global environmental issue because of the link between land degradation and a decline in agricultural production, but its causes are manifold. Regions prone to desertification are subjected to a rigorous and uncertain climate and biophysical systems are stressed between abundance and drought. By far the worst contributor to desertification, however, is human activity, through overcultivation and overgrazing, excessive irrigation, and deforestation. Drylands now cover 40 percent of the Earth's total land area and contain 20 percent of its population. Africa is by far the worst affected by desertification, with 75 percent of drylands now degraded. The situation is worsening worldwide, with the area of desertification increasing at about 60,000 sq kilometres (23,000 sq miles) per year.

A man-made tragedy
Fertile soil, crops, and species' biodiversity are the first casualties of desertification. People suffer as food and water supplies dwindle, and in the worst cases, land degradation can trigger famine, mass migration, and economic collapse. In 1968 drought and desertification in sub-Saharan Africa killed 250,000 people, the death of 12 million cattle, and a complete collapse of agricultural production in five countries.

153

DESERTIFICATION

Desertification leads to an estimated annual loss in agricultural production of US$42 billion, and is the leading cause of poverty in the world's most arid regions. Drylands are fragile ecosystems that respond quickly to climate change. For example, satellite imagery reveals that the southern boundary of the Sahara fluctuates annually by as much as 200 kilometres (125 miles). Desertification reduces the land's resilience to natural climate-variability. In the past, semi-arid areas recovered easily after long periods of drought. Increased human intervention and poor land management, however, has damaged and removed vegetation and made the soil less productive. Poor land management combined with severe drought can lead to extreme topsoil erosion, as in the 1930s 'Dust Bowl' in the Great Plains of the United States. An additional problem is the use of trees and bushes for firewood by indigenous people. With a growing population there is an increasing need for fuel, and so landscapes become depleted of trees. One frightening statistic is that 50 percent of all the wood used in the world is burnt for fuel. Once it has been destroyed, restoring the land is a long and slow process. Pervasive desertification has been taking place in the Sahel, parallel to the southern edge of the Sahara Desert. Other areas particularly affected by desertification are the sands of the Kalahari, southern Africa; Pakistan; parts of the western United States; the Aral Sea region; and Haiti in the Caribbean.

The pressure cooker

Climatic factors are the natural creators of arid and hyper-arid (annual rainfall less than 25 mm/1 inch) lands. Prevailing dry conditions are often the result of atmospheric stability associated with the presence of great high-pressure cells at around 30° latitude. Only occasionally do rain-bearing depressions penetrate into these zones. Deserts also form in the lee of mountains, or where land is subject to very dry continental winds, or even at the coast, when sea breezes do not release their moisture until they get farther inland. When rain does come, it is frequently heavy.

Human activities over recent centuries have caused, and continue to cause, extensive tracts of arid land to be

▼ Degraded soil is much more susceptible to desertification. This chart shows the changing contribution of various human activities to soil degradation by geographical regions. For instance, grazing practices are a significant contributor to soil degradation in Africa and Central America, but play an insignificant role in Europe. The collection of wood for fuel is the leading single cause of soil degradation in Africa and Oceania.

Grazing practices

Other agricultural practices

Industrialization

Deforestation

Fuelwood collection

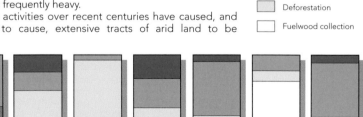

| Europe | Africa | N. America | C. America | S. America | Oceania | Asia |

▶ Dominating the north of Africa is the largest area of dry land on Earth: the Sahara Desert. Stretching across the Sahara are vast plains of sand and gravel, seas of sand dunes, and barren rocky mountains. Only 10,000 years ago, however, grasses covered the region. Now only two percent of the Sahara are oases, patches of land where crops will grow and where nearly 2 million people live. Oases are usually centered on natural water springs. Pictured above is the rocky land, spanning about 50 km (30 miles), near the Terkezi Oasis in Chad. The Sahara shrinks and grows. In the early 1980s, it crept south into the Sahel.

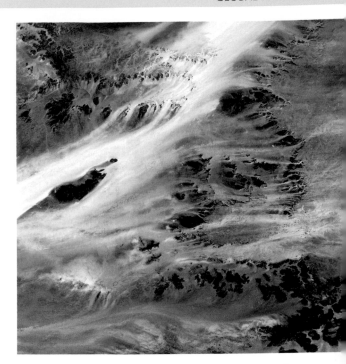

degraded. Changes normally occur slowly, although sand dunes can rapidly encroach on farmland if they are not anchored by fast-growing, drought-resistant trees, or stabilized by waist-high windbreaks across their crests. Belts of trees and shrubs can also cut down wind-erosion, which, along with water-erosion, is exacerbated by overgrazing, deforestation and bush burning. If the topsoil is blown away, degradation of the land is permanent. Even irrigation can cause problems, with water evaporating quickly in arid lands, leaving behind any salt that it may carry. This salt is not leached away into the deep soil, so its concentration rises rapidly in the upper layers, forming a white saline desert that ultimately has to be abandoned.

What makes a desert?

It comes as a surprise to most people that, despite the snow and ice that has accumulated over many years, the largest and driest desert in the world is the Antarctic. Most of Greenland, parts of Canada and Siberia, and many high-altitude mountain ranges are also technically desert. Deserts may be defined by low precipitation, high evaporation, or by the landforms or vegetation they contain. But most people think of deserts as rocky or sandy wastes, stretching to the horizon under a burning sun. There are deserts in all the continents except Europe, and an estimated 20 percent of

155

the Earth's surface is covered by arid land. Human activities are helping to expand these barren environments every day.

Among warm deserts there are huge variations to be found in landscape, vegetation, and other natural features. Deserts can be completely bare rock (called hamada) with, perhaps, a sprinkling of pebbles and stones (desert pavement), or they can be covered with sand dunes. Desert surfaces can consist of ash, lava, or salt; and they either have very little vegetation of any kind, or plants that are classified as desert types. These plants either have very deep tap-roots, or are xerophytes – plants such as cacti, specially adapted to life in a dry environment. Lichens, algae, and fungi may also grow under stones. All of the warm deserts are dry, lying within the arid and hyper-arid regions of the world. Average annual precipitation is below 25 cm (9 inches) and evaporation rates are high. Dry lands are not necessarily desert lands, and – like the vineyards of southern Spain – they may be productive. Arid and hyper-arid lands cover between 15 and 30 percent of Earth's land area, depending upon exactly how they are defined. Hyper-arid regions may not receive any rainfall at all in a year, and are thus indisputably deserts. Semi-arid and arid regions may be classified as desert according to the amount and type of their vegetation.

Shifting sands

Sandy deserts, in which the surface is composed of wind-blown dunes, are often devoid of vegetation, because the sand particles are constantly being moved on by the wind, and plants have nothing on which to anchor. Although the Sonoran Desert in Arizona and northern Mexico is teeming

▼ The shrinking of the Aral Sea is visible in these three images spanning more than 25 years: May 29, 1973 (left); August 19, 1987 (middle), and July 29, 2000 (right). Over the past 40 years, water has been diverted from the Amu Darya and Syr Darya rivers that feed the Aral Sea in order to irrigate millions of hectares for cotton and rice production in Central Asia. In the past few decades, the volume of the Aral Sea has decreased by 75 percent, the equivalent of draining Lakes Erie and Ontario, and its surface area has shrunk by 50 percent. The

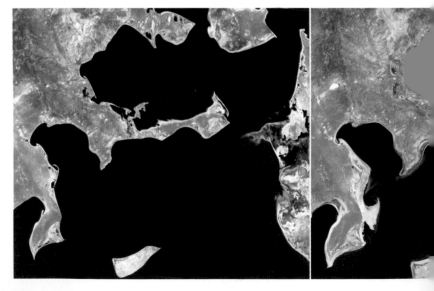

with plant life and supports a magnificent desert ecosystem, deserts normally have a lower biomass (the weight of living plants and animals) than any other landscape. Typically, a sand-dune desert has a biomass under 250 kg/hectare (1,350 lbs/acre), compared to a savanna's biomass of 10,000 kg/hectare (54,500 lbs/acre), or a tropical forest's biomass of more than 250,000 kg/hectare (1,350,000 lbs/acre).

If the deserts really are expanding, the threat is critical. They could enlarge if the climate changed or the desert edge was gravely mishandled. Both have happened and will probably happen again. In the course of the past 12,000 years, there have been times when climate change has transformed millions square kilometres from vegetation to desert. Human activity has also created deserts; in Iraq, for example, salt injected from irrigation schemes dating from before the time of Christ has endured in many millions of hectares of soil.

shoreline has receded up to 120 km (75 miles) from its former shore. Sea level has fallen by more than 16 metres (52 feet) in this already shallow sea. This is a drastic change, but, in the far distant past, the Aral Sea has completely dried up. It has also been much larger than it was in 1960. The controversy about the Aral Sea Region arises because the change is human induced rather than a natural cycle of environmental change. During natural cycles, changes occur fairly slowly, over hundreds of years. Human-induced environmental changes occur more rapidly.

Is desertification happening now?

At the time of the great Sahel drought of the late 1960s and early 1970s, some scientists asserted that the world was undergoing a real climatic change, and the strong consensus of climate-scientists is that global-warming will lead to increased desertification in Africa, the Mediterranean, and elsewhere. On the other hand, desert climates are fickle, and there are few meteorological stations in place to measure such climate shifts as they might affect deserts.

Meteorologists now concede, however, that rainfall in the West African Sahel was below the 30-year average in the late 1910s and in the 1930s, and that the period 1970–90 was dry by the standards of previous years. The cruel and rampant

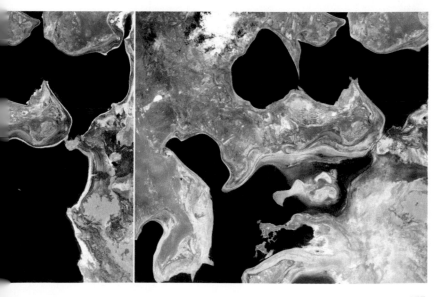

droughts that occurred in the Sahel and the Horn of Africa during this period are ample evidence of this. It is uncertain whether this long dry period has ended, or whether the abundant rains that fell previously were abnormal. For people living on the desert edge, drought will always be a fact of life, but we should not confuse short-term fluctuations with long-term climate change of the sort that could lead to major changes in the extents of the world's deserts.

The dangers of land misuse

Some scientists argue that desertification includes the loss of soil fertility brought about by persistent cropping of the same land, and even so-called 'green desertification' – the invasion of pastures by trees and shrubs (reducing their productivity for grazing cattle). These confusions of meaning have led to false moves in the fight against desertification. One recent plan, financed with Japanese aid, called for the planting of a massive 'green belt' from Mali to Chad, when most experts realized that the real problems occurred some distance further south. To avoid such confusion, many scientists prefer to call these persistent problems 'land degradation'.

Desertification can be exceedingly rapid when humans misuse the land. A tragedy is unfolding around the Aral Sea, the fourth largest inland sea in the world, in the central Asian state of Kazakstan. Between 1960 and 1989, the area of the Aral Sea shrank from 60,000 to 28,500 sq km (23,000–17,400 sq miles). From 1960 to 1995, the sea received less than 1,000 cu km (240 cu miles) of river water, which led to the lowering of the sea level by 17 m (56 feet) and a decline in the overall volume of the lake by 75 percent. Before 1960, the fishing industry employed 60,000 people and harvested 50,000 tonnes of fish. Now, the commercial fishing industry is dead. The salt content of the sea has risen to 40 grammes/litre (2.48 ounces/pint) from its original concentration of 10 grammes/litre (0.62 ounces/ pint). The salinity and shrinking area of the sea has killed off much marine life.

What caused the catastrophic shrinking of the Aral Sea? In the Soviet era, efforts were directed toward making the surrounding region a vast plantation for the growing of cotton. Irrigation networks diverted all of the natural incoming flow from rivers, and heavy use of pesticides

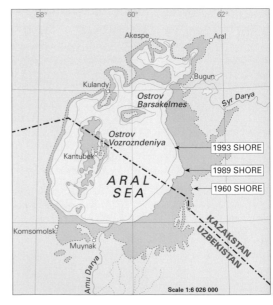

▼ The effect of the over-abstraction of water from the rivers Syr Darya and Amu Darya, which feed the Aral Sea, has been a dramatic 75% reduction in the Sea's volume. Fishing ports now lie more than 60 km (35 miles) from the Aral's shore, and boats are stranded in an ocean of sand. The extensive areas of dry seabed and alluvial deposits have become the source for large dust storms that cover surrounding land in blankets of saline dust. The increased salinity destroyed the reproductive cycle of fish stocks in the Aral Sea.

Scale 1:6 026 000

▲ In Mauritania, west Africa, a tree maintains a precarious hold on a landscape that is turning to desert around it. The aerial roots are not an adaptation to the desert conditions, but have occurred as the root system has been progressively exposed by wind erosion of the soil. Lateral root extensions are truncated in favour of plunging tap roots, which bring up moisture from deep below the surface. The open arrangement of the foliage is an adaptation to reduce the potential of wind damage.

contaminated the sea and the groundwater. Salts blown from the evaporating sea covered the ground for hundreds of kilometres, causing temperatures to climb and altering native and plant life. This modern-day ecological disaster, triggered by humans, has permanently damaged the environment and the health and life-expectancy of the local population.

Prevention and mitigation

Desertification is primarily a problem of sustainable development. It is a matter of addressing poverty and human need, as well as preserving the environment. Social and economic issues, including food security, migration and political stability, are closely linked to land degradation. The results of desertification in many parts of the world are probably not reversible, but there are some cures and palliative measures to slow further degradation. The timed and careful rejuvenation of marginal soils is necessary. There must be a return to drought resistant crops, such as sorghum and millet, rather than cash crops that require extensive irrigation. Programs of social forestry need to be introduced together with the availability of alternate fuel supplies. The bottom line is that solutions enforced from outside and food rescue missions only act as sticking-plasters in terms of addressing the fundamental problems of desertification.

Drought and Famine

The idea of drought – a long period without rain – is simple to understand, but hard to define in a useful way. If a drought were simply a shortage of rain, the Sahara would be in permanent drought and the Sahel would be considered well-watered. It is, perhaps, better to regard a drought as being 'less rain than expected', and to focus on how people come to be disappointed in their expectations of rain. Whatever definition is agreed upon, a drought is an extended period of rainfall deficit where the agricultural biomass becomes severely curtailed.

Can droughts be predicted?

Droughts happen erratically, which makes planning very difficult. For example, a dry spell lasting more than 20 years in the Sahel has had two 'dips' – in the early 1970s and again in 1984 – when rainfall was even lower than for the rest of the period. It is difficult to decide whether the long dry spell was simply a drought or evidence of a more long-term climatic change. Drought may occur in many parts of the world, and there have been severe droughts in Australia in 1902, 1912, 1915, 1965, 1967, and 1972. The worst Australian drought for two centuries began in 1983. In the early 1990s, north-east Brazil had its worst drought since 1583, and southern Africa had a terrible drought in 1992.

Undoubtedly there will be more droughts, both long and short, and although meteorologists do not know when they will arrive, some clues are emerging. The Biblical theory of seven lean years and seven fat years suggests that there is a regular drought cycle. This may prove to be partly correct, although such cycles (if they are shown to occur) will be much more complicated than a regular seven-year pattern.

▼ *This map shows the location and date of the worst incidents of drought and famine in the 20th century, based on the number of fatalities. Drought and famine are inextricably linked through the failure of crops due to lack of rain. Famine can also occur following a period of particularly heavy rain or because of poor food distribution, for example in times of war. During the terrible 1984 famine in Sudan and Ethiopia, the situation was exacerbated by war and the use of food as a political weapon. In general, famine hits poorest countries hardest, and many of them are dependent on international aid for relief programmes.*

■ Worst droughts and famines

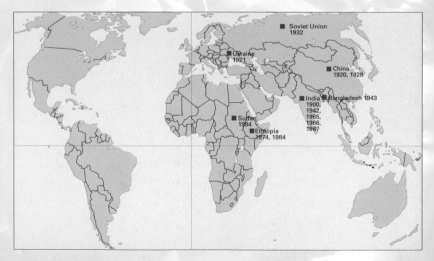

Soviet Union 1932

Ukraine 1921

China 1920, 1928

India 1900, 1942, 1965, 1966, 1967

Bangladesh 1943

Sudan 1984

Ethiopia 1974, 1984

WORST DROUGHTS AND FAMINE				
Region	Country	Year	Disaster	Number of fatalities
Nationwide	Soviet Union	1932	Famine	5,000,000
Shensi, Honan, Kansu	China	1928	Drought	3,000,000
–	Bangladesh	1943	Famine	1,900,000
Calcutta, Bengal	India	1942	Drought	1,500,000
Bengal	India	1900	Drought	1,250,000
South Ukraine, Volga	Soviet Union	1921	Drought	1,200,000
North	China	1920	Drought	500,000
–	India	1965	Drought	500,000
–	India	1966	Drought	500,000
–	India	1967	Drought	500,000
Wollo, Tigray, Eritrea, Shoa, Gonder, Harerge, Sidamo	Ethiopia	1984	Drought	300,000
Wollo, Tigray, Kangra	Ethiopia	1974		200,000
Countrywide	Sudan	1984	Drought	150,000

Waiting for rain

The distress that droughts bring is often the result of misplaced expectations. For example, by the end of the 1960s a decade of better-than-usual rains in the Sahel had persuaded people to plant crops and settle in areas that had previously been too arid. Populations grew rapidly and people saw a modest increase in their standards of living. Expectations rose, placing a greater demand for resources. Consequently when the rains failed, the drought had a far greater impact. The idea of drought gets complicated if we look in more detail at the problems of survival in desert margins. In wet years, for instance, hollows may be water-logged and produce poor crops, while in the dry years they may collect the only water there is, and produce the best crops. The soil type of an area affects how quickly water evaporates in dry spells and the impact of a drought also depends on the types of crop that are grown.

Coping with drought

The populations of dry lands have to learn to live with drought through careful management of resources. Drought is now a matter for national and even worldwide concern, and since the terrible drought-related African famines of the 1970s and 1980s, when millions of people died, there have been concerted efforts to prepare for the inevitable scourge. Scientists now use satellite images to measure the progress of rains in order to identify droughts before people begin to starve. This method gives accurate warnings, but very often aid-agencies lack the resources to respond in time. Other strategies to alleviate drought include improvements in transport and storage so that food can quickly reach affected populations. Despite these actions, catastrophic droughts – magnified by civil strife and population growth – hit parts of the Horn of Africa in the 1980s and 1990s, and continues to affect tens of millions of people in the region and much of sub-Saharan Africa.

During the 1930s, several years of drought occurred in the heartland grain-growing area of the United States, where dry weather and overcultivation produced the infamous 'Dust Bowl'. Extensive crop failures and famine led to the abandonment of thousands of farms and the migration of 300,000 people to California, a story familiar to the readers of John Steinbeck's novel *The Grapes of Wrath* (1939). Drought and famine of the United States is dwarfed, however, by the biblical droughts and famines that continue to afflict Africa.

The seven-year drought in the Sahel, 1968–75

Between 1968 and 1975 a prolonged drought struck the Sahel, in a wide swathe of sub-Saharan Africa, from Mauritania to Eritrea. Eighty to 90 percent of the people in the Sahel exist by subsistence farming and the consequences were tragic and devastating. The early years passed in the hope that the seasonal rains would come and the drought would end soon. By 1970, 3 million people were displaced and in need of emergency food-aid. Chronic malnutrition ensued, compounded by the inaction or inability of local governments to respond to the drought conditions. By 1972, the national governments were relying on international aid to feed 50 million people. The continuing drought brought about the economic collapse of Mauritania, Senegal, Mali, Niger, Chad, Sudan, Ethiopia, and Somalia. In 1974 airlifts distributed food to the starving, but the success ratio for

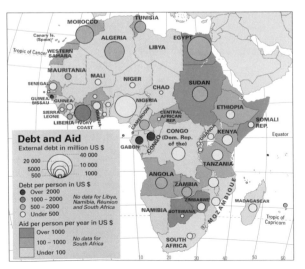

◀ Africa owes US$227 billion to western creditors. While loans to Africa can provide short-term relief from famine, in the long-term servicing the national debt contributes to food shortages. The money spent on servicing debt cripples many African economies. Other factors that lead to famine include extreme climate situations and health issues such as the millions suffering from HIV/AIDS. In addition, civil war and issues related to governance and economic policy can also be problematic.

Debt and Aid
External debt in million US $
40 000
20 000
10 000
5000
500
1000

Debt per person in US $
● Over 2000
● 1000 – 2000   *No data for Libya, Namibia, Réunion and South Africa*
◐ 500 – 2000
○ Under 500

Aid per person per year in US $
Over 1000
100 – 1000   *No data for South Africa*
Under 100

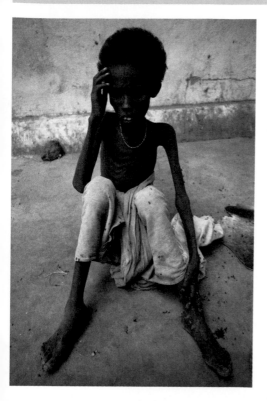

▲ *An emaciated child at a Red Cross refugee camp in Ethiopia during the famine of 1984–85. Three hundred died of starvation in Ethiopia despite one of the biggest aid campaigns in history.*

distribution was only 50 to 75 percent. All too frequently, because of the lack of basic infrastructure, the grain rotted in ports or was controlled in the black-market by warlords who used hunger to their advantage.

Drought in Ethiopia and the Sudan, 1984–85

The drought that struck the Sudan in 1984–85, led to terrible famine despite forewarning. In July 1983, Ethiopia was struck by a drought that gave early warning that Sudan would also suffer in the next few years. Management of the Ethiopian famine was complicated because the drought hit hardest in the rebel-held northern provinces of the country. Refugees trying to flee drought-stricken regions were brutalized by government troops and relief piled up in Ethiopia's eastern ports. The drought in Ethiopia spread to the Sudan, and the subsequent distribution of aid was hampered by inept railway and trucking difficulties, again leading to costly airlifts. An estimated 450,000 people died during the 1984–85 famine in Ethiopia and Sudan. Many more may have died without the fund-raising efforts of Band Aid and Live Aid.

The economics of drought

Unlike other natural disasters, drought and famine force people apart rather than together. Shortages of food and water lead to individual and group-conflicts in the struggle to survive. In Africa, for example, social upheaval continues today and the situation will continue to be difficult because of periodic droughts, desertification, and the steady increase in population. For developing countries, burdened by debt and dependent on foreign aid, mitigative and long-term recovery programs receive such a low priority that complete degradation seems inevitable. Elisabeth Dowdeswell, executive director of the United Nations Environment Programme (UNEP) succinctly summarized the problem in June 1993: "The front-line troops in this battle against desertification are generally impoverished and illiterate, overworked peasant farmers or pastoralists and most often women. Their priority is to feed their families, now". Even countries, such as India and Indonesia, which have established infrastructures to prevent starvation during times of drought, can face difficult times. The drought of 1982–83 in Indonesia, for example, produced a severe slowdown in the national economy as the country spent a large portion of its foreign reserves for the purchase of rice and wheat.

The causes of famine

It is worth stressing that famines are not caused solely by droughts. Flooding from tropical cyclones in the Indian sub-continent, for example, has destroyed rice and food crops. Cyclones can also increase the salinity of productive soils through storm-surge inundation. In 1876, for example, a storm surge moved from the Bay of Bengal up the River Meghna, between Calcutta and Dacca, drowning 100,000 people and killing a further 100,000 in the subsequent famine. Even without a storm surge, failure of the summer monsoons can lead to many deaths due to famine.

The Bangladesh famine, 1943

One of the worst famines ever recorded happened in 1943 in British-ruled eastern India (now Bangladesh), where it is esti-mated that 2 million people died of hunger. The famine was initially blamed on a shortfall in food production, although some economists now argue that even though food short-ages were a contributing factor, it was exacerbated by greed and hysteria during World War II. The supply of food was

▼ *Refugees at a refugee camp in Kassala, Sudan, wait for food distribution during the famine of 1984–85 which killed 150,000 in the Sudan and which affected c.150 million inhabitants of sub-Saharan Africa.*

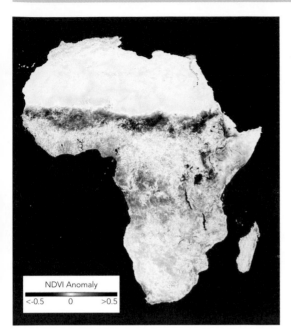

NDVI Anomaly

<-0.5   0   >0.5

▲ *The African drought of 1984–85 shows clearly in this Multi-spectral Drought Index image from August 1984. Dark reddish-brown areas indicate unhealthy vegetation relative to a normal year. The drought withered crops from the Sahel (along the southern border of the Sahara desert) to East Africa and hit Ethiopia, Sudan, and Somalia especially hard.*

deemed to have been of low priority for the British rulers at the time, leading to the hoarding of food by Indian traders who sold it at exorbitant prices.

Why is desert rainfall unpredictable?

Although deserts have little rain on average, on the occasions when rain arrives, the rate at which it falls can be dramatic, and it has been said that in deserts more people have drowned in rivers than have died of thirst. Arid regions experience the most unpredictable rainfall patterns in the world, and in general, the less it rains on average in a particular region the less predictable is the rainfall. Both Bakel and Dakar in Senegal, for example, lie on the same 500 mm (20 inches) isohyet (contour joining areas with the same average annual rainfall), yet a difference of 270 mm (10.6 inches) was recorded in 1972. Rain may fall only once every eight years in parts of the Sahara and the Middle East, and only once every 18 years in desert regions of Peru.

The reason for the unpredictability of rainfall patterns lies with local climates. Most deserts are located beneath semi-permanent anticyclones (areas of high pressure) into which moist air, rain-bearing frontal systems or tropical cyclones can only occasionally penetrate. When they do penetrate, rapidly rising hot desert air, which cools and condenses as it rises, causes highly localized rainfall. One consequence of such localized rainfall is that surface runoff may flow into only a few wadis (ephemeral desert watercourses), which leads to torrents of water in a relatively small area.

See also **Floods**, pages 90–105; **Desertification**, pages 152–59

Fires

Wildfire is an all-embracing term for bush fire, forest fire, or indeed any fire that starts and spreads in a non-urban (commonly wilderness) environment. Often such fires grow into conflagrations and spread to urban areas with punishing consequences. Natural resources are damaged, human settlements are destroyed, and the areas devastated by the fires are made more vulnerable to the subsequent effects of torrential rainfall, including flooding and landslides.

Causes of wildfire

Wildfires may be caused intentionally or accidentally by human action, but are typically triggered by lightning strikes. In the western USA, for example, many fires, especially in forests, are started by lightning. During a recent ten-year period, more than 15,000 such fires occurred across the whole USA. These resulted in damage costing several hundred million dollars and the destruction of some 800,000 hectares (2 million acres) of forest. Many regions of the world are susceptible to forest and bush fires, particularly those that experience a significant dry season in a year when conditions are especially hot. Some national weather services advise forestry departments regarding the type of weather that increases the risk of such fires. One factor is the occurrence of an El Niño, which places tropical countries in the western Pacific region at a significantly higher risk than normal because of the enhanced dry season experienced there. The vast pollution from fires in Malaysia and Indonesia during September 1997, devastating bush fires during Australia in late 1997 and early 1998, and widespread forest fires in Borneo during April 1998 were all attributed to the knock-on effects of the prevailing El Niño.

▼ In 1997, wildfires raged throughout much of Indonesia, consuming 9.7 million hectares (240 million acres) of land and creating a choking, thick haze over much of the southern hemisphere. The 'hot spots' (shown below) occurred in the provinces of Riau, Sumatra Utara, Sumatra Barat, South Sumatra and Jambi on the island of Sumatra, Java Barat and Java Timur on the island of Java, Kalimantan Barat, Kalimantan Tengah, and Kalimantan Selatan on the island of Borneo, and Irian Jaya on the island of New Guinea.

▲ *Spot fires in the forests of No Name Creek above Glenwood Springs, north-east Colorado, June 2002. In 2002, President George W. Bush declared a major disaster for the state of Colorado.*

Irian Jaya

The Indonesian wildfires, 1997

In September 1997, Indonesian companies cleared land for palm oil and pulp plantations by burning. The fires burned out of control, consuming more than 300,000 hectares (750,000 acres) of bush land on the Indonesian islands of Sumatra, Borneo, Sulawesi, and Java. These areas were already tinder-dry due to the severe drought brought about by El Niño conditions. In conjunction with the uncontrolled fires, a grey haze of thick pollutants and smoke engulfed urban centres, choking more than 70 million people. Fanned by winds across the Strait of Malacca, the blanket of smog covered much of Indonesia and Brunei, and stretched westward to Malaysia and Singapore. In the United States, a Pollutant Standards Index provides a measure of carbon monoxide, sulphur dioxide and other pollutants in the lower atmosphere. Levels seldom exceed 100, and readings of 300 to 400 lead to emergency conditions. In Kuching, south-west Sarawak, Malaysia, a comparable index reached 700. It is estimated that up to 2.6 billion tons of carbon were released into the atmosphere during the fires. For political reasons, criticism and calls for action from Indonesia were slow in coming. Indonesia's government subsidizes logging and plantation industries, thereby removing incentives to protect tropical rainforests, which are particularly vulnerable if the tracts of volatile peat beneath the forest-canopy catch fire.

The Wisconsin wildfire, USA, 1871

One of the worst forest-fires in US history has been virtually ignored because of a bizarre coincidence. The forest-fire took place in the virgin forests near Peshtigo, north-west

167

Wisconsin, on October 18, 1871. The expanding need and fever for lumber caused the rapid development of Peshtigo, but also unwittingly generated vast amounts of wood debris as potential fuel for a wildfire, while the introduction of the railroad provided locomotives as a prospective ignition source. The 2,000 residents of Peshtigo did not realize that they were at risk of an impending disaster, even though a prolonged summer drought had continually subjected the surrounding countryside to small fires produced by the spontaneous combustion of compacted and fermented dead vegetation and trees. On the afternoon of Sunday October 8, the hot, dry climatic conditions were just right for a number of individual fires to coalesce and burst into a gigantic tongue of flame engulfing Peshtigo in a fire tornado or firestorm. The explosion of superheated air completely consumed the town, destroying more than 400,000 hectares (1 million acres) of forest and taking 1,500 lives. Comparisons of such a natural firestorm have been made to the fire bombings of Tokyo, Hamburg and Dresden during World War II. The Peshtigo disaster in the Wisconsin woods is only poorly remembered today because it occurred on the same day, and almost at the same hour, as the Great Chicago Fire. In fact this, and a number of other allegedly inexplicable aspects of the two fires have led to speculation – at present completely unsubstantiated – that they were the result of a comet fragment exploding in the lower atmosphere over the US Midwest.

Wildfires in Australia
Australia is particularly vulnerable to bushfires because of the highly flammable nature of its vegetation, which makes them

◀ The varied fire seasons in Australia reflect different weather patterns. For most of southern Australia, the danger period is summer and autumn. For New South Wales and southern Queensland, the peak risk usually occurs in spring and early summer. Northern Australia experiences most of its fires in winter and spring.

Winter and spring
Spring
Spring and summer
Summer
Summer and autumn

AUSTRALIAN FIRE-DANGER RATING SYSTEM (FDRS) – GRASSLANDS		
Fire Danger Index	Fire Danger Rating	Difficulty of Suppression
0–2.5	Low	Head-fire stopped by roads and trucks
2.5–7.5	Moderate	Head-fire easily attacked with water.
7.5–20	High	Head-fire attack generally successful with water
20–50	Very High	Head-fire attack may succeed in favourable circumstances. Back-burning close to the head may be necessary.
50–200	Extreme	Direct attack will generally fail. Back-burns from a good secure line will be difficult to hold because of blown embers. Flanks must be held at all costs.

very difficult to contain and control. On December 15, 1997, Australian firefighters fought to control a massive bush fire in the north-west of the State of Victoria that destroyed almost 4,000 hectares (10,000 acres) of natural scrub in the Murray-Sunset National Park. Approximately 45 fires had started on the previous day, due largely to lightning strikes.

The McArthur Forest Fire Danger Index (FFDI)

The McArthur Forest-Fire Danger Index (FFIDI) is well-known to Australian bushfire managers. Meteorological and fuel-load variables contributing to the behaviour of a fire are integrated into a numerical index of fire danger on a scale of 0 to 100. A value of 1 signifies that environmental variations would extinguish the fire. A value of 100 is a worst-case scenario for a bushfire. During the period January 3–9, 1994, there were five days during which the index exceeded 50, indicating extreme fire-danger. The combination of circumstances that produced such ripe conditions were a prolonged drought (a rain deficit

▶ Australian bushfires burning on January 18, 2003. Brisk winds are sweeping smoke plumes eastward off the Australian coast north of Cape Howe. The agricultural valleys of the Murrumbidgee and Murray Rivers give way to the burning, darker bush areas of the mountains with the extreme eastern coastline of Victoria visible beyond.

of more than 100 mm/4 inches), a temperature of 35°C (95°F), a relative humidity of 15 percent, and a mean wind speed of 33 km/h (21 mph).

In January 1994, almost the whole of coastal New South Wales experienced weather that produced an extremely high risk of fire. Between December 27, 1993 and January 16, 1994, more than 800 fires destroyed about 800,000 hectares (2.2 million acres) of vegetation, and more than 200 houses – mainly in suburban areas, including the outskirts of Sydney. Two firefighters and two members of the public died due to the fires during this period. This loss was not as dramatic, however, as two other major events. On February 16 (Ash Wednesday), 1983, a wildfire killed 75 people and destroyed more than 2,500 properties in the Adelaide Hills and Outer Melbourne. On February 7 ('Black Tuesday'), 1967, bushfires around Hobart, south-east Tasmania, claimed more than 62 lives and razed more than 1,300 buildings to the ground. The fires were preceded by a season of above-average rainfall and a heavy growth of grasses. The grasses dried out in 1966–67, and controlled burns were used to reduce the fire risk. The fires were left burning because it was anticipated that they would be subsequently extinguished by expected rains. The rains never came, however, and soon the flames were licking at the outskirts of Hobart.

Building in wildfire-prone areas

An important message for town-planners and local authorities is that wildfires will continue to occur at regular intervals if urban development is permitted to encroach on surrounding forests and bush-land. Despite this, developments of this kind continue in parts of Australia, southern California, and other wildfire-prone regions. In 2003 this message was reinforced by events in south-east Australia. In January, a wildfire

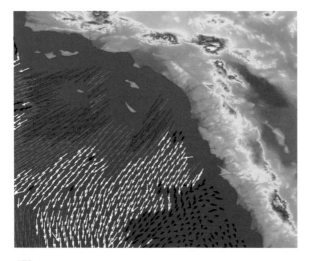

◄ Santa Ana wind event over California, USA. In this false-colour image taken on January 6, 2003, the arrows represent the direction of the surface winds over the ocean, with arrow-colours standing for wind speed. Red arrows show winds travelling greater than 8 m/sec (26 feet/sec); orange represents 6–8 m/sec (20–26 feet/sec); white shows winds of 4–6 m/sec (13–20 feet/sec); and black stands for less than 4 m/sec (13 feet/sec).

▲ *Firefighters work to control the Schoonover fires in Douglas County, central Colorado, USA, June 2002. The 2002 wildfires in Colorado were the costliest fires in the state's history.*

swept into the Australian capital of Canberra, destroying hundreds of homes and forcing thousands to flee. The Canberra region had been in the grip of drought for a year, and extremely dry conditions combined with lightning strikes to start fires in nearby parks and forest preserves. Nearly 20,000 hectares (50,000 acres) of forest were burned as fires advanced to the city. The conflagrations also claimed one of the world's major astronomical observatories at Mount Stromlo, destroying – among other instruments – the famous 1.3-m (50-inch) Great Melbourne Telescope. Total damage was estimated at more than US$134 million.

Wildfires in California

Dry winds are a key contributor to devastating fires because winds can affect a large region. More than 95 percent of all burned areas are produced by less than five percent of the total number of fires. Very strong winds will occur when a high-pressure air mass flows over a mountain range, descending as warm dry wind towards a low-pressure zone. The wind flows fast, commonly with speeds of 70 to 100 km/h (40–60 mph). These winds are broadly known as föhns, but they also have many local names. In California they are known, east of the Rockies as Chinook winds, in the south of the state as Santa Ana winds and in the San Francisco Bay area as Diablo winds. These hot, very low humidity winds, racing across dehydrated vegetation in California provide the perfect weather conditions for wildfires.

The Berkeley wildfire, USA, 1991

In October 1991, a devastating urban fire occurred in the hills behind Oakland and Berkeley, western California. In the steep-hilled regions of these communities, million-dollar homes command a sweeping view of San Francisco Bay. A five-year drought in the late 1980s dehydrated the native vegetation, while an unusual frost in December 1990 was followed by spring rains that produced a rapid growth of grass. This was followed by drought into October 1991. Consequently the amount of dry vegetation was very high. A fire of suspicious origin broke out, followed by Diablo winds that pushed the fire in different directions, taking 25 lives and destroying around 2,500 homes. When the fires were finally extinguished, 650 hectares (1,600 acres) had been razed and the cost in damage to property was in excess of US$1.5 billion. Southern California is all too commonly ablaze from fires exacerbated by the Santa Ana winds (see page 170), and between October 27 and November 4, 1993, more than 14 wildfires occurred in the region. The fires were started in a variety of ways, including from the sparks of wind-felled power lines, flames from camp-fires, and deliberately by arsonists. Fanned by the strong, dry winds, the firestorms created fire tornadoes that sent embers jumping into adjacent canyons to start new fires. The wildfires proved to be unstoppable and burned clear to the Pacific Ocean, where they provided a spectacular backdrop to surfers on the ocean. When the fires finally burned themselves out, more than 1,000 homes had been destroyed and the property

▼ *In November 1995, a member of the firecrew with California Department of Forestry uses a drip torch to burn the scrub-chaparral in the Mojave*

damage was in excess of US$1 billion. The annual Santa Ana winds in California always present the possibility of similar destructive fires.

Managing the wildfire threat: the US way

Wildfires are a serious and growing hazard over much of the United States, posing a considerable threat to life and property – particularly when they move from forest or rangeland into developed areas. Wildfires also constitute a natural process, and attempts at suppression in the past are now recognized to have created a larger fire hazard, as living and dead vegetation accumulates in areas where fire has been excluded. In addition, the absence of fire has altered or disrupted the cycle of natural plant succession and wildlife habitats in many areas. Consequently, United States' land management agencies are committed to finding ways, such as prescribed burning, to reintroduce fire into natural ecosystems, while recognizing that fire fighting and suppression are still important. The US Geological Survey (USGS) conducts fire-related research to meet the varied needs of the fire-management community and to understand the role of fire in the landscape. The USGS research includes fire management support, studies of post-fire effects, and a wide range of studies on fire history and ecology. Fire managers rely upon accurate and timely information to help reduce the wildfire hazard. Since the early 1990s, the EROS (Earth Resources Observation Systems) Data Center (EDC) in

Desert, near Hesperia, southern California, USA. Controlled fires are used regularly to prevent a wildfire burning out of control into built-up areas.

Sioux Falls, South Dakota, has produced maps for the 48 US contiguous states and Alaska that display plant growth and vigour, vegetation cover, and biomass production, using multi-spectral data from satellites of the National Oceanic and Atmospheric Administration (NOAA). The ability to measure the greenness of vegetation over time provides fire managers with vital information concerning vegetation conditions for any two-week period. EDC also produces maps that relate current vegetation conditions for the two-week period to average (normal) conditions for the same period during the previous seven years. The two types of image provide comprehensive growing season profiles for forests, rangelands, grasslands, and agricultural areas. They are used by fire and land managers to assess the condition of all vegetation throughout the growing season, to provide a foundation for planning for fire suppression, scheduling prescribed burns, or studying long-term vegetation changes resulting from human or natural factors. For example, the US Forest Service (USFS) uses greenness maps to generate national maps of selected fire weather and fire danger components of their Wildland Fire Assessment System.

▲ Smoke rises from the Mojave Desert after a prescribed burn, near Hesperia, southern California, USA. Prescribed burning is the intentional use of fire to reduce wildfire hazards, clear felled trees, control plant diseases, improve rangeland and wildlife habitats, and restore natural ecosystems. About 60,000 hectares (150,000 acres) of wildlands are treated each year in California using the method of prescribed burning.

The Fire Potential Index (FPI)

The Fire Potential Index (FPI) is a valuable fire-management tool that has been developed by USGS scientists in collaboration with scientists at the USFS. The FPI characterizes relative fire potential for forests, rangelands, and grasslands,

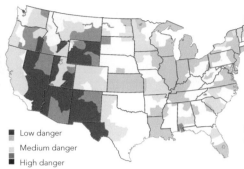

■ Low danger
■ Medium danger
■ High danger

▲ *Fire Potential Index map of the United States, based on data between July 20 and 27, 2000. The area most at risk is the south-west, especially New Mexico, Arizona, and Nevada.*

▼ *On June 15, 2002, a helicopter drops water in an attempt to douse spot fires in the forests of No Name Creek above Glenwood Springs, north-east Colorado, USA.*

both regionally and locally, so that land managers can develop plans for minimizing the threat from fires. The FPI combines multi-spectral satellite data with geographic information system (GIS) technology to generate 1-km (0.6-mile) resolution fire potential maps. Input data include the total amount of flammable plant material or fuel load (derived from vegetation maps), plus the water content of the dead vegetation, and the fraction of the total fuel load that is live vegetation. Water content of dead vegetation is calculated from temperature, relative humidity, cloud cover, and precipitation, and the proportion of living plants derives from the greenness maps described above. The FPI is updated daily to reflect the changing weather conditions and is posted by the USFS on their website. The Bureau of Land Management (BLM), Bureau of Indian Affairs, and USFS are working with the USGS to validate the model. Fire-management staffs in Oregon, Nevada, and California are using the FPI in their decision-making process daily to supplement their traditional information sources. They use these data to establish priorities across the area for prevention activities and to plan the allocation of suppression forces to improve the probability that any initial attack will control fires occurring in areas of high concern. The FPI is also being tested in Argentina, Chile, Mexico, and Spain with the support of the Pan American Institute for Geography and History.

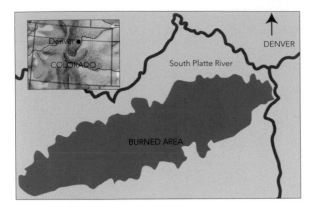

◀ Map showing the 4,700 hectares (11,600 acres) of burned area caused by a wildfire in the Buffalo Creek and Spring Creek watersheds in May 1996. Buffalo Creek lies in the Rockies, Pike National Forest, about 32 km (20 miles) south-west of Denver, Colorado.

The legacy of wildfires

Wildfires create enormous problems, even after the last ember is extinguished. In July 1994, a wildfire burned 800 hectares (2,000 acres) of forest and scrub on the steep slopes of Storm King Mountain, near Glenwood Springs, north-east Colorado. In September 1994, torrential rains triggered debris flows, which poured from this burned area and inundated a 5-km (3-mile) stretch of Interstate 70 with tons of mud, rock, and other debris. The flows engulfed 30 cars, sweeping two of them into the Colorado River, causing serious injuries but fortunately no deaths. Scientists from the USGS Landslides Hazards Program are studying the linkage between wildfires and debris flows at Storm King Mountain and at sites in several other States. During an intense wildfire, all vegetation may be destroyed; also organic material in the soil may be burned away or may decompose into water-repellent substances that prevent water from percolating into the soil. As a result, even normal rainfall may result in unusual erosion or flooding from a burned area, while heavy rains can trigger destructive debris flows, as happened at Storm King Mountain.

California wildfires, USA, 1997

In 1997, wildfires charred more than 120 hectares (300 acres) of southern California, leaving them bare before the heavy, El Niño-induced rainfall in the winter of 1997–98. Ten of these fires produced debris flows after the first major winter storm, and flooding dominated in eight areas, while only four showed little or no erosion or runoff. The relative importance of topography, vegetation conditions, and the amount and pattern of rainfall are being investigated at each of the sites to develop a model for debris-flow susceptibility from recently burned areas.

The Buffalo Creek wildfires, USA, 1996

Water supplies may also be significantly affected by wildfires. The loss of ground-surface cover, such as needles and

▶ Outer bark, inner bark, cambium, sapwood and heartwood of a tree. The cambium must survive in a fire for the tree to live.

▲ *Prescribed fire during the dry season (May–October) in the savannah of southern Africa. Africa is known as the 'continent of fire' because of its annual patterns of burning. About 90% of fires in Africa are caused by humans.*

small branches, and the chemical transformation of burned soils make watersheds more susceptible to erosion from rainstorms. In May 1996, a fire burned 4,800 hectares (12,000-acres) of the small Buffalo Creek and Spring Creek watersheds in northeast Colorado, which feed into the Strontia Springs Reservoir which supplies more than 75 percent of the municipal drinking water to the cities of Denver and Aurora, Colorado. Two months after the fire, a severe thunderstorm caused flooding in the burned area, killing two people. In addition, the Denver Water Department immediately experienced a deterioration of water-quality from floating burned debris and high levels of manganese. Two years after the fire, phosphate levels in the water remain high, and the Denver Water Department is concerned about loss of reservoir capacity and impaired water-quality. USGS researchers are studying the post-fire hydrogeology of Buffalo Creek and Spring Creek to understand the processes of runoff generation, sediment production, and the transport of sediment out of the watersheds and into the reservoir. Although the burned hill-slopes are showing signs of regrowth, sediment is still being eroded two years after the fires. Between September 1996 and August 1998, about 250,000 cubic metres (8.8 million cubic feet) of coarse sediment were trapped in a delta at the upper end of the reservoir. The post-fire accumulation rate is about 10 times that calculated by the engineers who designed it. Furthermore, this was not an unprecedented event: the results of stratigraphic studies on the Buffalo Creek watershed suggest that there may have been about seven similar fire-flood events in the last 2,000 years. Although the fire has had disastrous consequences for the city of Denver and surrounding communities, the post-fire evaluation is expected to help land managers along the Colorado Front Range better anticipate the effects of wildfire on other watersheds and other reservoirs.

The sequoia groves of California

In the giant sequoia groves of the Sierra Nevada, California, USA, cooperative research by the USGS and University of Arizona has used fire scars found in giant sequoia tree-rings to develop the world's longest and most detailed fire histories. The annual- and seasonal-resolution fire records span two millennia,

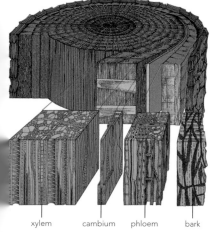

xylem   cambium   phloem   bark

and show that during most of that period, low- to moderate-intensity surface fires burned in parts of individual sequoia groves, on average, about every three to eight years. With the loss of fires set by Native Americans and the suppression of lightning fires that followed European settlement, most grove areas today have experienced a 100- to 130-year period without fire, a fire-free period that is unprecedented in the past 2,000 years.

The consequences of fire exclusion for sequoia groves are beginning to show. Almost no new giant sequoias have seeded in the last 130 years, because sequoia seedling establishment depends on fire to expose bare mineral-rich soil and to create clearings. The additional sunlight and soil moisture found in clearances are especially favourable for the growth of new trees. Fire exclusion has also allowed the growth of dense thickets of flammable, shade-tolerant plant species. Forest litter and woody debris have accumulated, causing a huge build-up of surface fuels, which has led to an increased hazard of intense wildfires sweeping through groves, severe enough to damage or even kill full-grown sequoias. This fire-history information is being used by managers to guide the restoration and preservation of sequoia ecosystems for future generations. Managers are also using low- to moderate-intensity prescribed fires to reduce hazardous fuel loads, to thin shade-tolerant tree species, and to open small holes in the forest canopy. The results are sequoia groves that are less vulnerable to high-intensity wildfires and as a result are experiencing their first abundant sequoia reproduction in more than a century.

▲ *A small prescribed grassland fire on August 15, 2000 in Kruger National Park, South Africa, set to coincide with the overpass of NASA's Terra spacecraft and research aircraft involved in the SAFARI 2000 field campaign.*

The environmental impact of wildfire

Prescribed fire has a long history in the south-eastern United States, where it has been used to improve forage quality, reduce pest populations, and decrease the likelihood of destructive wildfires. Fire has been so pervasive that most of the familiar habitats in the south-east United States require periodic fire to perpetuate themselves: if pine forests remain unburned for long periods, they are replaced by hardwood forests that do not support the flora or fauna native to the area. If left unburned for as little as five to ten years, pine forests accumulate large amounts of fuel, making them susceptible to destructive wildfires such as occurred in spring 2003 in northern Florida. Ground-cover vegetation may recover quickly from such wildfires, but the canopy of pine trees may be completely killed. This spells disaster for species such as the endangered red-cockaded woodpecker that depends on large, live pine trees for its nesting cavities.

Environmental impact in the Pacific Northwest

Fire is the dominant ecological disturbance in forests of the Interior Columbia River Basin in the Pacific Northwest. Historical fire-disturbance regimes in this region have varied widely with respect to fire frequency and severity, but the number of available fire-history studies is limited. It is known that fire-return intervals in the Interior Columbia River Basin during the past century are longer than in previous centuries because of landscape fragmentation (caused by timber harvesting, agriculture, and roads), fire suppression, and lack of deliberate burning as formerly practised by all inhabitants of the area. The lack of frequent fire means that forest fuels per acre are greater in many locations than they would have been during the past few centuries. Resource managers are reintro-

WORST WILDFIRES SINCE 1975				
Location	Country	Year	Killed	Affected
Heilongjiang province	China	May 1987	191	56,313
Victoria	Australia	February 16, 1983	75	11,000
Borneo, Sumatra, Kalimantan, Java, Sulawesi	Indonesia	August 1991	57	–
Terai	Nepal	March 1992	56	50,000
–	Sudan	April 19, 1998	47	–
Gdansk, Szczecin, Bydgoszcz, Katowice, Liegnit	Poland	July 1992	35	–
–	Nepal	March 1999	32	4,000
–	Russia	July 7, 1992	31	–
Hongqing	China	March 6, 1995	29	–
California	USA	October 20, 1991	26	6,933
Huvsgul, Bulgan, Arkhangai, Khentii, Tuv, Dornod, Uvs	Mongolia	March 1996	25	5,061

ducing fire into these landscapes to reduce fuel loadings and the intensity of future fires. Accurate estimates of historical fire-return intervals are necessary to implement reasonable forest management plans.

Using fire to protect native ecosystems

Over the last several decades prescribed and free burning under specified weather and fuel conditions has been used in urban bushlands, production forests, and some national parks. Certainly it is the least expensive management technique available to control native vegetation. It is also controversial. Fire was used in the early years of settlement in North America and Australia to aid in clearing operations. These early days were followed by a period when fires were viewed as something to be eliminated. Today, the use of fires arouses great concern among some critics. On the one hand, managers of forestlands are expected by society to maintain a pristine natural habitat avoiding human-caused fire. On the other hand, these same managers are asked to minimize the risk of fire outbreak, for which controlled burning plays a critical role. Repeated bush fires in Australia are pushing the pendulum towards fuel reduction.

Different methods of fire control: USA and Mexico

Fire suppression is viewed differently in the United States and Mexico. Chaparral (a dense, perennial thicket of shrubs of evergreen-oak) is indigenous to southern California and Baja California, Mexico. Younger plants do not burn easily but, after several decades of growth, dead-plant material acts as a fuel that burns easily and intensely. Chaparral fires often occur in southern California from September to November, when the hot and dry Santa Ana winds blow. In the United States, all fires are fought aggressively and often

▼ *Bitterroot inferno, Bitterroot National Forest, Montana, on August 6, 2000. The picture shows two elk standing in a stream, perhaps seeking shelter from the rapidly spreading flames. Toward the end of August 2000, the wildfires in Bitterroot Valley merged with wildfires in Mussigbrod in the Big Hole River drainage basin to burn more than 100,000 hectares (250,000 acres).*

▶ *Total forest area and area of protected forest in south-east Asia. The area of protected forest throughout the region is comparatively small in relation to the total forest area. The logging and controlled burning of forests provides valuable income to developing countries through the wood trade and creation of land for agriculture.*

PROTECTED FOREST IN SOUTH-EAST ASIA		
Country	Total Forest Area (sq km/square miles)	Protected Forest Area (sq km/square miles)
Brunei	3,454 / 1,334	1,029 / 397
Indonesia	911,337 / 351,867	193,177 / 74,586
insular Malaysia	101,621 / 39,236	11,421 / 4,410
Papua New Guinea	362,492 / 139,958	39,320 / 15,181
Philippines	62,768 / 24,235	2,550 / 985
Solomon Islands	26,687 / 10,304	0
TOTAL	1,468,359 / 566,934	247,496 / 95,558

at great expense. In Mexico, wildfires are allowed to burn with minimal human interference. Statistics show that fire-control efforts in the United States reduce the number of fires, but in comparison with Mexico, not the total amount of land burned.

The economic causes of wildfire

Deliberate deforestation by burning is a serious problem in Indonesia and also in Brazil where deforestation of the Amazon rainforest is proceeding at an alarming rate. The high poverty-rate in countries like Indonesia and Brazil create social needs that conflict with environmental needs. Deforestation provides families with farmland and loggers with jobs. Demand for wood creates economic reasons for the destruction of local forestry. Although schemes have been proposed to assist in the reduction of fires and regrowth in damaged areas, large timber concessions generally control forestry in endangered areas and rely on fast production and cheap employment in order to generate their large profits. Any reforestation scheme would necessarily involve a cut in profits, a sacrifice that most corporations, and indirectly, most governments, are not prepared to take.

Building to beat fire

One needs to be careful in attributing death and destruction from fires solely to nature. Bad decisions on the location of housing, landscaping, and building construction style are the key culprits. For this reason, a few simple procedures and building construction techniques are worth pointing out that can help to limit damage and save lives. The roof is the most vulnerable part of a house to the dangers posed by wind-blown embers. To minimize risk in fire-prone areas, therefore, a roof should be constructed of lightweight fire resistant materials, and should always be kept clear of leaves, pine needles, and other plant debris. Space around the dwelling to distances of 10–30 metres (30–100 feet), depending on the terrain, should be cleared of all dry grass, brush, and leaves. Trees should be kept well trimmed with low-lying branches cut off, so that ground fires cannot easily climb to the treetops.

Diseases

More than 2,000 years after the ancient Greeks laid the foundations of rational medicine, the world faces a rising tide of human disease. On the one hand, there are the so-called lifestyle diseases, such as cancer and heart disease that predominate in high-income countries. The World Health Organization (WHO) has warned of an explosion of these diseases within the first two or three decades of the 21st century. On the other hand, there is the inexorable toll taken by infection, with worldwide, infectious diseases now responsible for more than 13 million premature deaths each year.

Warning of 'lifestyle plagues', the WHO confirmed that the rich nations face a growing incidence of cancer, heart disease and strokes, chronic lung disease, and degenerative conditions such as arthritis and Alzheimer's. For example, the number of people with what is now acknowledged to be one of the leading 'lifestyle' conditions, diabetes, is predicted to rise to 300 million by 2025 (from 135 million in 1995). Meanwhile, developing countries face the 'double burden' of combating infectious disease while increasingly confronting the lifestyle illnesses of the affluent nations.

Disease trends

Dramatic changes are taking place in global patterns of communicable disease. The last three decades have seen the reappearance of many previously controlled diseases, including, anthrax, diphtheria, trench fever – a scourge of World War I infantry – plague, and whooping cough. In addition, more than 30 new diseases have been identified in humans, including: AIDS, Kawasaki, Lyme, Legionnaire's, Campylobacteriosis, toxic-shock syndrome, Ebola fever, a new strain of Hantavirus, Hepatitis C and E, and SARS (severe acute respiratory syndrome). There are a number of reasons for this changing epidemiological kaleidoscope, including poverty (globally the leading cause of ill-health and premature death), malnutrition, war, failure of public health measures, movement of populations, relentless urbanization, global warming and the impact of human activities on the environment. Leading British development groups have warned that 40 percent of the world's population lacks access to sanitation, and with the growth of megacities (populations in excess of eight million), many fringed with squatter settlements, sewage pollution is now one of the biggest causes of disease.

One million people travel between high- and low-income countries every week and, of course, air travel is now the fastest way of spreading infection. This was amply demonstrated in the case of SARS, a new, atypical form of pneumonia thought to have originated in China's Guangdong province. In November 2002, the first cases were identified and by spring 2003 the virus had migrated to Europe and North America, causing alarm at airports receiving flights from the Far East. By late May 2003, with more than 8,000

MOST SEVERE EPIDEMICS IN THE 20TH CENTURY				
Country	Date	Type	Name	Killed
worldwide	1917	Respiratory	Influenza	20,000,000
eastern Europe	July 1914	Rickettsial	Typhus	3,000,000
Russia	1917	Unknown	–	2,500,000
India	1920	Plague	Bubonic	2,000,000
China	1909	Plague	Bubonic	1,500,000
India	1907	Plague	Bubonic	1,300,000
worldwide	May 1957	Respiratory	Influenza	1,250,000
worldwide	late 1968	Respiratory	Influenza	700,000
India	1920	Diarrhoeal/Enteric	Cholera	500,000
India	1926	Smallpox	–	423,000
Bangladesh	1918	Respiratory	Influenza	393,000
India	1924	Diarrhoeal/Enteric	Cholera	300,000
Uganda	1901	Unknown	–	200,000
Niger	1923	Meningitis	–	100,000
China	1910	Plague	Pneumonic	60,000
Canada	1918–25	Respiratory	Spanish Influenza	50,000
Egypt	September 1947	Diarrhoeal/Enteric	Cholera	10,276
west Africa	October 1969	Arbovirus	Yellow fever	10,200
Peru	August 18, 1991	Diarrhoeal/Enteric	–	8,000
Ethiopia	September 1988	Meningitis	–	7,385
Nigeria	May 6, 1991	Diarrhoeal/Enteric	Cholera	7,289
New Zealand	November 1918	Respiratory	Influenza	6,700

probable cases on record and around 700 deaths, the SARS virus had been identified, the gene sequenced, and work had begun on a vaccine. Besides the risk of contagion among passengers, there is also evidence that disease pathogens (germs) are being spread round the world in aircraft sewerage. In 1997 a survey at two major US airports found that, of 40 samples pumped from international flights, 19 contained viruses that had survived the disinfectant used in aircraft tanks.

The big six
Only six diseases are responsible for nearly 90 percent of infection-related deaths among people under 44 years of age. The 'big six' are: AIDS, malaria, tuberculosis, measles, diarrhoeal diseases, and respiratory illnesses such as pneumonia. Some of these were thought to have been curbed, but a number of factors, including the emergence of new disease strains, have hindered control and eradication programmes. As a result, life expectancy in some of the world's poorest countries has fallen back to medieval levels. In Malawi, for example, average life expectancy is just 37 years.

DISEASES

Tuberculosis

The WHO called the resurgence of tuberculosis (TB), currently claiming 3 million lives a year, a 'global emergency'. About one third of the world's population is infected, with some 10 million new active cases emerging each year. On average, TB kills one person every 15 seconds. Furthermore, an unwelcome alliance has arisen between the TB bacillus (*Mycobacterium tuberculosis*) and HIV, the virus that causes AIDS, with HIV rendering a TB carrier 30 times more likely to develop active TB. While the quest continues for effective new vaccines and anti-tuberculosis drugs, many industrialized countries are experiencing marked increases of multi-drug resistant TB. WHO predicts that by 2020 nearly 1 billion people will be newly infected with TB.

Malaria

Malaria is the world's second-largest killer disease (after TB). Half a billion people suffer periodic attacks of malaria and the disease kills an estimated 2 million people each year. Forty years ago, when malaria was also widespread in the temperate zones of Europe and North America, there were hopes of eradicating it with a combination of DDT-saturation of mosquito-ridden areas and anti-malarial drugs. However, both the *Anopheles* mosquito and the parasite responsible for most deaths (*Plasmodium falciparum*) have developed resistance. Today, with more than 40 percent of the world's population living in high-risk areas, malaria is running out of control. Deforestation and changing agricultural practices have created new breeding grounds for mosquitoes and global warming is enabling the resurgence of the disease in sub-tropical and temperate zones where it had earlier been eradicated.

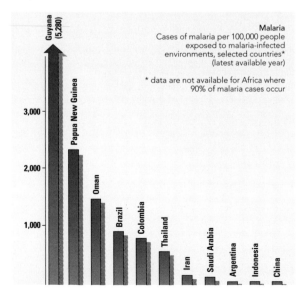

Malaria
Cases of malaria per 100,000 people exposed to malaria-infected environments, selected countries* (latest available year)

* data are not available for Africa where 90% of malaria cases occur

◀ *Malaria is the world's most significant tropical parasitic disease, killing more than 1 million people a year. More than 90% of all malaria cases are in sub-Saharan Africa, where malaria kills a child every 30 seconds. Children living in remote rural areas without clean drinking water or adequate health facilities are the most susceptible. In 1997, the economic cost of malaria in sub-Saharan Africa was an estimated US$2 billion (1997). Shifting populations, changing climate and weather patterns are increasing its reach.*

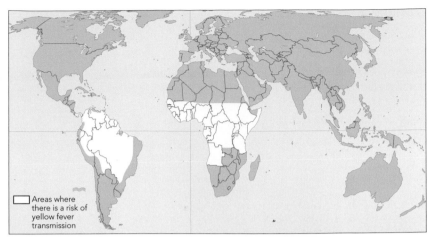

Areas where there is a risk of yellow fever transmission

▲ *Occurences of yellow fever are isolated to sub-Saharan Africa (where it is endemic) and tropical South America. In Africa, the case fatality rate is around 23%, and infants and children are at greatest risk. In South America, most cases occur in young men working in the forested areas of Bolivia, Brazil, Colombia, Ecuador, and Peru, but the disease is spreading to urban areas. The case fatality rate is currently 65%.*

The reappearance of mosquito-borne diseases such as malaria and dengue fever in territories where local populations have no immunity raises the possibility of major epidemics – rapidly developing outbreaks that affect great numbers of people. The global prevalence of dengue fever, a severe flu-like illness, has mushroomed in recent decades, and the disease is now endemic (constantly present) in more than 100 countries. In 2001, some 390,000 cases were reported in Brazil alone, including more than 670 cases of the potentially lethal form, dengue haemorrhagic fever.

Measles

Other diseases that rapidly reach epidemic proportions include measles, which gives rise to more than 30 million cases a year and kills nearly 1 million children; typhoid fever (17 million cases a year, approximately 600,000 deaths), which is contracted from food or water contaminated with the *Salmonella typhi* bacterium; and typhus, a louse-borne disease often associated with wars and major disasters.

Yellow fever

The mosquito-borne yellow fever virus is also extending its range, and is now endemic in much of South America and tropical Africa. In the early 1990s, the disease appeared in Kenya, the first case in east Africa for more than a quarter of a century. There are also fears that the disease could move into Asia, although there is some evidence that antibodies to dengue fever, which is endemic in Asia, could provide some protection against yellow fever.

Yellow fever is one of a long list of haemorrhagic fevers, two of which – lassa and ebola – attract headlines in the developed world wholly disproportionate to the threat they pose. Ebola, identified in 1976, is the more deadly of the two, being fatal in up to 90 percent of cases. In the 2002–03

185

outbreak in the Republic of Congo, which is thought to have resulted from the consumption of contaminated bush-meat, more than 120 people and hundreds of gorillas succumbed. Haemorrhaging (internal bleeding) is also a complication of Rift Valley fever, which is primarily a disease of livestock. Thousands of people were affected by the epidemic that ravaged north-east Kenya in 1997–98; the worst outbreak for two decades, leading to at least 300 deaths.

Modern-day epidemics

Diseases causing sizeable epidemics (that is, involving more than 10,000 cases) over the past 30 years include anthrax (Zimbabwe, 1970s), cholera (Latin America, 1991), dengue fever (Havana, 1981; Delhi, 1982, 1996; Brazil, 2001), diphtheria (Russia, 1995), hepatitis A (Shanghai, 1989), hepatitis C (parts of North America, 1991), meningitis (São Paulo, Brazil, 1974; Sahel countries, 1996), Rift Valley fever (Egypt, 1977; Kenya, 1997–98), typhus (Burundi, 1996–98), and visceral leishmaniasis (southern Sudan, 1985–87).

Real and potential pandemics

Three diseases at large in the world today have pandemic potential – AIDS, cholera, and influenza. A pandemic is an epidemic that spreads rapidly to affect vast numbers of people in many different countries. Originally confined to southern Asia, cholera began to spread across the world from 1817, in what would be the first of a series of pandemics. The outbreak in Latin America in 1991 was the first to have struck the Americas in a century.

Cholera

Cholera is a water-borne disease characterized by violent diarrhoea and vomiting that often strikes in the wake of wars or major disasters. In 1996 scientists discovered that the toxin that can render this disease rapidly lethal derives not from the cholera bacillus (*Vibrio cholerae*) itself but from a virus that uses the bacillus as a means of gaining entry into cells. With antibiotic treatment, the death rate from cholera is less than one percent, although, worryingly, drug resistance is increasing.

AIDS

Although TB and malaria currently affect more people, AIDS is well on its way to eclipsing the Black Death as the

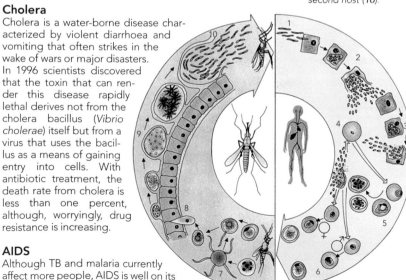

▼ *An infected mosquito injects thousands of* plasmodium *organisms into the bloodstream when it bites a human (1). These penetrate liver cells, multiply and cause cell rupture (2). Released organisms may re-infect liver cells (3), but usually progress to infect red blood cells (4,5). Male and female parasites shortly appear (6). Another mosquito bites the human and takes infected blood (7). Fertilization occurs within the mosquito, the 'embryo' penetrating the stomach wall (8). Within the resulting cyst (9), thousands of organisms develop. The cyst ruptures, and the released organisms travel to the salivary glands, from where they are injected into a second host (10).*

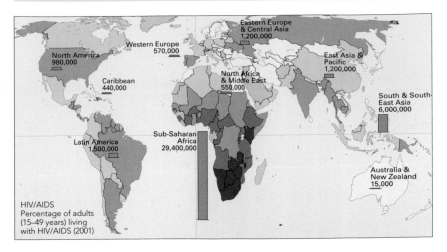

HIV/AIDS
Percentage of adults
(15–49 years) living
with HIV/AIDS (2001)

	15–40%
	5–15%
	0.5–5.0%
	0.1–0.5%
	Under 0.1%
	No data
	Total number of people with HIV/AIDS by region (2002)

▲ AIDS is a fatal disease caused by the retrovirus HIV, which attacks the human immune system. There are two distinct viruses: HIV-1, which has spread worldwide; and HIV-2, which is concentrated almost entirely in West Africa. Both viruses cause AIDS. There are three main means of tranmission: through sexual contact; from mother to baby during birth; and through contact with contaminated blood. The virus can remain dormant for up to 10 years.

biggest killer in history. In the 14th century, bubonic plague swept through Asia and Europe killing some 40 million. Today, only two decades since the AIDS virus was discovered, 42 million people are infected with HIV. Sub-Saharan Africa is worst hit, with an estimated 29.4 million people known to be carrying the virus, but the HIV pandemic is also sweeping relentlessly across eastern Europe and Asia. India, for example, already has nearly 4 million people living with HIV and 1.2 million AIDS orphans.

With resistant HIV strains on the increase, trials continue to find one or more effective vaccines and curative drugs, although some authorities feel that physical methods may prove more effective in curbing infection. These include safe-sex practices, in particular the use of condoms, and application of one or more of the microbicide gels, foams, creams, or suppositories now being developed to annihilate the virus at its point of entry into the body. Without treatment with the anti-viral drugs currently available, most people infected with HIV develop AIDS and die within about ten years. Already, AIDS has caused 22 million deaths and epidemiologists warn that the disease will have claimed 65 million lives by the year 2010.

Contaminated needles are implicated in the spread of HIV, and also of the hepatitis B and C viruses. While there is now an effective vaccine against hepatitis B, an epidemic of liver disease is becoming apparent with approximately 200 million people infected with hepatitis C; a virus only identified in 1989 and against which a number of vaccines are now being developed.

Influenza

The 20th century saw three flu pandemics: in 1918 (a minimum of 20 million deaths and possibly as many as 40 million), 1957 (1 million), and 1968 (700,000). The Center for Disease Control and Prevention (CDC) in Atlanta, Georgia, has predicted

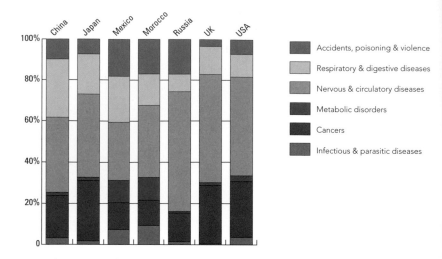

China Japan Mexico Morocco Russia UK USA

- Accidents, poisoning & violence
- Respiratory & digestive diseases
- Nervous & circulatory diseases
- Metabolic disorders
- Cancers
- Infectious & parasitic diseases

that, when the next flu pandemic strikes, 40 million people in the US alone could require treatment of whom as many as 200,000 could die. The flu virus owes its success to its mutability (ability to mutate). New strains sweep round the world every 10 to 40 years, one of the most recent being the avian flu virus (H5N1) first identified in humans in Hong Kong in 1997. Fearing the onset of a fourth pandemic, the authorities ordered the slaughter of hundreds of thousands of chickens. In the event, only 18 people became infected (six of whom died) before the outbreak petered out. SARS, a new strain of pnemonia, is proving more difficult to control.

More diseases on the increase
Another avian virus causing increasing problems in humans is the West Nile virus, which can lead to potentially fatal encephalitis. It is present in many bird species, but is usually transmitted to humans by mosquitoes. Endemic in the Middle East, Africa and Asia, West Nile virus affected more than 500 people in an outbreak in Bucharest, south-east Romania, in 1997, and by 1999 had reached the western henisphere, spreading out from New York City, where it claimed seven lives.

Two similar viral forms are Japanese encephalitis, which kills about 15,000 people a year and leaves many more disabled, and Nipah virus, which in 1999 caused an outbreak in Malaysia that killed more than 100 people. The Nipah virus, which has the fruit bat as its natural host, is a relative of the Hendra virus first isolated in Queensland in 1994.

Bacterial meningitis (mainly the A strain but sometimes also C) remains epidemic in the countries of the Sahel, the arid territory south of the Sahara. The disease is broadly seasonal, reappearing each December in what is known as the 'meningitis belt' and subsiding with the onset of the rains in May and June.

▲ Infectious and parasitic diseases, such as malaria, which claimed 2.1 million lives in 1995, remain a scourge in the developing world. Respiratory infections and injury claim more lives in developing countries, which lack the drugs and the medical staff to deal with them. Developing countries lack the basic services taken for granted in developed nations. For example, in 1990–95 in sub-Saharan Africa, only 31% of the population had access to safe drinking water. By contrast, circulatory diseases and cancer are the main causes of death in rich, industrialized countries. In the mid 1990s in the United Kingdom, circulatory diseases, which cause heart attacks and strokes, accounted for nearly 50% of all deaths, and cancer accounted for nearly another 25%.

Death in the tropics

The leading tropical diseases continue to exact a formidable toll. The WHO warned that, by the year 2010, the big five alone – malaria, leishmaniasis, sleeping sickness, lymphatic filariasis, and schistosomiasis – will claim 4 million lives a year. A single-celled parasite (*Leishmania*), transmitted by sandflies, causes Leishmaniasis, which infects more than 1 million people. The visceral form of the disease is believed to have killed around 100,000 people during a two-year (1985–87) epidemic in the Sudan.

Sleeping sickness

Sleeping sickness (African trypanosomiasis), transmitted by the tsetse fly and known as Nagana when it develops in cattle, was almost eradicated in the 1960s but is now spreading faster than AIDS. Reported to have reached epidemic levels in Congo, Angola, Sudan, and Uganda, it kills up to 400,000 a year. A pan-African campaign was launched following the eradication of the tsetse fly from the east African island of Zanzibar in 1997 (where meat and dairy output has since doubled). Furthermore, a major pharmaceutical company has agreed to make available the drug melarsoprol, which to date represents the only safe treatment for sleeping sickness.

Filariasis and schitosomiasis

Filariasis is a tropical disease caused by nematodes (roundworms) infecting the lymphatic system. The larvae are spread by mosquitoes leading to infection that causes inflammation and ultimately blockage of the lymph vessels, giving rise to the painful and unsightly swelling of the tissues known as elephantiasis. Blood flukes (genus *Schistosoma*) are responsible for schistosomiasis, which develops as a

▼ *The influenza virus viewed under a microscope. Influenza causes 10,000–40,000 deaths every year in the US alone. A modern-day influenza pandemic could kill far more than the 20 million people who died in the 1918–19 outbreak. Influenza spreads rapidly in seasonal epidemics and is expensive in terms of hospital and other health-care costs. It is more common in high-risk groups like the very young and the elderly.*

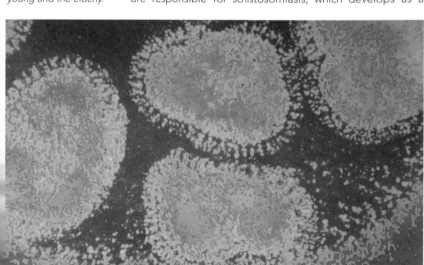

generalized illness with fever, diarrhoea, vomiting, respiratory problems, and a long-term risk of liver damage. Eggs from infected individuals undergo larval development in freshwater snails and so the disease is contracted from contaminated waterways. There have been reports of tourists becoming infected through bathing in Lake Malawi.

More tropical diseases

There are other tropical diseases, including leprosy, Chagas' disease, and river blindness, which, while not necessarily fatal, nonetheless leave populations in chronically poor health and further undermine poor economies. A successful multi-drug treatment regimen has brought a 90 percent reduction in the incidence of leprosy, although the bacterium (*Mycobacterium leprae*) still infects many thousands every year. Leprosy remains endemic in Brazil, Madagascar, Mozambique, India, Burma, and Nepal, with some 75 percent of cases concentrated in India.

The bio-terrorism threat

Real gains have been been made against poliomyelitis, with cases down from 350,000 in 1988 (when a global eradication campaign was launched) to 480 in 2002. The Americas were declared polio-free in 1994, but a setback occurred with outbreaks first in Haiti and then in the Dominican Republic (where two victims died) in 2000–01. Both outbreaks were traced to mutant forms of the virus used in the oral vaccine. This episode has called into question the eradication of polio, which the WHO had hoped to achieve by 2005, and pointed up the need for continued vaccination. There is also a fear that the polio virus, like the anthrax bacillus and the

▼ *Decontamination of an FBI agent after leaving the American Media offices in Boca Raton, south-east Florida, USA. In 2001, a spate of anthrax scares at high-profile locations in the United States highlighted the potential dangers of bio-terrorism. Anthrax is an acute infectious disease caused by the spore-forming bacterium Bacillus anthracis. It most commonly occurs in wild and domestic animals, but it can also occur in humans when they are exposed to infected animals or spores.*

smallpox virus, could feature in acts of bioterrorism. The spectre of the return of smallpox, the only human disease ever to have been eradicated worldwide, is such that, in the United States, vaccination is being offered to key personnel.

The bacterium responsible for plague (*Yersinia pestis*) is also thought to be a candidate for germ warfare. It gives rise to two forms of plague: bubonic and (the often rapidly fatal) pneumonic. Reservoirs of plague persist in rodent colonies in Africa, Asia and parts of the western hemisphere, causing up to 3,000 cases a year. The last serious outbreak was in India in 1994, when the pneumonic form claimed 855 lives. Resistant strains have been reported in Madagascar. Today, the genes of *Y. pestis* have been sequenced and a genetically engineered vaccine is being developed.

New arrivals in the developed world
In Britain, the outbreak of variant CJD, the human form of bovine spongiform encephalopathy ('mad cow disease'), has remained much smaller than feared, with only 125 deaths and a further seven suspected cases reported by spring 2003. In 2003, with the number of new cases falling, researchers at Imperial College, London, reduced its worst-case estimate of UK deaths from vCJD from 50,000 to 7,000.

The classical form of Creutzfeldt-Jakob disease, first described in the 1920s, is a rare disease which is largely sporadic. It is one of a group of diseases caused by prions, rogue proteins that destroy the brain. The variant form (vCJD), which was only identified in 1996, follows a similar degenerative course, although the pathological changes seen in brain tissue are somewhat different; it, too, is invariably fatal. To date, the most likely explanation for the vCJD cases occurring is exposure to the BSE agent.

A silent epidemic that is causing increasing concern in developed countries involves infection with one or other of the so-called 'superbugs'. Drug-resistant pathogens are universal and a problem, especially in hospitals and nursing homes, where they are implicated in many deaths. Most notorious is methicillin-resistant *Staphylococcus aureus* (MRSA), a bacterium that is showing some resistance even to powerful antibiotics of last resort such as vancomycin and linezolid.

Hitherto MRSA has threatened vulnerable groups such as the very young, the frail elderly, people who have suppressed immune systems, and patients weakened by serious illness or injury. Now, however, there is evidence that a new strain of the bacterium is moving beyond the institutional setting and infecting healthy people in the community, apparently spread by skin contact. The US Center for Disease Control (CDC) in Atlanta, Georgia, has identified outbreaks in a number of US cities, including New York, Boston and Miami, and there are fears that the new strain will spread outside the United States.

Water Pollution

At the time of the 1972 United Nations Conference on the Human Environment held in Stockholm, south-east Sweden, the greatest threat to the marine environment was perceived to be water pollution. Waste discharged from ships, as well as urban and industrial effluent from land-based sources, were all seen as contributing to a significant reduction in the health and quality of the marine environment. Although marine pollution is still considered a major cause of concern, it is now recognized that other human activities, including large-scale commercial fishing and the extensive modification of coastal environments, may be having just as great an impact on the quality of the seas and oceans.

Coastal pollution

Although the open ocean remains relatively clean, the greatest problems of pollution and contamination are found in coastal areas. Many coastal habitats are being lost irretrievably to the construction of harbours and industrial installations, the development of coastal settlements and cities (including tourist facilities), and an increase in mariculture. By the time of the 1992 United Nations Conference on Environment and Development, held in Rio de Janeiro, Brazil, land-based pollution was considered to be the major source of pollution in the marine environment. Of even greater importance, however, was the overriding need to develop more rational management of human uses of the coastal zone and inshore resources.

Marine pollution

Contaminants enter the sea either through direct discharge, or indirectly through rivers and the atmospheric transport of particles in aerosols and gases. Around 80 percent of all marine pollution is derived from land-based sources, a further 10 percent results from marine dumping, and the remaining 10 percent from maritime operations, such as ship-based discharge of sewage. Most of the materials entering the ocean remain in the continental shelf areas, and in semi-enclosed bays and seas where they may be deposited in sediments and re-suspended at a later date during storms or dredging operations. In some semi-enclosed areas, such as the North Sea, the build-up of contaminants has reached unacceptably high levels, resulting in algal blooms, toxic red-tides, and viral deaths of marine mammals.

Chemical pollution

In the 1960s, more than 40 people died in town of Minamata, south-west Japan, as a result of eating fish contaminated with mercury that had built up from 30 years of dumping. Many of the town's 50,000 inhabitants suffered pins and needles, a lack of feeling in the limbs, slurred speech, and tunnel vision. Minamata disease first alerted the world to the fact that mercury dumped in the sea was not dispersing, but rather was accumulating in the bodies of marine animals.

▼ Many human activites pollute the world's water and damage the environment. Some pesticides, for example, do not decompose after they have been sprayed on fields and may transfer to rivers when it rains (1). If rainfall is sufficiently heavy, open fields are subject to field erosion (2). This impoverishes the land and may cause rivers to silt up. Salt used to grit roads during the winter can be washed into rivers

▶ People generate huge amounts of rubbish (8), which can create toxic runoff. Seepage of buried industrial waste (9) is more dangerous. Some factories expel industrial waste directly into rivers (10). Pollution is also generated by the sludge farmers put on their land (11). Liquid manure contaminates rivers (12). Sewage is also dumped into the sea (13) and eaten by fishes (14).

(3), harming the wildlife. Reservoirs are created at the expense of agricultural land (4), while our homes (5) are full of chemicals used for cleaning purposes. Filter beds (6), used to remove household chemicals from water, can often be rendered ineffectual by chemicals such as bleach. In addition, a large percentage of untreated domestic sewage flows straight into the sea (7), contaminating tidal mud.

Other heavy metals that are present in industrial waste, such as lead used in some paints, petrol, and cadmium used for bright pigments and zinc-smelting, are notorious poisons. In addition, the effect of two or more heavy metals, or other poisons, is usually greater than the sum of their individual effects. In the recent past, heavy metals such as mercury, cadmium, and lead were considered among the most pervasive pollutants. It is now recognized that some marine organisms naturally concentrate these elements, and high concentrations may not necessarily reflect man-made pollution. Nevertheless, pollution by such elements remains a concern in areas of high-industrial discharge. Anti-fouling agents such as organo-tin compounds are known to have major effects on the reproductive biology of shellfish, and some countries have banned their use. Other dangerous pollutants, such as the chlorinated hydrocarbons, of which DDT is an example, are insoluble and cannot be broken down by organisms. For this reason they accumulate in the fatty tissue of animals low down in the food chain and, as these animals are eaten by their natural predators, the concentration of DDT increases and continues to do so as it

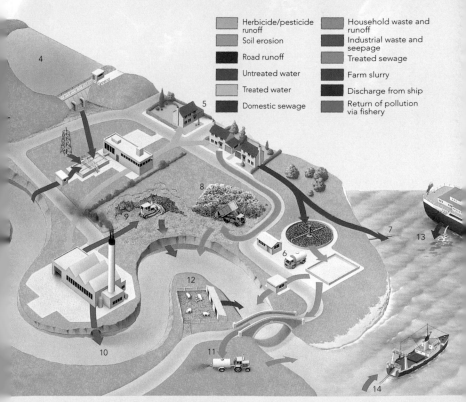

Herbicide/pesticide runoff

Soil erosion

Road runoff

Untreated water

Treated water

Domestic sewage

Household waste and runoff

Industrial waste and seepage

Treated sewage

Farm slurry

Discharge from ship

Return of pollution via fishery

passes higher up the food chain. In the end, animals from shrimp to fish to carnivorous seabirds are put at risk. Chlorinated hydrocarbon pesticides may cause problems along tropical coastlines, but the concentrations of these materials declined in the developed world following control and restriction of their use. PCBs (polychlorinated biphenyls) are another harmful pollutant. They are used in manufacturing paints, plastics, adhesive-coating compounds, hydraulic fluids, and electrical equipment. They have similar effects to DDT but are more persistent, gradually collecting in seafloor sediments, where they are then slowly released into the overlying water.

Oil pollution

Maritime activities have considerably less impact now than in the past, mainly due to the introduction of international conventions limiting the discharge of wastes at sea. Nevertheless maritime accidents, such as the1989 *Exxon Valdez* oil-spill (40,000 tonnes) disaster in Prince William Sound, Alaska, and the 1990 *Mega Borg* supertanker spill (42,000 tonnes) in the Gulf of Mexico had serious and well-publicized local impacts. Although oil may be considered a highly visible contaminant of the marine environment, particularly following tanker disasters, it is generally of less concern than many other materials. Floating oil is usually less damaging than oil that comes into direct contact with bottom-dwelling organisms, either in the inter-tidal or sub-tidal areas. Damage from such accidents is not usually irreversible, although recovery may be slow. Bio-remediation was successfully used as a method of oil abatement after the *Mega Borg* spill, with oil-consuming bacteria being mixed with the nutrient-rich seawater and spread over the oil slick.

▼ *Map showing the areas of greatest water pollution in the world. The numbers correspond to major oil tanker disasters, which are listed in a table on the opposite page.*

Severely polluted sea areas and lakes

Less polluted sea areas and lakes

Areas of frequent oil pollution by shipping

⑨ ○ Major oil tanker spills

▲ Major oil rig blow-outs

▼ Offshore dumpsites for industrial and municiple waste

— Severely polluted rivers and estuaries

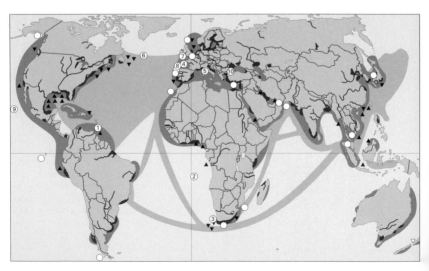

► *Satellite image of the north-west coast of Spain, November 21, 2002. Several dark-coloured fingers of oil are visible reaching through white waves towards the cliffs along the shoreline. The area pictured here is just north of Cape Finisterre. The oil tanker, containing 77,000 tonnes of oil, sank some 210 km (130 miles) due west of Cape Finisterre.*

Nutrients

Current discharges of sewage, both treated and untreated, not only represent a potential health hazard to bathers and seafood consumers, but more importantly are increasing the rate of primary nutrient production in coastal waters. Sewage and agricultural runoff are high in nitrogen and phosphorus, which encourage phytoplankton production in coastal waters. These high inputs cause rapid growth, or blooms, of phytoplankton, resulting in unsightly algal scum on tourist beaches. When the algae die and sink to the bottom of the sea, the resulting bacterial decomposition uses up available dissolved oxygen, causing de-oxygenation of deep waters, which in extreme cases will kill fish. Furthermore, the species of algae in the blooms often produce toxic substances that may be taken up by shellfish, rendering them unfit for human consumption.

Fit for drinking?

A comparatively new water-pollution problem that threatens freshwater and underground drinking supplies is nitrate. There are three main causes for the increase of nitrate in fresh water: the use of nitrate fertilizers, discharges from sewage plants, leakage from cesspools and septic tanks, and intensive livestock farming, producing waste rich in nitrates. Landfills, where urban wastes are buried, are also of particular concern for introducing pollutants into the hydrologic environment. It is easy to blame farmers and industrialists for polluted water, but our unblemished fruit and vegetables owe a lot to pesticides. Moreover, industries use chemicals to produce the cars, coloured toilet paper, and many other luxury products that we consume.

POLLUTION FROM OIL TANKERS		
Tanker name	Tonnes spilt	Year
1 Atlantic Express	287,000	1979
2 ABT Summer	260,000	1991
3 Castillo de Bellver	252,000	1983
4 Amoco Cadiz	223,000	1978
5 Haven	144,000	1991
6 Odyssey	132,000	1988
7 Torrey Canyon	119,000	1967
8 Urquiola	100,000	1976
9 Hawaiian Patriot	95,000	1977
10 Independenta	95,000	1979

Ozone Depletion

The ozone layer is a region of the Earth's atmosphere in which the gas ozone (O^3) is concentrated. Ozone levels are greatest at altitudes of between 21 and 26 kilometres (13–16 miles), and result from reaction between oxygen and incoming sunlight, forming a layer that absorbs much of the solar ultraviolet radiation, thereby shielding the Earth's surface. Aircraft, nuclear weapons, and some aerosol sprays and refrigerants all yield chemical agents that can break down high-altitude ozone, leading to a marked increase in the level of potentially harmful ultraviolet radiation reaching the surface of the Earth.

Global sunscreen

The diffuse, gaseous, ozone layer, 14–45 kilometres (9–28 miles) -thick, is all that protects us from the Sun's harmful ultraviolet radiation, and without it, terrestrial life could not exist. Recent observations have shown that pollution of the atmosphere could be destroying this vital layer. Scientists have detected an 'ozone hole' over Antarctica, which appears seasonally, extending over an area the size of the United States. Were this hole to spread, the consequences would be disastrous for both animal and plant life. Without sunlight, Earth would be a barren planet. Solar radiation warms the Earth's surface and is harnessed by plants by means of photosynthesis. But some wavelengths of light emitted by

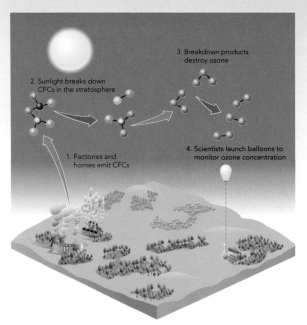

2. Sunlight breaks down CFCs in the stratosphere

3. Breakdown products destroy ozone

1. Factories and homes emit CFCs

4. Scientists launch balloons to monitor ozone concentration

◄ Process of ozone depletion due to the release of chlorofluorocarbons (CFCs) into the atmosphere. CFCs drift slowly into the stratosphere and are broken down by the Sun's ultraviolet radiation into chlorine atoms that destroy the ozone layer. In 1990, growing concern about the environmental effects of CFCs led to an international agreement that sought to reduce and eventually phase out the use of CFCs.

▲ *Commercial logger cutting down a tree in the rainforest of Gabon, west Africa, in 2002. Forests help contain increases in carbon dioxide by converting carbon into cellulose and releasing oxygen through photosynthesis. The destruction of the rainforests leads to the build-up of vast amounts of greenhouse gases such as carbon dioxide, methane, ozone, and nitrous oxide in the atmosphere.*

the Sun are less beneficial to life: indeed, ultraviolet light is an effective sterilizing agent and is used in hospitals to kill microorganisms. Much of this radiation is filtered out in the stratosphere before it can wreak its destructive effects. Under normal circumstances, the concentration of the ozone that absorbs the ultraviolet light is constant, but in recent decades this has changed.

Chlorofluorocarbons (CFCs)
In the 1970s and 1980s, it became clear that human activity was disturbing this delicate equilibrium. Most notably it was determined that chlorine gas released into the atmosphere by human activities was depleting the levels of stratospheric ozone. Chlorine atoms are released in the form of chlorofluorocarbons (CFCs), which are widely used as coolant fluids in refrigerators, to make bubbles in foamed plastic, and in aerosols. After their release, CFCs take many years to rise into the stratosphere. At these altitudes, ultraviolet radiation is sufficiently intense to split CFC molecules and liberate chlorine atoms, which can then attack ozone. A single chlorine atom can result in the destruction of many thousands of ozone molecules before it is finally removed from the stratosphere, and small increases in the levels of chlorine released can therefore cause enormous changes in the chemistry of the upper atmosphere. Emissions of CFCs have been rising rapidly in recent decades, and because CFCs remain in the stratosphere for lengths of time ranging from 65 to 130 years, immediate reduction in their use is essential.

Supersonic transport
In the early 1970s, the thrust, on both sides of the Atlantic, to build and fly supersonic transport (SST) passenger aircraft caused some stratospheric specialists to voice concern. To

achieve speeds of Mach 2, such aircraft were required to cruise in the lower stratosphere – the very region where ozone is most highly concentrated. The prime concern of the scientists was that reactive nitrogen in the SST exhausts might speed up the natural decay of ozone and lead to significant depletion. As it turned out, only a small number of *Concorde* SSTs were constructed, the first making its maiden commercial flight to the Gulf in 1976. Since then, the impact of these few aircraft has been insignificant.

The hole in the ozone layer

In 1985, scientists discovered that the ozone layer was not being depleted gradually across the planet, but rapidly and seasonally in one particular area: the Antarctic. The amplified impact of CFCs in Antarctica is a result of the unique meteorology of that region. During the southern winter the cold, heavy air high over the ice cap is prevented from mixing with the warmer, strong winds that whirl around the continent. Within this thin, cold air, at temperatures around −90°C (−130°F), icy particles form clouds known as polar stratospheric clouds (PSCs). In the dark polar winter, atmospheric chemistry is at a virtual standstill. But some reactions still take place on the surfaces of the cloud particles, slowly preparing the chlorine held in 'reservoirs' to make a rapid escape when the sun begins to shine in the southern spring. This sudden springtime 'flush' of chlorine rapidly depletes the stratospheric ozone layer over the Antarctic.

Arctic difference

The Arctic is quite different: it is much more susceptible to the incursion of frontal disturbances deep into its interior, particularly through the Norwegian Sea. This means that, in most years, the stratosphere above it does not become cold enough for the formation of PSC and, therefore, does not suffer a similar annual depletion. On occasion, however, some unusually cold winters have led to ozone depletion within the Arctic stratosphere.

▶ *Impact of stratospheric ozone depletion on increased UV at the Earth's surface. The key health effects from exposure to increased UV-B due to ozone depletion include skin cancer, cataracts, and accelerated aging of the skin.*

Northern hemisphere   Southern hemisphere

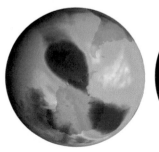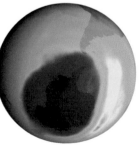

◀ *Total atmospheric ozone concentration in the northern and southern hemispheres (Dobson units, 2000). The false colour images show the total atmospheric ozone concentration in the northern hemisphere (March 2000) and the southern hemisphere (Sept 2000), with the hole in the ozone layer clearly identifiable at the centre. The colours represent the ozone concentration in Dobson units (DU).*

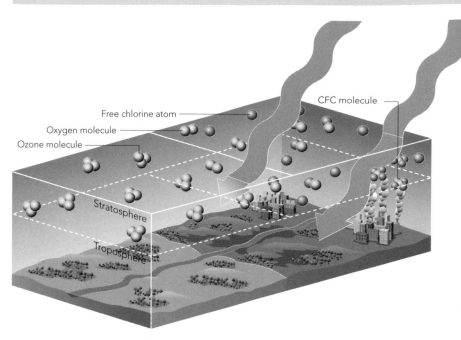

CFC molecule

Free chlorine atom

Oxygen molecule

Ozone molecule

Stratosphere

Troposphere

▶ *Strong circulating winds isolate the air in the middle and lower stratosphere over Antarctica. Air in the upper stratosphere and lower mesosphere of Earth's atmosphere descends into the polar vortex. In winter, the stratospheric circulation above the Antarctic is more-or-less a smooth westerly flow, centred near the pole. When springtime solar radiation starts to increase in September and October, the circulation breaks down, becoming wavy and letting in ozone-rich air from higher latitudes. This raises the concentration of gases to a safer level until circulation cuts off again.*

The vanishing screen

Each October since 1979, the thickness of the ozone layer here has decreased by up to 50 percent or more, and the resulting ozone 'hole' is constantly expanding. The thickness of the ozone layer is measured in Dobson units, a hundred of which correspond to 1 millimetre (0.04 inches) of compressed ozone. In spring, when the hole is at its largest, the ozone value may drop to as low as 250 Dobson units. In the southern summer, the thickness of the layer builds to about 350

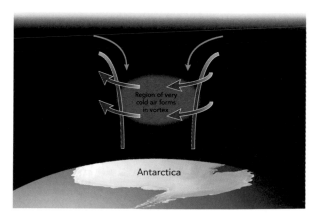

Region of very cold air forms in vortex

Antarctica

199

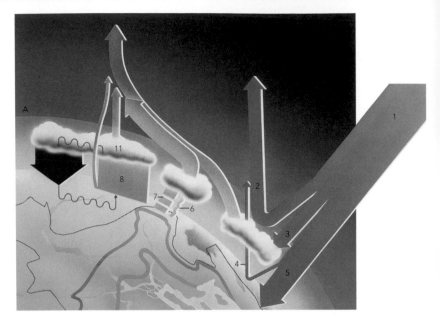

Dobson units. The ozone hole is repaired in this way because the polar stratospheric clouds evaporate in the warmth of the summer, and fresh air returns to the Antarctic from other latitudes, allowing ozone levels to recover.

Protecting Earth's atmosphere

An international agreement to halt ozone depletion through legislated reductions in the use of CFCs was ratified by 170 countries as part of the 1987 Montréal Protocol, and this effort is proving successful. In the upper atmosphere, CFCs initiate a chain of chemical reactions that lead to the production of chlorine and the destruction of ozone. The burden of ozone-depleting chemicals in the lower atmosphere has been decreasing since 1994 as a result of the Montréal Protocol and researchers now predict that the Antarctic ozone hole should close by the year 2050. With the banning of CFCs the recovery is assured, but greenhouse gases could lengthen the process. Greenhouse gases warm the lower atmosphere but cool the stratosphere allowing ice crystals to form, and these catalyze the destruction of ozone by CFCs. In the context of environmental protection, limiting the production of CFCs has been one scientific recommendation listened to and acted upon by policy-makers at a global level.

Life in a destructive light

Increased levels of ultraviolet radiation, especially ultraviolet-B (290–320 nanometre wavelengths), are expected to cause

▶ *The Earth's limb. When viewed from the side, the Earth looks like a flat circle, and the atmosphere appears like a halo around it. This glowing halo is known as the limb. From a side view, the layers of the atmosphere appear like layers in a cake, allowing instruments to see the lower layers of the stratosphere. This is important because most of the recently observed ozone change, like the 'ozone hole', occurs in the lower stratosphere.*

◄ *Greenhouse gases (A) are fairly transparent to the near infra-red, visible and shorter wavelength light that brings most of the Sun's energy (1), though about 25 percent is reflected by the atmosphere (2), and 25 percent is absorbed by it (3). About five percent is reflected from the Earth (4), which absorbs the rest (5). Some of this absorbed energy rises again in thermals (6), or in the heat of evaporated moisture (7). The rest is reradiated (8) as long wavelength infra-red rays.*

marked increases in sunburn, skin cancer and in eye problems such as cataracts. For every one percent decrease in ozone, there may be as much as a five percent annual increase in the incidence of non-malignant skin cancers in humans.

Warming the planet

Burning fossil-fuels such as coal expels more greenhouse gases into the atmosphere. At the same time, cutting down vast areas of tropical forest reduces the amount of oxygen being recycled into the atmosphere. Consequently, human activities are conspiring to dramatically raise the levels of heat-trapping gases in the atmosphere. Furthermore, the destruction of the forests – leading in many cases to an expansion of urban areas or of arid, eroded deserts – also modifies the land surface and thus affects the climate by altering the amounts of the Sun's energy that is absorbed and reflected. If there were no moisture or carbon dioxide in the atmosphere, Earth's average temperature would be only −18°C (0°F). The presence in the atmosphere of small quantities of carbon dioxide and several other gases helps to trap the Sun's heat. This natural insulation is vital to our survival, but the levels of these insulating gases have increased by a third since the 19th-century Industrial Revolution, trapping more heat and warming up the atmosphere. The overwhelming consensus among the world's leading climate scientists is that the dramatic rise is the result of human's polluting the Earth. At present, pollution concentrations are set to double in the course of the 21st century, with dire consequences. According to the worst predictions, the global temperature could rise by 2–3°C (4–6°F) over the next couple of decades. If this happens, the world will be warmer than at any time during the past 2 million years.

Acid Rain

Acid rain is rain that is highly acidic because of sulphur dioxides, nitrogen oxides, and other air pollutants dissolved in it. Normal rain is slightly acidic, with a pH of 6. The pH scale ranges from one for extremely acidic to 14 for extremely basic or alkaline, with seven being neutral. The pH scale is a negative logarithmic scale: a pH value of 4 is ten times more acidic than a pH of 5 and 100 times more acidic than a pH of 6. Vinegar has a mean pH value of 3, while stomach acid has a value of 1.5. Acid rain typically has a pH value of 2.8, but values as low as 1.8 have been detected. Automobile battery acid has a pH value of 1.

The causes of acid rain

The main instigator of acid rain is the introduction of sulphur into the environment either by volcanic eruptions or from human activities, usually from industry. The formation of acid rain is directly related to the burning of fossil fuels. The primary culprit that we are most familiar with is the burning of coal in power plants for producing electricity, although petrol consumption also adds to the problem. When sulphur-containing fossil fuels are burned, sulphur dioxide is released which can mix with moisture to form sulphuric acid droplets in the atmosphere, contributing to environmental

▼ Map showing regions with high concentrations of acid rain. The coloured areas – those places with high levels of acidity (low Ph levels) – are often located away from the dotted areas – those regions with high emissons levels. This is because pollution is dispersed by the wind. Norway, for example, receives far more pollutants than they produce, much of them from Britain.

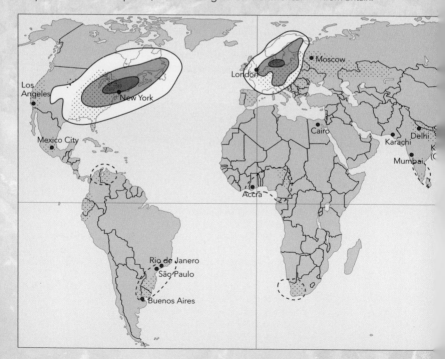

▶ *Branches from healthy and unhealthy trees. The branch from a tree in the Black Forest of south-west Germany (left) shows needle loss and yellowed boughs caused by acid rain.*

 Main areas of sulphur and nitrogen emissions (from the burning of fossil fuels)

• Major cities with levels of air pollution exceeding World Health Organization guidelines

 pH less than 4.0 (most acidic)

pH 4.0–4.5

pH 4.5–5.0

 Potential problem areas

degradation. These droplets can combine to form a haze layer (a sulphate aerosol) that can produce lung disease. This haze also modifies the atmospheric reflectivity, and as a result, changes the amount of solar energy brought into the Earth's climate system, usually cooling the surface. Even though there are some open questions on causes, sulphate aerosols, acid rain, and smog effect major physical, biological, health, and social problems.

The effects of acid rain

For many aquatic organisms that live in waters exposed to such extremes of acidity, the corrosive environment produced by acid rain spells death. The acid even eats away at the surfaces of buildings and statues in towns. In European forests, the trees are more vulnerable still. Damage to forests by acid rain has affected more than half of all trees in the Czech Republic, Germany, Greece, the Netherlands, Norway, Poland, and the United Kingdom. Acid rain also adversely affects human health and causes smog.

Air pollution

We are daily poisoning the air we breathe. Many automobile exhausts emit tetra-ethyl lead, which is added to petrol to prevent engine-knock. Tetra-ethyl lead concentrates in air and dust. This is especially harmful in cities, and a study in Turin, north-west Italy, showed that 30 percent of the lead in the inhabitants' blood came from petrochemicals. Lead in the blood can cause stomach pains, headaches, irritation, coma, and death. And very low levels of lead can affect the brains of growing children. There is growing international pressure to ban the use of leaded petrol, but lead is only one of the harmful substances – many of them carcinogenic – regularly pumped into the air as a by-product of our highly industrialized society.

ACID RAIN

Upsetting nature's balance

The comparatively recent rapid industrialization in Europe and North America has added tremendous quantities of acidic pollutants to the atmosphere, and taller chimneys allow pollution to spread to distant, previously unaffected areas. The pollutants produce lifeless lakes, dying forests, and contaminated soils. Food chains may be disrupted in forests, as the leaves of damaged trees become deficient in

calcium through leaching processes. For instance, caterpillars eat affected leaves, and nesting-birds eat caterpillars. These birds produce very thin and easily damaged eggshells or no eggs at all, and the bird population accordingly declines.

Some soils are more vulnerable to acidification than others. Laterite soils of many tropical regions, for example, are highly sensitive to acidification. Tundra soils and soils that contain high levels of calcium and sodium are the least susceptible.

◄ Most sulphur (1) leaves factory chimneys as the gaseous sulphur dioxide (SO_2), and most nitrogen (2) is also emitted as one of the nitrogen oxides (NO or NO_2), both of which are gases. These gases may be dry deposited – absorbed directly by the land, by lakes, or by the surface of vegetation (3). If they are in the atmosphere for any time, the gases will oxidize (gain an oxygen atom) and go into solution as acids (4).

Sulphur dioxide will become sulphuric acid (H_2SO_4) and the nitrogen oxides will become nitric acid (HNO_3). The acids usually dissolve in cloud droplets and may travel great distances before being precipitated as acid rain.

Catalysts such as hydrogen peroxide, ozone and ammonium help promote the formation of acids in clouds [5]. More ammonium (NH_4) can be formed when some of the acids are partially neutralized [6] by airborne ammonia (NH_3). Acidification increases with the number of active

hydrogen (H^+) ions dissolved in an acid (7).

Hydrocarbons emitted by – for example – car exhausts (8) will react in sunlight with nitrogen oxides to produce ozone (9). Although it is invaluable in the stratosphere, low-level ozone causes respiratory problems and also hastens the formation of acid rain.

When acid rain falls on the ground, it dissolves and liberates heavy metals and aluminium (Al) (10). When it is washed into lakes, aluminium irritates the outer surfaces of many fish. Eventually their gills become clogged with mucus, and they die.

As acid rain falls or drains into a lake, the pH of the lake falls. Perfectly neutral water would have a pH of 7, and each drop of one point on the pH scale means that acidity has increased tenfold.

Naturally occurring water always contains dissolved substances that make it slightly acid or alkaline even without man's intervention. Experiments in Canada indicate that minnows (11)

and shrimps (12) begin to disappear when the pH reaches six. Trout (13), which feed on them, also begin to decline. At pH 5.6, the exoskeletons of crayfish (14) soften and become overrun with infestation. All that is left is a clear lake with a lush carpet of green algae (15) and moss. Alkaline soils containing calcium carbonate can help neutralize acid rain, and some countries add lime or limestone to protect vulnerable lakes.

Forests suffer the effects of acid rain through damage to leaves, through the loss of vital nutrients, and through the increased amounts of toxic metals liberated by acids, which damage roots and soil microorganisms.

205

ACID RAIN

CHART OF PH LEVELS						
	pH 6.5	pH 6.0	pH 5.5	pH 5.0	pH 4.5	pH 4.0
trout	●	●	●	●		
bass	●	●	●			
perch	●	●	●	●	●	
frog	●	●	●	●	●	●
salamander	●	●	●	●		
clam	●	●				
crayfish	●	●	●			
snail	●	●				
mayfly	●	●	●			

◄ *Table of freshwater species and their pH-tolerance levels. Acid rain can change the pH level of a body of water. This has dramatic consequences for wildlife. For example, the death of a mayfly in water of pH 5.0, can affect the population of frogs, which have a higher tolerance level, because mayflies are a major food supply.*

Dying forests
As mentioned earlier, the environmental consequences of acid rain include damage to vegetation, lake ecosystems, drinking water, and human structures. Forests suffer the effects of acid rain through damage to leaves, through the loss of vital nutrients, and through the increased amounts of toxic metals liberated by acids, which leach out nutrients and damage roots and soil microorganisms. Vast tracts of evergreen trees in Germany and red spruce trees in Vermont, north-east USA, have been killed by acid rain.

Polluted lakes
Lake ecosystems have been damaged by acid rain. The life-cycles of fish and other aquatic animals are disrupted because acid rain interferes with the natural recycling of nutrients. Aquatic plants may not grow so that animals that feed on the plants have little to eat. This adverse effect is passed up the food chain to fish and other animals. Fish that were once abundant and used for food and sport fishing in the lakes of Sweden have disappeared as a result of an increase in acidity. Scientists have traced acid rain problems in Scandinavian lakes to airborne pollutants from Germany, France, and Great Britain. Acid precipitation problems are also prevalent in the north-eastern United States and Canada. Prevailing winds push the emission of sulphur dioxide from industrial plants in the Ohio Valley, east-central USA, in a north-westerly to north-easterly direction. Typical distances for the transportation of sulphur dioxide before deposition range from 200 to 600 kilometres (120 to 370 miles). Some lakes in the north-eastern USA now have a pH of less than 5.

▶ *Acid rain has eroded this stone sculptured head at the top of St Stephens Church, Stamford, Lincolnshire, east-central England. Acid rain affects stone primarily in two ways: dissolution and alteration. When acids in polluted air react with the calcite in marble and limestone, the calcite dissolves.*

Polluted water supplies
Acid rain can contaminate supplies of drinking water by dissolving and thus liberating toxic metals in the soil. The corrosion of underground drinking-water pipes is another source of danger. One very serious consequence is the harm caused to the liver and kidneys of young children by the accumulation of high levels of copper.

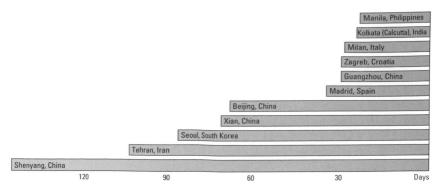

Days				
				Manila, Philippines
				Kolkata (Calcutta), India
				Milan, Italy
				Zagreb, Croatia
				Guangzhou, China
				Madrid, Spain
		Beijing, China		
		Xian, China		
	Seoul, South Korea			
Tehran, Iran				
Shenyang, China				
120	90	60	30	Days

▲ *This bar-chart shows the number of days each year (averaged over four to 15 years in the 1970s–1980s), when sulphur dioxide levels exceeded the WHO threshold of 150 microgrammes per cubic metre (about a ten-millionth of an ounce per cubic foot) in the world's most air-polluted cities.*

Corrosive rain

Acid rain can damage many building materials, including steel, paint, plastic cement and masonry. Human-made structures, particularly those constructed of limestone, sandstone and marble, are especially vulnerable. Structures on the Acropolis in Athens, Greece, have decayed over the past 100 years because of air pollution. The problem is severe, requiring that many monuments and statues be periodically coated at great expense or placed in glass enclosures. Building degradation is also taking place in many urban cities of the eastern seaboard of the United States and in Europe.

Acid fog

The consequences of acid rain are not solely restricted to Europe and the eastern United States. The problem is moving westward in the form of acid fog. Unlike acid rain, which forms high in the atmosphere and can travel long distances, acid fog forms when water vapour near the ground mixes with pollutants and forms acid. This acid collects around particles of smog and if the humidity is high enough an acid fog can develop. Acid fog with a pH of 3, ten times more acidic than acid rain in the eastern United States, has been observed in Los Angeles, California. These acid fogs pose a considerable hazard to health.

Smog

Smogs occur when pollutants accumulate in a shallow layer of cold air trapped under warmer air (a situation known as a temperature inversion). Where poor-quality coals are used widely, as in Eastern Europe, sulphurous smogs often envelop cities in cold winters. The London smog event of December 1952 was a landmark event and a wake-up call to the pollution hazards from burning coal as a heating fuel. Between December 4 and December 10, 1952, it was estimated that 4,000 people in London died from the sulphur dioxide in the air and the acid fog. London was famous for its fog, but at the time little was known about the combined impact of coal burning. Switching to natural gas has not eliminated London's fog but the debilitating combination of fog and pollution from coal burning has been removed. Such smogs have been largely eliminated from Western Europe and North America, only to be replaced by photochemical smogs in summer, caused by hydrocarbons and nitrogen oxides from vehicle exhausts reacting with sunlight to form eye-stinging ozone.

Los Angeles, California, enclosed between mountains and the sea, suffers severe photochemical smogs in summer. With its population increasing by 1 million every four years, smogs were expected to worsen; but tough new controls were introduced in 1989 in an effort to eliminate smog by the year 2007. Unfortunately, cities situated in a topographic bowl surrounded by mountains are susceptible to smog problems. Cities such as Los Angeles and San Diego, in California, Phoenix, Arizona, and Mexico City continue to have severe air-quality problems from time to time.

Future prospects

Thousands of kilometres of rivers and thousands of lakes in the United States, Canada, and Europe are in various stages of acidification. For instance, many rivers in Nova Scotia,

▼ Smog obscures the south-east coast of China, January 7, 2002. In late December 2001 and early January 2002, most of south-eastern China was covered by a thick greyish shroud of aerosol pollution. The smog was so thick that some regions of China are obscured in this satellite image. Hong Kong is the large brown cluster of pixels toward the lower left-hand corner of the image. The island of Taiwan, due east of mainland China, is also blanketed by the smog.

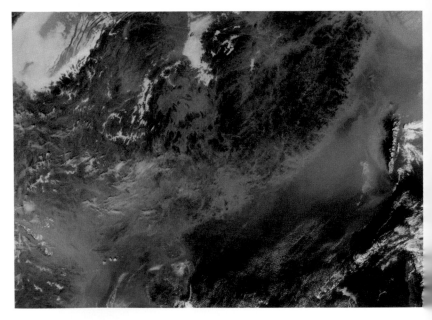

south-east Canada, cannot support healthy populations of Atlantic salmon. More than 200 lakes in the Adirondack Mountains of the eastern United States can no longer sustain fish. The problem of Scandinavian lakes has already been mentioned.

Acid-rain buffers

Since the early 1980s, some progress has been achieved in tackling the problem of acid rain. One solution is to rehabilitate the lakes with periodic additions of lime. This procedure is known as 'buffering' or the neutralization of acids. Known buffers are calcium carbonate or calcite, which removes the hydrogen ions in the acid by forming neutral bicarbonate ions. However, this solution is expensive and requires long-term, continuous effort.

Reducing pollutants

The only long-term solution to the problem of acid rain is to minimize the production of acid-forming pollutants into the atmosphere. This can be done in a number of ways. Energy conservation in itself can produce lower emissions. Another key aspect is to treat coal before, during, and after burning to capture the sulphur dioxide before it is released into the environment. However, this is costly and can place heavy burdens on low-income countries. The reduction of nitrogen oxide is more difficult because it is produced by the burning of petrol in automobiles. A number of countries have signed international agreements to reduce emissions of sulphur and nitrogen oxides, especially from large coal-fired power stations. It is encouraging that the reduction of pollutants is slowly becoming an international priortity. Environmentalists have strongly suggested, however, that such promised reductions do not go far enough. Soils and lakes of many regions are now so acidified that their effects will last for many decades to come.

Land Contamination

Fouling the Earth

Contaminated land is a widespread problem of unknown dimensions in most industrialized countries, and increasingly in developing nations. At Lekkerkerk, south Holland, Netherlands, for example, about 300 houses were built on an old refuse dump that contained organic solvents and other wastes. At another site near Utrecht, the former home of an asphalt works, tar penetrated the soil to depths of 45 metres (150 feet). Reclaiming the site cost many millions of dollars and involved isolating the vitiated earth by sinking steel plates to the full depth of contamination. The polluted soil was then excavated and incinerated to burn off the tars.

The Love Canal chemical site

Between 1942 and 1953 nearly 22,000 tonnes of chemical waste were buried in a waste disposal site at Love Canal, Upper New York state, eastern USA. The site was sold to the local board of education for just one dollar with the warning that it should not be disturbed. In fact, the warning went unheeded and a whole new neighbourhood was built. In 1976, local residents noticed the appearance of a foul-smelling liquid, and people fell ill. In 1980 about 700 families were evacuated. Love Canal has since become a synonym for the ecological hazard of contaminated land.

Chemical waste

Waste or the dumping of chemicals has contaminated many sites, such as old military bases. The treatment of soils to

▼ *Aerial view of the chemical plant responsible for the Love Canal disaster, New York state, USA. From 1942 to 1953, the plant buried toxic waste at a disposal site in the Love Canal neighbourhood. In 1980, about 700 families were forced to relocate after evidence emerged of the health risks of their exposure to the toxic waste.*

uranium 238	
Half-life 4.47 bn yr	α
Thorium 234	
24.1 days	β
Protactinium 234	
1.17 min	β
Uranium 234	
245,000 yr	α
Thorium 230	
80,000 yr	α
Radium 226	
1,600 yr	α
Radon 222	
3.82 days	α
Polonium 218	
3.05 min	α
Lead 214	
26.8 min	β
Bismuth 214	
19.7 min	β
Polonium 214	
0.00016 s	α
Lead 210	
22.3 yr	β
Bismuth 210	
5.01 days	β
Polonium 210	
138.4 days	α
Lead 206 (stable)	Radiation types

remove contaminants, however, is a very costly process. Contamination of the soil and groundwater by leaking underground-tanks is a particularly serious environmental concern in urban areas, often requiring a dramatic response. In 1983 the US federal government evacuated and purchased the entire town of Times Beach, eastern Missouri – a small community of 2,400 residents. It had been discovered that oil sprayed on the local roads contained dioxin, a colourless, chlorine-bearing hydrocarbon that is extremely toxic to humans and other mammals. The required dosage that is detrimental to human health is not yet established, but the chemical is a known carcinogen at very low concentrations.

Buried and forgotten

The millions of tonnes of tars, solvents, pesticides and domestic rubbish discarded each year by modern, consumer society are primarily dumped in landfill sites that are often any convenient hole in the ground. As rain seeps into these rubbish heaps, it forms a toxic liquid (or leachate), which percolates into the underlying soil and contaminates ground-water. In such sites, migration of the leachate was once considered to be a good thing: the idea being that the poisons, which become more dilute the further they migrate from the site, would be broken down by bacteria or become attached to soil particles at low concentrations. But the strategy has not worked. Western Germany, for example, has 35,000 problem sites, while Denmark has an estimated 2,000 landfill sites that have seriously contaminated surrounding groundwater. New landfill sites are designed to prevent leachate from forming or, if this fails, to prevent the leachate from migrating. These sites will eventually be sealed off with a low-permeability clay layer, impermeable plastic liners around the base and sides, and an impermeable cap.

Landfill sites

In all landfill sites, anaerobic bacteria, which thrive in the compacted, air-free layers of rubbish, digest organic matter and produce a combination of methane and carbon dioxide gases. The methane that escapes out of the top of the site or

▶ The half-life of a radioactive element is the time taken for half of the existing amount of the substance to decay into some other element. This element may, in turn, be radioactive, with its own, different, half-life. The diagram shows the half-life of Uranium-238 (the parent radio-nucleide) and of each

of its products (the daughter radio-nucleides). Each daughter decays into another daughter until the process reaches lead-206, which is stable and non-radioactive. The degree of isolation required for radioactive waste depends on the lifetime of the waste concerned, and on the lifetimes of its daughters.

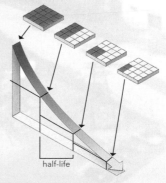

half-life

LAND CONTAMINATION

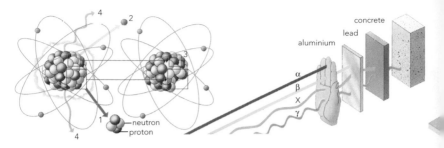

the sides not only contributes to global warming, but as an explosive gas that can seep into houses with potentially disastrous consequences. New landfill sites are engineered to collect the methane, which can be used in the same way as natural gas - which is exactly what it is. Organic waste, including domestic sewage, is separated from other materials so that anaerobic bacteria can be used to generate methane in a controlled environment. Any sludge that remains after the bacteria are finished can make a safe, sterile fertilizer. If the sludge is mixed with straw or any low-grade organic waste, its high nitrogen content can feed other bacteria, which will break down the organic waste creating pleasant smelling manure or compost that can be used on the land. In China, this is exactly what happens to organic waste and sewage in almost every village. The most toxic waste, which cannot legally be dumped at landfill sites in the countries of origin, often finds its way to dumping grounds in the developing countries. More than 40,000 tonnes of industrial waste is shipped to these countries every year.

Nuclear waste

Low-level nuclear waste is buried at 15 principal sites in the United States. These wastes are buried, under a philosophy of 'dilute and disperse', in areas where the hydrological and geological conditions are believed to curtail the migration of radioactivity. Not all of these buried sites have, however, been successful in providing the needed environmental protection. The disposal of high-level radioactive wastes that are left in spent-fuel assemblages from nuclear reactors is a very serious problem. Disposal in the polar ice caps or the deep ocean has been considered but installation in stable bedrock seems to be the best long-term solution. The US Department of Energy is considering the existing nuclear reservation at Yucca Mountain, southern Nevada, south-west United States, as a repository for high-level nuclear waste beginning in 2010.

There is currently only one major designated facility for disposal of low-level nuclear waste in the United Kingdom. This is the Drigg facility, which is close to the Sellafield nuclear reprocessing plant at Seascale, Cumbria. Sellafield is the site of the world's first commercial-scale nuclear power station, Calder Hall, opened in 1956.

▲ *Many elements are naturally radioactive, which means there is always background radiation even when there is no man-made or accidentally generated radioactivity in the vicinity. Alpha radiation occurs when an unstable atomic nucleus emits an alpha (1) particle (which is a helium nucleus – two protons and two neutrons). Alpha (α) radiation is stopped by flesh. Beta (β) radiation occurs when an electrically neutral neutron emits a negative electron (which is the beta (2) particle) and becomes in the process a positive proton (3). A thin sheet of aluminium (Al) can stop beta particles. X-rays and gamma (γ) rays are both forms of electromagnetic radiation (types of light), created when a nucleus loses energy without undergoing structural change (4). X-rays can be stopped by a sheet of lead (Pb), while high-energy gamma rays will penetrate thin sheets of lead, but may be stopped by a layer of concrete.*

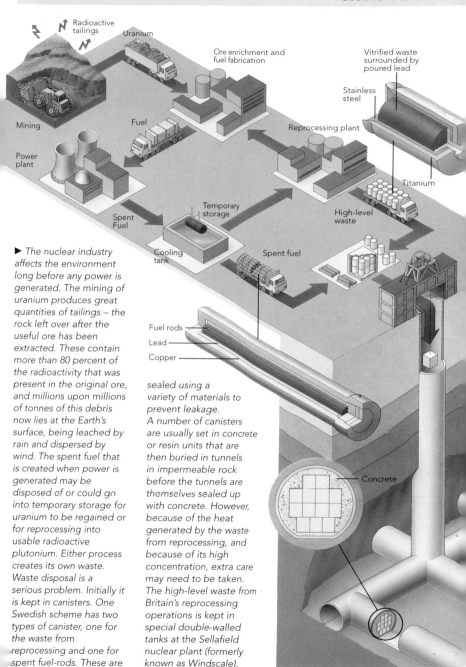

Radioactive tailings

Uranium

Ore enrichment and fuel fabrication

Vitrified waste surrounded by poured lead

Stainless steel

Mining

Fuel

Reprocessing plant

Titanium

Power plant

Spent Fuel

Cooling tank

Temporary storage

Spent fuel

High-level waste

Fuel rods

Lead

Copper

Concrete

▶ The nuclear industry affects the environment long before any power is generated. The mining of uranium produces great quantities of tailings – the rock left over after the useful ore has been extracted. These contain more than 80 percent of the radioactivity that was present in the original ore, and millions upon millions of tonnes of this debris now lies at the Earth's surface, being leached by rain and dispersed by wind. The spent fuel that is created when power is generated may be disposed of or could go into temporary storage for uranium to be regained or for reprocessing into usable radioactive plutonium. Either process creates its own waste. Waste disposal is a serious problem. Initially it is kept in canisters. One Swedish scheme has two types of canister, one for the waste from reprocessing and one for spent fuel-rods. These are sealed using a variety of materials to prevent leakage. A number of canisters are usually set in concrete or resin units that are then buried in tunnels in impermeable rock before the tunnels are themselves sealed up with concrete. However, because of the heat generated by the waste from reprocessing, and because of its high concentration, extra care may need to be taken. The high-level waste from Britain's reprocessing operations is kept in special double-walled tanks at the Sellafield nuclear plant (formerly known as Windscale).

Habitat and Species Loss

The wide variety of plant and animal systems, genetic strains and the ecosystems that support them are known as the Earth's biodiversity. The maintenance of biodiversity is a major aim of conservationists concerned about ecological stability and biological research. It is estimated that less than 10% of the Earth's surface is host to nearly 75% of its species. Many of the world's most species-rich habitats, such as rainforests and wetlands, are also the most threatened by human development. Speaking on International Biodiversity Day (May 22, 2003), United Nations Secretary-General Kofi Annan stated: "Biodiversity is an essential heritage for all humankind, stopping its loss, and guaranteeing the continued functioning of the earth's ecosystems – both marine and terrestrial – should be a high priority for everyone."

Pressures on the rainforests

Rainforests present a wide array of resources in areas of the world that are frequently beset by poverty and rapidly expanding populations. Demographers predict that by the end of the century 80 percent of the Earth's population will be living in a country with tropical forests. Despite an already wide spectrum of wealth in these countries, all are striving for a better standard of living. Some countries, such as Malaysia, Brazil, and Indonesia, are now at various stages of industrialization, while others, notably in tropical Africa, are still struggling to find the path to development. During the 21st century, increasing pressure on forests will arise from the needs of the people in these countries, notably homes, roads, food, educational and recreational facilities, electricity and industrial consumer goods. In many ways, the natural resources of the tropical forests are the raw materials for this development, but will they still exist?

▼ A view from a tower above the Amazon rainforest canopy, north of Manaus, north-west Brazil. Most photosynthesis occurs in the canopy, which absorbs as much as 90% of the sunlight falling on the forest. The canopy is also the most productive part of the forest. Each year, a tropical rainforest produces about 10–12 tonnes of new growth per hectare (22–27 tons per acre). In 2001, logging and fires destroyed 15,787 sq km (6,095 sq miles) of the Amazon rainforest. Scientists estimate that 42% of the rainforest will either be totally deforested or heavily degraded by 2020.

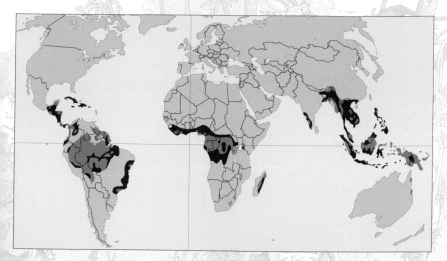

■ Former areas of rainforest

■ Existing rainforest

▲ Map showing the former and current areas of rainforest. 'Hot spots' of deforestation in south-east Asia include north-east India, Burma, Cambodia, Laos, central and northern Vietnam, southern China, and Sumatra and Kalimantan in Indonesia. Cameroon and Gabon are 'hot spots' of deforestation in central Africa. In South America, the eastern and southern portions of the Amazon basin are the main 'hot spots of deforestation. Other sites include the foothills of the Andes in Peru and Ecuador, and the coastal forests of Colombia, Ecuador and Guyana. Only fragments of forest remain in Central America, and most of these are shrinking or under threat.

Logging the forests

Much of the land clearance during recent decades has been haphazard, taking place spontaneously without any form of control or planning. Landless settlers have hacked down and burned countless thousands of square kilometres of either undisturbed or logged forest. They gain access to previously virgin forest by using roads built by governments or by logging or mining companies. The frequent result is severe environmental degradation. All too regularly, the type of shifting cultivation that the settlers use is unsustainable. The ecosystem is destroyed forever, and the cleared land has to be abandoned after a few years. The settlers are forced to move on, only to repeat the process elsewhere. With the ever-increasing population pressure in countries with rain forest, it is inevitable that this type of deforestation will continue. Poverty, population growth, and unequal land ownership are the fundamental causes of this ad hoc land conversion and destruction. It is this sort of wastage that cannot be allowed to continue. The tropical forest resource is still very large, particularly in South America and parts of Central Africa: but it is far from infinite. Once trees have been cut down and the soil has been eroded over very large areas, there is little chance of the forest ever regenerating satisfactorily. It is not only the impoverished who are placing demands on the rainforests. It is also the rich industrialized countries that provide the demand that drives the trade in tropical timber and the markets for beef cattle that graze on pastures that were once rainforest.

The Ivory Coast, a major West African exporter of timber, is about to be completely 'logged-out' and expects to begin importing wood in the next two or three years. In south-east Asia, timber production from the Philippines has declined through over-exploitation, a pattern now being repeated in parts of Malaysia. So far, the Amazon Basin has remained comparatively untouched, although the situation here is also deteriorating rapidly. Commercial logging is often seen as the major cause of deforestation in rainforests, but in fact it is almost never directly responsible for forest loss. Indirectly, it has more malign effects, permitting migrant settlers to move into the forest along the loggers' roads and complete the deforestation illegally.

Attitudes towards the logging industry are polarized. The view taken by some western pressure-groups, such as Friends of the Earth and the World Rainforest Movement, is that loggers are responsible for mass destruction of forests, both directly through their logging operations, and indirectly by creating access for landless peasants. Other groups such as the IUCN and the World Wide Fund for Nature (WWF) regard the timber trade itself as holding the key to saving the world's tropical forests, despite its poor track-record in the past. The point is that if the forests die, so does the lucrative trade in tropical hardwoods, which is certainly not in the interest of the logging companies.

'Shifting' agriculture

Slash-and-burn is an emotive phrase that more often than not brings to mind pictures of destruction, of vast areas of the smouldering stumps of trees put to the torch as peasant farmers clear the forest for cultivation. But indigenous peoples of the rainforests throughout the tropics have used this technique for generations as part of a life-giving, sustainable forest agriculture system. Known as 'shifting' or 'swidden' agriculture, this is often the only way in which the nutrient-poor rainforest soils can support crops.

Today, the problem is that as population pressure increases, the natural limitations of the shifting system are not respected. As the land is used more and more intensively, the fallow period becomes shortened, which leads to the overworking of the soil, decreasing soil fertility, and reducing crop yields. In addition, migrant settlers, who are unfamiliar with the forest,

▼ *These Landsat images from 1975 to 2000 show the deforestation (left to right) of an area of tropical dry forest to the east of the city of Santa Cruz, eastern Bolivia. Since the mid 1980s, a large agricultural development effort (the Tierras Baja project) and the San Javier scheme for the resettlement of people*

do not generally plant the wide variety of crops used by the traditional shifting cultivators, which removes what is essentially a natural pest-control system. Planting monocultures makes the crop more susceptible to pest infestations. Furthermore, the cleared plots are frequently much larger than those of the indigenous people, which means that the forest regeneration during the fallow period takes significantly longer.

A combination of increasing population pressure and ignorance of suitable farming techniques has led to severe land degradation throughout the tropics, and vast areas of scrub and unproductive grassland, 30,000–40,000 sq km (11,500–15,500 sq miles) in Papua New Guinea alone, bear witness to this. In Laos, current estimates suggest that between 2,000 and 3,000 sq km (750–1,500 sq miles) of forest are lost each year to the army of shifting cultivators. If present rates continue unchecked, all Laotian rainforest will have disappeared by the year 2030. It is widely recognized that this sort of uncontrolled and unsustainable shifting agriculture represents the biggest threat to the future of the rainforests. In many countries, governments encourage landless peasants in areas of high population-density to move into less-developed forest areas. These people are thus essentially 'shifted' cultivators.

After logging and shifting cultivation by landless settlers, cattle ranching is the third and final phase in degradation of the forests. During the last 30 years, the spread of beef cattle ranching has posed a particularly serious threat to the rainforests of Latin America. The clearing of huge areas of forest has been given special tax advantages by governments in Central America and Brazil, and aid grants from the World Bank, to produce beef for domestic consumption and export to the North American and West European fast-food markets. The combined beef herds of Nicaragua, Honduras, Guatemala and Costa Rica doubled to 9.5 million head of cattle between 1960 and 1980; during the same period, 25 percent of the forest in these countries was cleared. Today, the process is continuing even faster.

The impact of mining and hydroelectric power

To many tropical nations, their forests are not just a source of timber and land. They may conceal considerable mineral wealth and, by damming the forest's rivers, they may provide a vital source of renewable energy in the form of hydroelectric power.

As a direct threat to rainforests, mining is a relatively minor cause of deforestation, although access roads, and the generally increased level of development in the region of mines, frequently attract landless settlers. The Amazon Basin certainly contains enormous mineral and oil wealth, as do parts of New Guinea, the Philippines, and Indonesia.

from the Altiplano (the Andean high plains) has lead to this area's deforestation. The rectangular, light coloured areas are fields of soya beans cultivated for export, mostly funded by foreign loans. The dark strips running through the fields are windbreaks, which are advantageous because the area's soil is prone to wind erosion.

HABITAT AND SPECIES LOSS

Probably the largest and most ambitious mining project being developed in a rainforest is the Brazilian Grande Carajás programme. Costing an estimated US$70 billion, it will cover an area in eastern Amazonia the size of France. At the core of the project are the enormous deposits of iron ore that lie under the forest. At least 18 pig-iron smelting plants are being set up. The first, at Marabá in the northern state of Pará, started production in March 1988. These smelters will be fuelled with charcoal produced from virgin rainforest. When all 18 smelters are on stream, the charcoal they burn will consume a staggering 2,300 sq km (900 sq mi) of virgin forest each year.

One feature of rainforests, as their name suggests, is that they have an extremely high annual rainfall, which feeds some of the world's great rivers including the Amazon, the Congo, and the Orinoco. But harnessing this energy means building dams and flooding large areas of forest. Although many tropical rainforest habitats are adapted to seasonal flooding, the creation of a reservoir usually entails large-scale, extreme and permanent change. Apart from the sheer loss of forest, dams often cause major ecological problems. Silting is a serious concern and may be exacerbated by deforestation of the watershed. For example, the Ambuklao dam, east Luzon, Philippines had its life-expectancy reduced from 60 to only 32 years due to the accumulation of silt in the reservoir. In addition, the build-up of nutrient accumulate promotes rapid growth of algae that upsets the ecological balance and can result in the death of fish. The static waters of reservoirs additionally provide excellent breeding grounds for snails, mosquitoes, and other insects.

Endangered species
Animals or plants threatened with extinction as a result of such activities as habitat destruction and overhunting are

▶ *Number of species classified as endangered or threatened in the United States (1999). Endangered species include the puma (cougar), brown pelican, and loggerhead turtle.*

▶▶ *The gorilla is an endangered species native to the forests of equatorial Africa, but has suffered from destruction of its habitat and trophy hunting.*

▼ *Percentage of mammal species classified as threatened (1996). Many scientists believe we are currently experiencing a period of mass extinction of species.*

More than 20%
15–19.9%
10–14.9%
Less than 10%
No data available

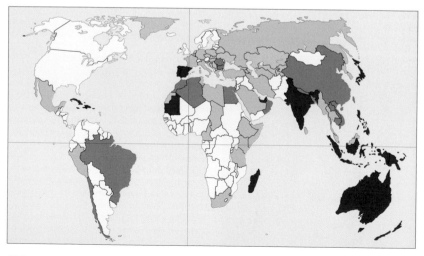

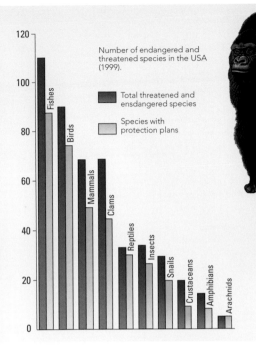

Number of endangered and threatened species in the USA (1999).

▇ Total threatened and endangered species

▢ Species with protection plans

Fishes
Birds
Mammals
Clams
Reptiles
Insects
Snails
Crustaceans
Amphibians
Arachnids

▼ *The black and white ruffed lemur (Varecia variegate) is a subspecies of lemur found in the rainforests of Madagascar. It is classified as endangered on the IUCN Red List.*

known as endangered species. Before the 19th century, roughly one species became extinct a year – but in the last 100 years the extinction rate has accelerated and we are now losing our wildlife at a rate of several species a day. In 1948 the International Union for the Conservation of Nature and Natural Resources (IUCN) was founded in Geneva, Switzerland, to protect endangered species. The IUCN publishes the Red Data Book, which currently lists more than 1,000 animals and 20,000 plants considered endangered. The Convention on International Trade in Endangered Species of Wild Flora and Fauna (CITES) was signed in 1975. CITES seeks to prevent international trade in c.30,000 species. In the United Kingdom, the Wildlife and Countryside Act (1981) gives legal protection to a wide range of wild animals and plants. In the United States, the Endangered Species Act (1973) gives legal protection to a wide range of wild animals and plants.

Annually, international wildlife trade is estimated to be worth billions of dollars and to include hundreds of millions of plant and animal specimens. The trade is diverse, ranging from live animals and plants to a vast array of wildlife products derived from them, including food products, exotic leather goods, wooden musical instruments, timber, tourist curios, and medicines. Levels of exploitation of some animal and plant species are high and the trade in them, together with other factors, such as habitat loss, is capable of heavily depleting their populations and even bringing some species close to extinction. Many wildlife species in trade are not endangered, but the existence of an agreement to ensure the sustainability of the trade is important in order to safeguard these resources for the future.

NUMBERS OF THREATENED SPECIES OF ANIMALS

The table shows the threatened-status categories for major taxonomic groups of animals in 2000.

Class	EX	EW	subtotal	CR	EN	VU	subtotal
Vertebrates							
Mammalia	83	4	**87**	180	340	610	**1,130**
Aves	128	3	**131**	182	321	680	**1,183**
Reptilia	21	1	**22**	56	79	161	**296**
Amphibia	5	0	**5**	25	38	83	**146**
Cephalaspidomorphi	1	0	**1**	0	1	2	**3**
Elasmobranchii	0	0	**0**	3	17	19	**39**
Actinopterygii	80	11	**91**	152	126	431	**709**
Sarcopterygii	0	0	**0**	1	0	0	**1**
subtotal	**318**	**19**	**337**	**599**	**922**	**1986**	**3,507**
Invertebrates							
Echinoidea	0	0	**0**	0	0	0	**0**
Arachnida	0	0	**0**	0	1	9	**10**
Chilopoda	0	0	**0**	0	0	1	**1**
Crustacea	8	1	**9**	56	72	280	**408**
Insecta	72	1	**73**	45	118	392	**555**
Merostomata	0	0	**0**	0	0	0	**0**
Onychophora	3	0	**3**	1	3	2	**6**
Hirudinoidea	0	0	**0**	0	0	0	**0**
Oligochaeta	0	0	**0**	1	0	4	**5**
Polychaeta	0	0	**0**	1	0	0	**1**
Bivalvia	31	0	**31**	52	28	12	**92**
Gastropoda	260	12	**272**	170	209	467	**846**
Enopla	0	0	**0**	0	0	2	**2**
Turbellaria	1	0	**1**	0	0	0	**0**
Anthozoa	0	0	**0**	0	0	2	**2**
Subtotal	**375**	**14**	**389**	**326**	**431**	**1,171**	**1,928**
Total	**693**	**33**	**726**	**925**	**1,353**	**3,157**	**5,435**

Source: 2000 IUCN Red List of Threatened Animals (www.redlist.org)

▲ **Categories:**

EX – extinct: a taxon is extinct when there is no reasonable doubt that the last individual has died.
EW – extinct in the wild: a taxon is extinct in the wild when it is known only to survive in cultivation, in captivity or as a naturalized population (or populations) well outside the past range. A taxon is presumed extinct in the wild when exhaustive surveys in known and/or expected habitat, at appropriate times (diurnal, seasonal, annual), throughout its historic range have failed to record an individual.
Surveys should be over a time frame appropriate to the taxon's life cycle and life form.
CR – critically endangered: a taxon is critically endangered when it is facing an extremely high risk of extinction in the wild in the immediate future.
EN – endangered: a taxon is endangered when it is not critically endangered but is facing a very high risk of extinction in the wild in the near future.
VU – vulnerable: a taxon is vulnerable when it is not critically endangered or endangered but is facing a high risk of extinction in the wild in the medium-term future.
LR – lower risk: a taxon is lower risk when it has been evaluated, does not satisfy the criteria for any of the categories critically endangered, endangered or vulnerable. Taxa included in the lower-risk category can be separated into three subcategories:

1. conservation dependent (**cd**): taxa that are the focus of a continuing taxon-specific or habitat-specific conservation programme targeted towards the taxon in question, the cessation of which would result in the taxon qualifying for one of the threatened categories above within a period of five years.
2. near threatened (**nt**): taxa that do not qualify for conservation dependent, but that are close to qualifying for vulnerable.
3. least concern (**lc**): taxa that do not qualify for conservation dependent or near threatened.
DD – data deficient: a taxon is data deficient when there is inadequate information to make a direct, or indirect, assessment of its risk of extinction based on its distribution and/or population status. A taxon in this category may be well studied, and its biology well known, but appropriate data on abundance and/or distribution are lacking. Data deficient is therefore not a category of threat or lower risk. Listing of taxa in this category indicates that more information is required and acknowledges the possibility that future research will show that threatened classification is appropriate. It is important to make positive use of whatever data are available. In many cases, great care should be exercised in choosing between DD and threatened status. If the range of a taxon is suspected to be relatively circumscribed, if a considerable period of time has elapsed since the last record of the taxon, threatened status may well be justified.

LR/cd	LR/nt	DD	total
74	602	240	2,133
3	727	79	2,123
3	74	59	454
2	25	53	231
0	5	3	12
4	35	17	95
12	96	251	1,159
0	0	0	1
98	1,564	702	6,208
0	1	0	1
0	1	7	18
0	0	0	1
9	1	32	459
3	76	40	747
0	1	3	4
0	1	1	11
0	1	0	1
0	1	0	6
0	0	1	2
5	60	7	195
14	177	513	1,822
0	1	3	6
0	0	0	1
0	0	1	3
31	321	608	3,277
129	1,885	1,310	9,485

Because the trade in wild animals and plants crosses national borders, the effort to regulate it requires international cooperation to safeguard certain species from overexploitation. CITES was conceived in the spirit of such cooperation. Today, it accords varying degrees of protection to more than 30,000 species of animals and plants, whether they are traded as live specimens, fur coats, or dried herbs.

Island dwellers

Conservation started with attempts to preserve appealing animals. More recently there has been a growing concern for entire habitats, to protect a wide range of life-forms in balanced systems. At least 25 percent of Earth's species are threatened through loss of habitat. Island dwellers are especially at risk in the modern world, and more than half the world's threatened and endangered birds come from islands. Sailors and settlers have in the past brought their own livestock to islands, as well as less welcome passengers. Pigs, deer, rats, cats, stoats and ferrets have all wreaked havoc with native populations by competing with, or preying on them. Rats are the most deadly immigrants. Where they become endemic they are impossible to wipe out, and often the only solution is to move native creatures to another island.

Global change, coastal wetlands, and threatened habitats

The potential impacts of climate change are of great practical concern to those interested in coastal wetland resources. Among the areas of greatest risk in the United States are low-lying coastal habitats with easily eroded substrates, such as the northern Gulf of Mexico and south-east Atlantic coasts. Coastal wetlands are affected by large-scale climatic shifts. For example, rates of subsidence (the sinking of land below sea level) and sea-level rise (or 'eustacy' caused by thermal expansion of water and melting of polar ice caps and glaciers) are not being balanced by accretion (sediment accumulation) in many Gulf Coast wetlands. Such imbalances cause increased flooding, saltwater intrusion into freshwater wetlands, and erosion of the coastline. Although many coastal wetlands have maintained their relative elevation in response to gradual increases of 1 millimetre (0.04 inches) per year in sea level over the last several hundred years, these rates are projected to increase two- to four-fold within the course of the 21st century. It is vital to know whether the communities of submerged aquatic vegetation found in marine, estuarine, and coastal freshwater environments provide the critical habitat for fish, shrimp, wintering waterfowl, and endangered species such as sea turtles and manatees. This biodiversity must be maintained and protected.

Declining fish resources

Although marine resources currently provide between five and 10 percent of total world food production, they supply between 10 and 20 lpercent of the world's animal protein. In a report published in 1967, the Food and Agriculture Organization of the United Nations stated, "at the present rate of development few substantial stocks of fish accessible to today's types of gear will remain in another 20 years". We now have ample evidence that this statement was indeed correct, and many stocks of fish have declined throughout the world's fisheries. It has been estimated that the sustainable harvest of marine living resources is probably no more than 100 million tonnes a year. This level has been reached over the last few years, and it is believed that around 90–95 percent of the world's fish stocks are now fished at, or beyond, the maximum sustainable levels.

The processes controlling the size of fish populations and patterns of recruitment are not sufficiently known in order to regulate the harvest within sustainable limits. The recovery of North Sea fish stocks during World War II led to the assumption that fishing effort was the principal regulator of fish stocks. It is now realized that inter-annual variations in ocean characteristics, including variations in current patterns, upwelling and salinity, affect the survival of juvenile fry and

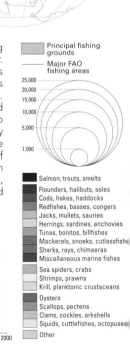

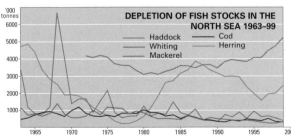

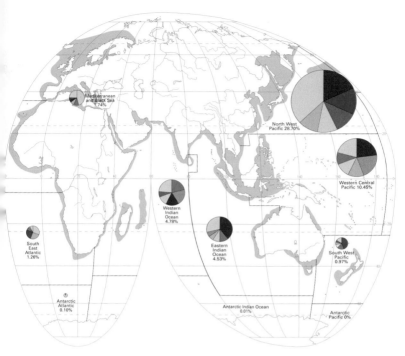

◀▲ *The ability to meet world demands for fish from natural stocks has reached its peak and is going into decline. An increased demand based on growing human populations is pressurizing the fish industry to turn increasingly to aquaculture, or fishfarms, in order to meet quotas. In 2003, a ban was proposed on cod fishing in the North Sea with overfishing pushing the formerly abundant species close to extinction.*

hence the size of the stock. As a result of declining fish stocks, some governments have taken action to control and, in some instances, reduce the numbers of fishing vessels operating in different fisheries. Some fisheries have closed, and in others, the numbers of fishing vessels and frequency of fishing have been curtailed in order to reverse stock declines.

In the past, when the numbers of fishermen were low and fishing technology was less sophisticated, the concept of open access to fisheries was workable. Unrestricted access to fisheries is no longer feasible in the face of accelerating growth in world populations and the subsequent demand for seafood products. Already the world's harvest of seafood is less than consumer demand, and this shortfall will increase if stocks continue to be overexploited. Clearly an urgent need exists to manage the oceans' living resources in a more sustainable manner than in the past.

Management is also dependent on climatic variations. The waters off the Peruvian coast are among the most productive fisheries in the Pacific, and the concentration of anchovetta in the productive zone of upwelling off the South American coast makes these waters a suitable target for large-scale industrial fishing. During normal years, larger catches of up to 20 million tonnes are obtained, but in years when an El Niño event occurs, production declines and the fishing industry stagnates.

223

Global Warming

Our planet's climate is constantly changing, naturally warming up and cooling down naturally in response to an wide range of interconnected astronomical, geological, meteorological and oceanographic factors. Over the past century, however, a warming trend has become apparent that is difficult to explain in terms of natural variations. In 1996 the Intergovernmental Panel on Climate Change (IPCC) issued a report stating that, "The balance of evidence suggests a discernible human influence on global climate through emissions of carbon dioxide and other greenhouse gases." The report acknowledged that average global temperatures have risen by about 0.6°C (1.2°F) since the mid 19th century, but there were grounds for caution in ascribing this warming largely or solely to human activities. Uncertainties persisted for a while due, for example, to discrepancies between measurements of temperatures around the world. Furthermore, our incomplete understanding about how climates change of their own accord, and our limited knowledge about human interference, how this varies in different parts of the world and how it differs from natural climatic variability, made interpretation of the data difficult. Now, however, there is no doubt that global warming is being driven by human activities and very few, notwithstanding the Machiavellian and those with vested interests in ignoring the problem, would deny this.

Polluting the Earth's atmosphere

Human interference with nature is nothing new, at least since people turned from hunting and gathering to agriculture more than 10,000 years ago. At first, human actions seemed to have no ill-effects because the systems that regulate the global environment were able to absorb damage. But from the late 18th century, the Industrial Revolution and the population explosion have caused pollution on a scale that threatens to overwhelm the Earth's ability to cope.

▼ The greenhouse effect means raised temperatures at Earth's surface as a result of heat energy being trapped by gases in the atmosphere. As the Sun's rays pass through the atmosphere, some heat is absorbed but most of the short-wave solar energy passes through. This energy is re-emitted by Earth as long-wave radiation, which cannot pass easily through the atmosphere. More heat is retained if there is a cloud layer. In the past 100 years, more heat has been retained due to increased levels of carbon dioxide (CO_2) caused by the burning of fossil fuels. Tiny particles of CO_2 form an extra layer, which acts like the glass in a greenhouse. The effect is componded by damage to the ozone layer caused by chlorofluorocarbon (CFC) emissions.

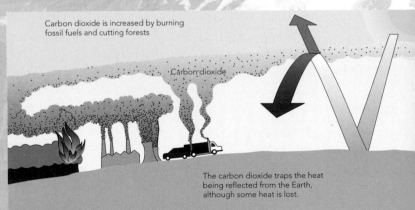

Carbon dioxide is increased by burning fossil fuels and cutting forests

Carbon dioxide

The carbon dioxide traps the heat being reflected from the Earth, although some heat is lost.

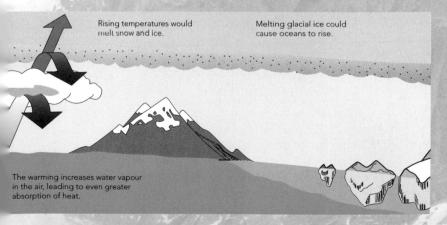

▲ *Plumes of smoke and steam rise from a petrochemical complex in Scotland. Such plants emit greenhouse gases such as carbon dioxide (CO_2), methane (CH_4), and nitrogen dioxide (NO_2) into the atmosphere, which contribute to global warming.*

In the 20th century, nature suffered enormously at the hands of our industrial society, from the dumping of industrial and agricultural wastes in rivers and seas, accidents at nuclear-power stations, and the creation of acid rain through the release of sulphur dioxides and nitrous oxides by the burning of fossil fuels. Chlorofluorocarbons (CFCs) from aerosol sprays, fridges and other sources have damaged the ozone layer in the stratosphere, the planet's screen against ultraviolet radiation. In many tropical areas, deforestation is making productive land barren, while in the dry grasslands bordering deserts, the removal of plant cover is causing desertification. Most importantly, the release of greenhouse gases, particularly carbon dioxide, but including methane and others, are now widely held to be the cause of the rapid

Rising temperatures would melt snow and ice.

Melting glacial ice could cause oceans to rise.

The warming increases water vapour in the air, leading to even greater absorption of heat.

warming experienced over the last 100 years. If allowed to continue unchecked, global warming will ultimately lead to large-scale melting of the polar ice sheets and the flooding of fertile coastal plains. Extreme meteorological events, such as storms and floods have been forecast to increase, while some models suggest that it might affect ocean currents so that north-western Europe, which owes its mild climate to the Gulf Stream, could expect bitterly cold winters. Other predictions, some more rational than others, include a growth in cloud cover leading to increased reflection of solar energy back into space and the start of a new Ice Age. It is now certain that human activities have placed the Earth in this precarious situation. The question is, do we possess the will and the ingenuity to respond to this crisis in planet management?

Greenhouse gases

In its simplest terms, global warming is an overall increase in the Earth's surface temperature. The world has always undergone periodic fluctuations in temperature, but it is now clear that the rapid accumulation of greenhouse gases in the atmosphere due to human activities is responsible for a further rise in temperature over the Earth.

Greenhouse gases are also produced naturally. Carbon dioxide, the primary greenhouse gas, is used by plants in photosynthesis at a level that is normally balanced by that produced in organisms during respiration. The burning of forests and fossil fuels has, however, increased overall levels in the past 200 years, which now stand about 30 percent higher than they did before the Industrial Revolution.

Carbon dioxide only accounts for around half of the so-called greenhouse effect that is leading to global warming. The rest is accounted for by gases including methane, produced by anaerobic bacteria that live in such diverse habitats as waterlogged land, rubbish tips and the intestines

▼ *Because the Sun is very hot, most of its energy reaches Earth in the form of short-wave radiation (yellow arrows). Since Earth is very much cooler, the outgoing energy emits at longer-wave infra-red radiation (orange arrows). The artwork on the left shows the percentages of what happens to Earth's energy. Natural greenhouse gases exert a profound effect on Earth's climate (right). These gases are transparent to most incoming short-wave radiation, but function as an opaque shield to some of the infra-red radiation retransmitted by Earth, preventing these waves escaping from our atmosphere. Predictions suggest that an increase in greenhouse gases may cause temperatures to rise by 1.5–4.5°C (2.5–8°F) by 2100.*

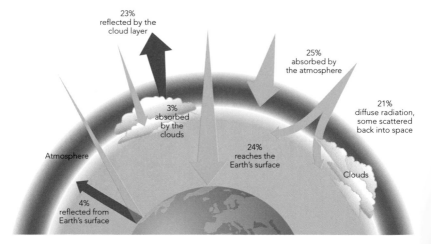

23% reflected by the cloud layer

25% absorbed by the atmosphere

21% diffuse radiation, some scattered back into space

3% absorbed by the clouds

24% reaches the Earth's surface

Atmosphere

Clouds

4% reflected from Earth's surface

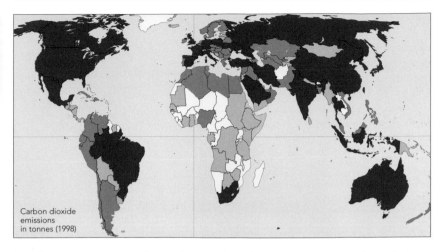

Carbon dioxide
emissions
in tonnes (1998)

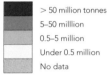

> 50 million tonnes

5–50 milllion

0.5–5 million

Under 0.5 million

No data

▲ According to the
World Resources
Institute, the United
States was responsible
for 30% of the world's
total carbon dioxide
emissions in the 1990s.

of animals, notably cattle. An increase in cattle and sheep farming has led to a dramatic rise in methane production.

Ozone, which forms an important layer between 15 and 50 km (10 and 30 miles) above the Earth, is also a greenhouse gas, although its most important function is to absorb ultra-violet light and so prevent it reaching the Earth's surface. Water vapour also has a 'greenhouse' role to play, and although in the form of clouds it can keep the Earth's surface cooler by blocking the sun's rays, it can also help keep it warmer by acting as an insulating blanket retaining the heat that does penetrate.

Chlorofluorocarbons (CFCs) are greenhouse gases used commercially in refrigerators, aerosols and foam plastics. They are very persistent, lasting for 60 years or more, and in

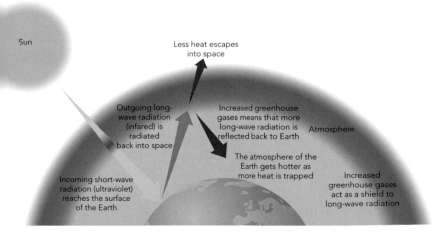

Sun

Less heat escapes
into space

Outgoing long-
wave radiation
(infared) is
radiated
back into space

Increased greenhouse
gases means that more
long-wave radiation is
reflected back to Earth

Atmosphere

The atmosphere of the
Earth gets hotter as
more heat is trapped

Incoming short-wave
radiation (ultraviolet)
reaches the surface
of the Earth

Increased
greenhouse gases
act as a shield to
long-wave radiation

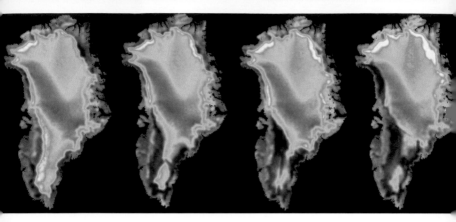

addition to contributing to global warming, they also deplete the ozone layer through a series of chemical reactions. This allows additional ultraviolet radiation to reach the Earth. To prevent this harmful effect, the use of CFCs is being phased out through an international agreement, called the Montreal Protocol, signed in 1987.

Greenhouse effect

The greenhouse effect is caused by short-wavelength radiation striking Earth's surface and being converted to heat, which has a longer wavelength. Greenhouse gases absorb this longer wavelength radiation, preventing it being reflected back into space. As such they act in the manner of a greenhouse, which accumulates heat beneath its glass exterior. The greenhouse effect is neither new, nor entirely malign. Indeed, it is the greenhouse gases that maintain the Earth's surface temperature at an average of 15°C (59°F) rather than the 218°C (424°F) it would be without them. Now, however, the accelerating levels of greenhouse gases are enhancing the natural greenhouse effect, triggering climate change at a rate that is too rapid to allow our society and much of the planet's flora and fauna to adapt.

The Earth Summit

The problem of global warming is of such concern that there is now international action to reduce the emission of greenhouse gases. The first Earth Summit, the United Nations Conference on Environment and Development in Rio de Janeiro (1992), was followed by a second in New York (1997). The Summit proposed a target for reducing carbon-dioxide emissions in developed countries to 15 percent below their 1990 level by the year 2010. In 1997, the Kyoto Protocol set a further recommendation of a 5.2 percent reduction in greenhouse gas emissions (from 1990 levels) by 2008–12. The US only agreed to maintain its level of emissions. The failure of the US government – by far the world's greatest polluter – to

▶ This image from NASA's Terra spacecraft in March 2000 shows concentrations of carbon monoxide (CO) at altitudes of 4,500 m (15,000 feet). Red colours indicate highest levels of CO (450 parts per billion). Blue colours indicate lowest levels of CO (50 ppb). CO is an air pollutant that also produces ozone, a greenhouse gas that is a human-health hazard. The most dramatic features are the immense clouds of carbon monoxide from grassland and forest fires in Africa and South America.

◀ In summer, the melting of the Greenland icesheets releases large amounts of freshwater into the ocean, and year-to-year variations can have a significant impact on global sea-level. Long-term changes in the patterns and extent of melting reflect the effects of climate variability; and Greenland is considered a sensitive indicator of global warming. Four images are shown at five-day intervals in 1999. Blue and white colours indicate surfaces which are cold and dry, while red and black indicate wet snow surfaces experiencing melting. As summer progresses, the area of melting expands inland and northward. A large pale and dark blue region in the central, high-elevation part of the ice sheet survives each summer without melting. This is known as the dry-snow region, and its area is a measure of the stability of the ice sheet. In the past 30 years, there has been a clear reduction in the extent of this zone, especially in the south-west.

ratify the agreement, however, has left the initiative dead in the water. Greenhouse-gas concentrations continue to rise and prospects for any effective reduction in the near future are bleak.

The consequences of global warming

Global warming is one of the most debated topics in our generation, but the time for debate is now long passed. Even if we dramatically slashed greenhouse gas emissions today, inertia would ensure that temperatures continued to rise for centuries and sea levels for thousands of years. Global warming is not simply a matter of a warmer climate; it is also predicted to lead to widespread economic, social, and environmental changes. Concern about global warming focuses on two principal consequences – a rise in sea level and a rise in temperature.

Sea levels have risen by about 2 cm (0.8 inches) over the last hundred years, although the detailed picture is complicated by various effects. South-east England, for example is undergoing tectonic subsidence, as is the Tokyo region of Japan, where this is related to earthquakes. Venice, Italy, on the other hand, is sinking because of the extraction of groundwater. However, if greenhouse gas emissions remain unmitigated, the rate of sea-level increase is forecast to reach 60 cm (24 inches) per century.

The melting poles

Current sea-level rise is the result of a combination of melting glaciers and small ice caps and thermal expansion of warming ocean waters, but acceleration will be driven by large-scale melting at the poles. Today, there is approximately 25 million cu km (6 million cu miles) of ice on the surface of the Earth. Melting of the Greenland Ice Cap, for example, would result in a sea-level rise of 7.4 m (24.3 feet), leading to major inundation of low-lying coasts worldwide. This may require a temperature rise of just 4°C (7°F), a figure that could be exceeded globally within the next 200 years. Even so, the process of glacial collapse is so slow it would take several hundred years for the ice to slide into the sea. Conversely, when/if the current interglacial period ends, the growth and expansion of land and sea ice sheets would result in a sea-level fall of perhaps 140 m (460 feet).

For countries such as Bangladesh, rising sea levels pose a far more urgent problem. In just 50 years, a combination of sea-level rise and land-level fall are predicted to result in a 1.8 m (5.9 feet) rise. This will see the loss of 16 percent of the country.

The rising sea

The oceans are slower to warm than the land, and will delay the rise in global temperature. By the 22nd century, however, mean temperatures could have risen to

5.8°C (10.4°F). Because of thermal expansion the sea could rise by 9 cm (3.5 inches) to 0.88 m/2.9 feet (estimate for 2100). Sea level is expected to rise about 60 cm (2 feet) along the US Gulf and Atlantic coasts in the next century. It could rise further because of the partial melting of mountain glaciers and polar ice sheets. Unless they are protected, cities like Amsterdam, Bombay, Hong Kong, Los Angeles, New York, Tokyo, and Sydney could disappear by the year 2100. Existing coastal defences will have to be raised and reinforced at a cost, for example, of US$3–9 billion in the Netherlands and US$6–7 billion in Britain. Poorer nations cannot afford such sums and will be dependent on international assistance.

Environmental consequences of sea-level rise

In the shorter term, the principal outcome of a continued rise in sea level is an increase in the depth of coastal waters. This rise will cause inland and upstream salinity intrusion, both of which affect fresh and brackish-water wetlands. Uncertainty surrounds the influence of global warming on the frequency and intensity of storm events, but any rise in sea level has the potential for increasing the severity of storm surges and tsunami, particularly in areas where coastal habitats and barrier shorelines are exposed.

The changing global climate

A worst-case global temperature rise of up to 6°C (11°F) is forecast for the year 2100, a rise ten times higher than that experienced over the last hundred years. Even the average-case scenario visualises a 4°C (7°F) rise, with land temperatures rising by even more than this. Drought, heatwaves, and wildfires will be far more prevalent than they are now, and access to water will be a critical issue. In just over 20 years, five billion people will live in countries with inadequate water supplies, leading to civil strife and wars over access to water. Regions that are currently dry are forecast to become even drier, with prospects bleak for sub-Saharan Africa, the southern Mediterranean and Australia. Broadly speaking, wet regions are forecast to get wetter, with more rain falling in shorter bursts leading to increased flooding. Increasingly intense windstorms are also forecast.

The environmental consequences of temperature rise

Models of global warming predict that higher latitudes will warm up more than lower latitudes, and the

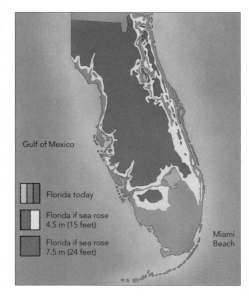

▼ *This map shows the dramatic effects of possible sea-level rise on the extent of the state Florida, south-east United States. Sea-level rise is one of the effects of global warming. If the sea-level rises by 4.5 m (15 feet), the entire Everglades would be submerged, as would the cities of Miami and Fort Lauderdale. If the sea-level rises by 7.5 m (24 feet), the whole of Florida south of Lake Okeechobee would be underwater, except for an island around Lehigh Acres. The city of Palm Beach and the Kennedy Space Center on Cape Canaveral would be inundated. Sea-level rise on this scale would affect more than 7 million residents of Florida.*

Gulf of Mexico

Florida today

Florida if sea rose 4.5 m (15 feet)

Florida if sea rose 7.5 m (24 feet)

Miami Beach

▲ On August 13, 2002, a camera aboard the International Space Station captured the collapse of the Kolka Glacier on Mount Kazbek, southern Russia. Although scientists have predicted the possibility of large glacial collapses as the climate warms, no one predicted that tragedy would strike the mountain village of Karmadon so soon. On September 20, the collapse of a hanging glacier from the slope of Mount Dzhimarai-Khokh onto the Kolka Glacier triggered an avalanche of ice and debris that went over the Maili Glacier terminus then slid more than 24 km (15 miles). The avalanche buried small villages in the Russian Republic of North Ossetia, killing dozens of people.

effects are likely to be greater in winter than summer. The warming of the tropical oceans would increase the geographical spread, frequency, and intensity of both hurricanes and droughts. The tracks followed by rain-bearing storms will change and crop yields in the United States, central Europe, and the Ukraine are expected to fall dramatically, causing worldwide shortages of food. Warmer conditions may expand crop production in Canada, Siberia, and Scandinavia, but they have poorer soils and yields will be low. Warmer conditions in the Arctic Ocean may mean the pack-ice becomes a seasonal feature, melting in the summer and reforming during the winter. Some Arctic ice-sheets have melted by 15 percent since 1980, and even the vast west Antarctic ice sheet may suffer substantial melting.

Natural variations in temperature

The temperature rise over the last century is not uniform. From 1910 to 1940, the Earth's mean temperature rose by 0.5°C (1°F), before greenhouse gases were added to the atmosphere. In the decade from 1940 to 1950, the mean temperature decreased by 0.15°C (0.27°F). In the past 25 years, the mean temperature has again risen, increasing by about 0.5°C (1°F). Many factors influence the global climate in addition to human activities, and these must be accounted for in any model of the Earth's climate and in forecasts of future warming. Most important among these are variations in solar output and what happens to this energy when it reaches our planet (see artwork, pages 226–27). Much is simply radiated back into space, and we rely on this to keep the planet cool. But even the energy that reaches the Earth's surface varies in intensity at different times, and there are additional terrestrial factors that affect the climate. These include the direction and speed of ocean currents, variations in atmospheric composition, cloud cover, and volcanic activity. Volcanic gases and solar luminosity can account for much of the temperature changes in the 19th century and the significant global cooling that took place between 1945 and 1950, and again between 1960 and 1970.

Predictions about the magnitude of global warming are based on general atmospheric circulation models and the observation that greenhouse-gas concentrations have risen by 30% since the Industrial Revolution. The various models used to forecast the future and its consequences are, however, far from perfect and are particularly weak in terms of predicting the effects of climate change at regional and local levels. It is also important to be aware that predictions can be affected by natural events such as large volcanic eruptions that can modify the warming trend, at least temporarily.

▼ Emissions of greenhouse gases continued to increase in the 1990s, but not uniformly. With the dangers of ozone depletion caused by CFCs, many countries banned them and the pie charts show a dramatic drop in CFC emissions. The graph shows that even with immediate drastic cuts in greenhouse gas emissions, global temperatures are set to rise 2.5°C (5°F) by the year 2050.

Volcanoes and the Earth's climate

The seasonal fluctuations in weather are well understood but details of the climatic response to external causal factors are open to debate. Debate revolves about whether the Earth's climate system is deterministic, stochastic, or chaotic. In a **deterministic** system there is direct cause-and-effect in a more or less one-to-one manner. The effect on global warming from volcanic eruptions is a good example. In 1963 Mount Agung on Bali, southwest Indonesia, erupted explosively, ejecting large volumes of sulphur dioxide gas into the stratosphere. Here it combined with water vapour to form a fine mist of sulphuric acid aerosols that spread worldwide and fell out slowly over a five-year period. The result was a

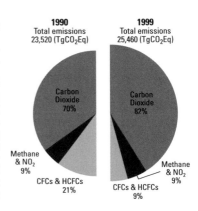

1990
Total emissions
23,520 (TgCO₂Eq)

Carbon Dioxide 70%

Methane & NO₂ 9%

CFCs & HCFCs 21%

1999
Total emissions
25,460 (TgCO₂Eq)

Carbon Dioxide 82%

Methane & NO₂ 9%

CFCs & HCFCs 9%

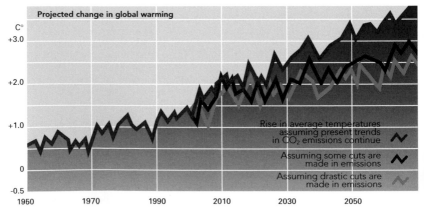

Projected change in global warming

Rise in average temperatures assuming present trends in CO₂ emissions continue

Assuming some cuts are made in emissions

Assuming drastic cuts are made in emissions

► *Aerial view of the north side of the crater on Mount Pinatubo, Philippines, with a small explosion in progress on June 22, 1991. Volcanic eruptions send up vast quantities of sulphuric acid aerosols that cause a temporary reduction in Earth's mean temperature. The eruption of Mount Pinatubo in 1991 caused a fall of about 0.2°C (0.4°F) in the average temperature on Earth in 1992 and 1993.*

decrease in the Earth's mean temperature by about 0.1°C (0.2°F). Similarly, in 1991, the gas cloud from the eruption of Mount Pinatubo, Luzon, Philippines produced a globally averaged fall in the mean surface temperature of the Earth in the next two years of about 0.2°C (0.4°F).

A **stochastic** system behaves in a statistical or probabilistic manner. The individual outcome of a throw of a dice cannot be predicted but the probability of an individual outcome can. These are known as the odds. Many elements of weather forecasts, particularly rainfall and snowfall are stated in terms of probabilities. The final type of behaviour is termed chaotic. In a **chaotic** system, there is a tendency to cluster around certain states. Examples are the ice ages, the interglacial periods, and the behaviour of large climate signals such as the El Niño-Southern Oscillation. To complicate matters, the Earth's climate system may well incorporate elements of all three types of behaviour, making detailed forecasting problematical.

The problem of global warming is further complicated by the discovery that the greenhouse effect may be slowed down by the large upswell of cold water to the surface in the eastern Pacific Ocean. The increase in global temperatures may be enhancing east to west winds in the southern Pacific Ocean which pushes warmer waters westward. The result is that the ocean dynamics in the equatorial Pacific may delay and reduce global warming.

The social and political effects of global warming

History shows that there have been wide fluctuations in the Earth's mean global temperature, some caused by discrete events such as eruptions, others due to external factors such as reductions in solar output. The winters of 1783–84 were unusually cold in Europe, due to the Laki eruption in southern Iceland. In addition, the Asama volcano in central Honshu,

Japan produced a violent eruption which, by itself, has been attributed as the cause of the severe cold years of the mid 1780s. Some social and climatic historians have argued that these colder years contributed to the crop failures and the social unrest of the era, triggering the onset of the French Revolution in 1789. Causes and effects of climatic change are difficult to prove on a short time-scale, but one cannot dispute that the consequences may be famine, political upheaval, and mass migration. The climatic interval known as the 'Little Ice Age' (c. 1550–1850) is widely held to reflect a period of reduced solar output, that had a dramatic impact on social and living styles of much of Europe. As the Little Ice Age drew to a close, a slow global-warming trend began. In 1845 Ireland, which depended upon and harvested a single crop, potatoes, was struck by potato blight, a devastating infestation triggered by wet and warm climatic conditions. The pendulum had swung in the other direction. As a result of the crop failure, about one million people died of famine and malnutrition. A further 500,000 people immigrated to the United States.

One aspect of human activity that may have a significant impact on the greenhouse effect and resulting climate change is the large-scale burning of forests, for example in the Amazon and Indonesia. This creates aerosols capable of altering temperature, rainfall and cloudiness, effectively creating a 'biogeophysical feedback' that has very important implications for the level and rate of future warming. Just as

▼ *Every year, large areas of grasslands burn during the dry season in southern Africa. In 2000, the burning season was extremely large. The heaviest burning was in western Zambia, southern Angola, northern Namibia, and northern Botswana. Some of the blazes had fire fronts 30 km (20 miles) long that lasted for days. SAFARI 2000 field-campaign scientists studied the extent of these fires and the impact of the rising smoke on air pollution, climate change, and clouds.*

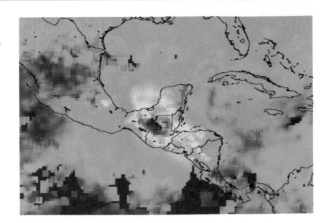

▶ Forest fires in Central America produce high concentrations of carbon monoxide (CO) in the lower atmosphere. This image shows CO levels as high as 360 parts per billion by volume of air (shown in red) on the Yucatán Peninsula. The orange and yellow colours indicate high levels of CO over Honduras, El Salvador, and Nicaragua. CO pollution is also carried northeastward over the Gulf of Mexico. Carbon monoxide is a by-product of the incomplete burning of fossil fuels. It is a hazardous air pollutant and producer of ozone.

the United States is reluctant to jeopardize its relationship with and reliance on oil companies in order to reduce its greenhouse-gas emissions, so other countries are equally reluctant to introduce measures to protect the rainforests. Without financial incentive, many governments will continue to pollute without thought for the future of life on our planet.

El Niño

El Niño, which means 'Christ Child' in Spanish, is the periodic easing or reversing of the trade-winds over the southern Pacific Ocean. El Niño forms part of the so-called ENSO (El Niño – Southern Oscillation) climate pattern in the southern hemisphere. It takes its name from a tendency to develop around Christmas. During a normal year, westward blowing trade winds force warm surface waters to accumulate in the western equatorial Pacific. These warm waters evaporate easily forming the clouds that bring heavy rainfall to the surrounding areas. The western Pacific's atmosphere is kept warmer, since the rainfall releases heat, and directs the jet stream to flow from north Asia to California.

Atmospheric and oceanic circulation

The El Niño phenomenon appears to be related to changes in atmospheric circulation, and in particular to a weakening of the westerly winds which drive the southern arm of the South Pacific Gyre, a near–circular pattern of currents in the southern Pacific Ocean. El Niño causes the warm surface waters that have accumulated in the western Pacific to flow back and warm the coastal waters of South America by up to two or three degrees Celsius. The consequences of such a

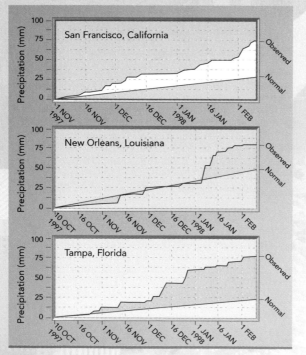

◄ The 1997–98 El Niño greatly increased the rainfall in the US cities of San Francisco, New Orleans, and Tampa. This was because an El Niño invariably strengthens the tropical jet stream that brings wet weather to North America. The three-month period between November 1997 and January 1998 was the wettest on record in the Pacific Northwest.

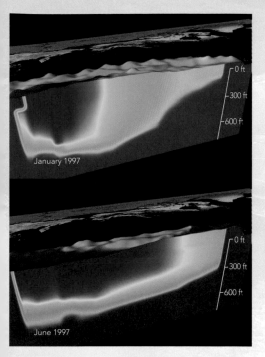

major change in the interaction between wind and sea are not confined to the Pacific Basin. These interactions also appear to be linked to other changes in atmospheric and oceanic circulation in the southern hemisphere. The dramatic results of these changes are reduced rainfall in Australia, weakening of the Indian monsoons, changes in the Kuroshio Current off southern Japan, shifts in wind patterns in the South Atlantic, with consequent changes in the orientation of coastal dunes, and droughts in south-east Asia. It even may be implicated in modified rainfall patterns as far away as Africa. In addition to affecting the onset of monsoons and the frequency, severity, and tracks of Pacific storms, El Niño influences the location of anchovy, tuna, shrimp, and other commercial fish populations. It also affects the occurrence of regional droughts, forest fires, floods, mudslides and tropical cyclones in many parts of the world. An El Niño nearly always strengthens the tropical jet stream that transports wet storms into North America, although the pattern of flow is variable. Sometimes, for example, the jet stream veers to the north, avoiding California, and other times it splits in two with the southern track drenching the state.

▲ These two thermal images show the temperature beneath the eastern Pacific Ocean in January and June 1997, during the 1997–98 El Niño. Red represents 30°C (86°F), blue is 8°C (46°F). The thermocline is the border between the dark blue at the bottom and the cyan. The thermocline exists at 20°C (68°F). The images also reveal the sea surface-height (represented by bumps). The rise in sea-level and the warming of the ocean indicates a strengthening of the 1997–98 El Niño event.

The South Pacific Gyre and the Peruvian Upwelling

Under normal conditions, the South Pacific Gyre dominates water circulation in the southern Pacific Ocean. Surface water flows eastwards under the influence of the trade winds as the South Equatorial Current, passes down the eastern coast of Australia (as the East Australia Current) and turns eastwards at the latitude of Sydney under the influence of the westerly winds. The Antarctic Circumpolar Current then moves eastwards towards Latin America where a major branch, the Humboldt Current, travels northwards along the coast of Chile towards Peru. The high Andes block the passage of the westerlies, deflecting them northwards, which not only adds to the speed of the Humboldt Current, but also causes the surface waters to move away from the coast. As they do so they form part of the eastward-moving South Equatorial Current, and subsequently cold, nutrient-rich water is drawn to the surface in the Peruvian Upwelling.

237

Off the coast of Peru, this water stimulates the production of phytoplankton and a community of comparatively large, multi-cellular phytoplankton develops. The large size of these primary producers, compared with the smaller, single-celled diatoms characteristic of nutrient-poor, open ocean water, means that they can be eaten directly by a small fish known as the anchovetta. These in turn form the diet of larger predatory fishes and numerous seabirds, whose breeding colonies on the Latin American coast have resulted in the deposition of guano, mined during the last century as phosphate fertilizer. Furthermore, the anchovetta were extensively fished from small purse seiners, and the catch processed to produce fish meal for domestic animal and poultry feed. The fisheries production of the Peruvian upwelling reflects both the high rates of primary production in the area, and the efficiency of the food chain, showing a reduced number of linkages between the primary producers and the top predator, in this case man.

Physical changes
During the last decade, extensive research on the El Niño phenomenon has shown that the surface currents of the

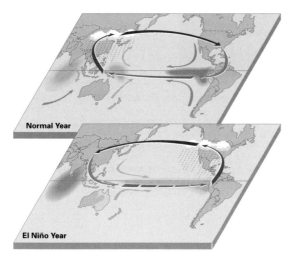

Normal Year

El Niño Year

▲ In a normal year in the Pacific Ocean (top), south-easterly trade winds drive sun-warmed surface waters westwards off the coast of South America into a pool off northern Australia. High cumulus clouds form above these warm waters, bringing rain in the summer wet season. Cooler, nutrient-rich waters rise to the surface off South America, supporting extensive shoals of anchovetta on which a vast fishing industry depends. The weather over this cold-water region is dry. Every three to seven years, a change occurs in the ocean-atmosphere interaction. The climatic pattern is reversed – an event known as El Niño. The trade winds ease and the warm surface waters which have 'piled up' in the western Pacific flow back to warm the waters off South America by 2–3°C (4–5°F), or even as much as 7°C (12°F). The warm waters off South America suppress upwelling of the cold nutrient-rich waters, spelling disaster to the fishing industry. During an intense El Niño, the south-east trade winds reverse direction and become equatorial westerlies, resulting in climatic extremes in many regions of the world, such as drought in parts of Australia and India, and heavy rainfall in the south-eastern United States. An intense El Niño occurred in 1997–98, with resultant freak weather conditions across the entire Pacific region.

EL NIÑO COSTS 1982–83	
Flooding	
US Gulf States	US$1,270 million
Ecuador/northern Peru	US$650 million
Bolivia	US$300 million
Cuba	US$170 million
Hurricanes	
Hawaii	US$230 million
Tahiti	US$50 million
Drought/fires	
Australia	US$2,500 million
southern Africa	US$1,000 million
Mexico/Central America	US$600 million
Indonesia	US$500 million
Philippines	US$450 million
southern Peru/western Bolivia	US$240 million
southern India/Sri Lanka	US$150 million

South Pacific Gyre are weaker during El Niño years, and the westward-flowing Equatorial Counter-current dominates the eastward-moving South Equatorial Current. During their 15,500 km (9,500 mile) -long journey across the Pacific Ocean, the surface waters of the South Equatorial Current become progressively warmer, leading to the formation of a pool of warm water in the western Pacific. In addition, the movement of the water results in higher sea levels in the western Pacific region, and lower sea levels along the Latin American coast. When the flow weakens or is reversed, the water levels change on each side of the Pacific Basin. During El Niño years, mean sea level in the western Pacific may be as much as 14 cm (5.5 inches) below normal, while along the Latin American coast it may be as much as 50 cm (20 inches) higher than usual. Warm waters from the western Pacific dominate the surface water off the coast of Peru, causing the end of the upwelling and a collapse in the biological productivity of the region, since the nutrients are no longer brought to the surface.

El Niño is characterized by the formation of a finger or wedge of warm water along the equator that stretches for thousands of kilometres from Ecuador to the International Date Line in the western Pacific Ocean. Trade winds, which usually flow from east to west across the equator, grow weaker. The normal strong, easterly flow of wind is called the Walker Circulation, which oscillates (the Southern Oscillation) in strength every 3–5 years. The reasons for this weakening in intensity are inexplicable but are suggestive of a chaotic system. As a result, the usual upwelling of cold water along the coast of South America weakens, and warm water takes its place. Some of the greatest El Niños are characterized by a complete reversal in the direction of the trade winds, as happened in both 1972 and 1982.

The 1982–83 El Niño

The 1982–83 El Niño was one of the most intense of the past century. Not predicted and not even recognized by scientists in its initial stages, this El Niño caused thousands of deaths and more than US$13 billion in damage worldwide. Flooding was severe in many South American countries, and torrential rains triggered severe landslides that killed 600 people in Peru and Ecuador. Furthermore, the warm waters punished the fishing industries of these countries, with catches dramatically reduced. Further afield, drought was prevalent in Indonesia, the Philippines, southern India, and many parts of Africa. Australia experienced one of its worst-ever droughts that, combined with rampaging bushfires, cost an estimated US$2.5

billion. El Niño also led to snowstorms in the deserts of the Middle East, and typhoons in Hawaii and Tahiti.

The 1997–98 El Niño

The 1997–98 El Niño was the strongest on record, and it developed more rapidly than any El Niño of the past 40 years. The scientific community had made tremendous advances in forecasting El Niño in the 15 years since the 1982–83 El Niño took the world by surprise. Many computer models correctly forecast that 1997 would be unusually warm in the tropical Pacific. On the other hand, the forecast models missed the rapid onset, the great magnitude, and the sudden demise of the 1997–98 El Niño. The rapid build-up of the El Niño allowed scientists to see its impacts on weather, marine ecosystems, and fisheries very quickly. The United States felt the effects of the El Niño quite badly. In the Pacific Northwest, for example, the three-month period from November 1997 to January 1998 was the wettest on record. Mudslides and flash floods devastated communities from California to Mississippi, storms pounded the Gulf Coast, and tornadoes ripped through Florida. In March 1998, temperatures soared to record levels in continental USA. The effects throughout the rest of the world were extraordinarily diverse. Indonesia and surrounding regions suffered months of severe drought. Forest fires broke out in Sumatra, Borneo, and Malaysia. In South America, great swathes of the Amazon rainforest burned. Temperatures soared to 42°C (108°F) in Mongolia, while Kenya's rainfall was 100 cm (40 inches) above normal. Storms battered Madagascar, and Central Europe suffered record flooding.

By the time it had finished its course, the 1997–98 El Niño had killed an estimated 2,100 people, and caused at least US$33 billion dollars in property damage.

▼ *Typical thermal and rainfall anomalies (December to February) during a strong El Niño.*

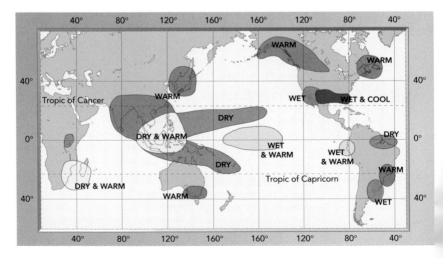

▲ *A man attempts to rescue belongings from a car buried by a mudslide, triggered by El Niño-induced rains, January 1982, Boulder Creek, west-central California, USA.*

The mysteries of El Niño

The cause of the slackening of the winds and the warm, swirling ocean currents is still a matter of scientific debate. Some researchers believe that the phenomenon is a natural random fluctuation of the Earth's climate, while others argue that the increasing frequency and severity of El Niño events may be triggered by anthropogenic global warming. Climate forecasting remains complex and, to some extent, controversial and does not always provide a realistic simulation of the present climate. Given the known natural variability in the climate of our planet and the large fluctuations in temperature that have occurred in the historical past, a link between El Niño events and global warming remains to be firmly established.

Ecological and economic impacts

During the 1982 83 El Niño, the catch of anchovetta by the fishing fleets of western South America fell by 60 percent. As fish stocks decline, the birds that depend on them for food also fall in numbers. Following the 1972–73 El Niño, the populations of cormorants, boobies and brown pelicans declined to around six million birds, from an estimated 30 million in 1950. After the 1982–83 El Niño, a further decline reduced their numbers to just 300,000. Loss of income due to a breakdown in the fishing industry constitutes just a small part of the total financial losses that can be attributed to an El Niño, the economic consequences of which are severe across much of the planet. Elevated water-levels along the Latin American coast increase the frequency of malaria, while inland flooding results in disruption of agriculture and the destruction of coastal infrastructure. Economic impacts also occur elsewhere in the world, with agriculture being adversely affected in the semi-arid regions of Australia, and subsistence food production being reduced in south-east Asia. Although difficult to estimate with any accuracy, a bad El Niño year is likely to cost the global economy tens of billions of US dollars.

TOGA and WOCE

The occurrence of El Niño events is irregular – some sources say it can occur every three to five years, others state every two to seven. Indeed, there is some worrying evidence to suggest that the frequency and severity of the event may have increased during the last few decades. Due to the widespread changes to the local climate and sea-level conditions that El Niño brings to certain regions of the tropics, and the subsequent substantial economic losses suffered by some countries, two international programmes have been established to monitor this phenomenon. The Tropical Ocean Global Atmosphere programme (TOGA) and the World Ocean Circulation Experiment (WOCE), have been set up with the aim of collecting data on the circulation of ocean currents and the interaction between the oceans and the atmosphere, with a view to modelling how the system works and hopefully predicting its occurrence. While scientists are now able to forecast the onset of an El Niño event in the short term, long-term predictions remain impossible. To view changes in the surface temperature of the Pacific Ocean, as observed by the Topex-Poseidon satellite, and to look for signs of a developing El Niño, go to: *http://topex-www.jpl.nasa.gov*

▶ *The top image shows sea surface-height ocean conditions on October 3, 1997, as the warm water associated with El Niño (in white) spreads northward along the entire coast of North America all the way to Alaska. The white and red areas indicate unusual patterns of heat. In the white areas, the sea surface is between 14 and 32 cm (6–13 inches) above normal. In the red areas, it is about 10 cm (4 inches) above normal. The bottom image shows the sea surface-height conditions for the 1999 La Niña. The low sea level or cold pool of water along the equator is clearly seen (purple and blue).*

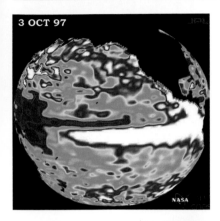

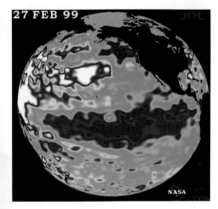

La Nina

La Nina is another periodic disruption of the ocean-atmosphere system in the tropical zone of the Pacific Ocean. It is, in effect, the reverse of an El Niño event, whereby unusually cold surface waters accumulate in the central and eastern Pacific Ocean. As with El Niño, La Nina affects global weather patterns, generally in an opposing sense, but the impact is usually less devastating. La Nina events tend to peak between El Niños, and one of the strongest occurred in 1988–90. Associated strong, easterly trade winds brought severe flooding to Brazil, China, Bangladesh, Indonesia, and Thailand, while in December 1988 a severe tropical cyclone struck Bangladesh – much later in the year than the normal cyclone season. In Australia, the summers of 1989–90 brought the heaviest rainfall in 25 years, together with unprecedented flooding of many rivers.

When the cooler water moves into the equatorial Pacific Ocean, wind systems change and different weather patterns are brought across North America. La Nina brings cold air and enhanced rainfall to north-western North America, while warmer temperatures and below average rainfall prevail over most of the rest of the continent. The winter of 1999–2000 was La Nina-driven – with heavy rainfall in the Pacific northwest and numerous wildfires feeding on the dried out El Niño-fed vegetation in the American south-west. La Nina is now believed to be as important as ENSO events in producing the extremes in flooding and drought over much of the Earth.

◀ Waves from the El Niño storm of 1983, batter beach houses on Laguna Beach, south-west California, USA.

Meteorites and Comets

A meteorite is a rocky or metallic object that survives its fall to Earth from space. About 30,000 meteorites are known, around 24,000 of which were found in Antarctica, 4,000 in the Sahara Desert, and 2,000 elsewhere. When an object enters the atmosphere, its velocity is greater than Earth's escape velocity (11.2 km per second/7 miles per second) and, unless it is very small, frictional heating produces a fireball. This fireball may rarely, and momentarily, rival the Sun in brightness. For example, at 1300 hrs on June 25, 1890, a brilliant fireball was visible over a large area of the Midwest of the United States, resulting in rare chondrite meteorite fragments reaching the surface at Farmington, east Kansas.

If a fragment of rock or metal (known as a meteoroid while still in space) enters the atmosphere at a low angle, deceleration in the thin upper atmosphere may take tens of seconds. On April 25, 1969, a fireball was visible along its 500 km (300 mile) -long south-east to north-west trajectory across much of England, Wales, and Ireland. As commonly occurs, towards the end of its path, the fireball fragmented. Sonic booms were heard after its passage, and two meteoritic stones were recovered, some 60 km (40 miles) apart – the larger at Bovedy, Northern Ireland, which gave its name to the fall. In 1868, a meteorite fell at Pultusk, east-central Poland. After fragmenting in the atmosphere, it is estimated to have had a total weight of 2 tonnes spread across an estimated 180,000 individual fragments. Large meteoroids of more than about 100 tonnes that do not break up in the atmosphere are not completely decelerated before impact. On striking the surface at hypersonic velocity, their kinetic energy is released, causing them to vaporize and produce explosion craters, such as Meteor (or Barringer) Crater in Arizona.

▼ *Halley's comet is the brightest and probably most famous short-period comet (it orbits the Sun every 76 years). Comet 1P Halley has been observed at each return since 240 BC, and it was first reliably noted in Chinese annals from the winter of 1059–1058 BC. It is named after the second British Astronomer Royal Edmond Halley (1656–1742), who was the first to calculate its orbit. When it gets close to the Sun, the Sun's heat causes the comet to burn off some of its dust and ice and the comet's tail becomes visible (white streak below). A second blueish tail is caused by reflected gas particles. On May 20, 1910, Earth actually passed through the comet's tail. It will next return in 2061.*

NEAs, NEOs, and PHAs

A Near-Earth Asteroid (NEA) has an orbit that crosses or approaches that of the Earth. Many such 'close-approach' asteroids have been found, and have been subdivided into three groups. **Amor asteroids** have orbits that cross that of Mars, but not that of the Earth. **Apollo asteroids** cross the Earth's orbit and have mean distances from the Sun greater than one astronomical unit (AU). One AU equals c. 150 million km (90 million miles). **Aten asteroids** have paths that lie mainly inside that of the Earth, so that their orbital periods are less than one year. One member of the Aten group, 2340 Hathor, is only 500 m (1,640 feet) across. At present, the holder of the 'approach record' is 1994 XM1 (yet to be named), which brushed past Earth on December 9, 1994, at a distance of a mere 112,000 km (70,000 miles). Although it is no more than 7 to 12 metres (23–39 feet) across, this object would have been sufficient to obliterate a city if it had scored a direct hit.

A **Near-Earth Object (NEO)** is an asteroid or comet with an orbit that brings it close to the orbit of the Earth. By analogy with the classes of orbit that comprise the NEAs, the criterion for an NEO is that the perihelion distance (closest distance to the Sun) be less than 1.3 AU. It is usual, though, to regard NEOs as including only those objects with smaller perihelia, making very close approaches to the Earth (and possibly impacts) feasible in the near term. A **potentially hazardous asteroid (PHA)** is an asteroid with an orbit that brings it very close to the orbit of the Earth, making a collision feasible in the near term, the object being large enough to cause significant damage in such an event. The limit set for the minimum orbit intersection distance is generally taken as being 0.05 AU. The minimum size is regarded as being between 110 and 240 m (360–790 feet), based upon observed absolute magnitude (measure of visibility) and estimated albedo (a measure of reflectivity). Sometimes the term 'potentially hazardous object' (PHO) is used in order to incorporate threatening comets as well as asteroids.

METEORITES/COMETS

Although most 'close-approach' asteroids are tiny on a cosmic scale, they carry sufficient energy to cause global catastrophe if they strike the Earth. One, 4179 Toutatis, was observed using radar and found to be a twin object, respectively 4 km and 2.5 km (2.5 and 4.5 miles) across, touching each other and moving round a common centre of gravity in 10.5 days. New 'close-approach' asteroids are being found regularly, and it seems that they are much more common than previously thought, so that occasional impacts cannot be ruled out. Indeed, in 2001 the Spaceguard Organization in Britain established itself at an existing observatory in Wales, especially to observe 'close approach' asteroids and to act as an information centre.

Ancient craters and meteorites

On a flat plateau off Highway 99, between Flagstaff and Winslow, central Arizona, United States, is what has been described as 'the most interesting place on Earth'. It is a huge crater, 1,265 m (4,150 feet) across, the walls of which rise 37–50 m (120–165 feet) above the surrounding plain. The outer slopes are quite gentle, but the inner slopes are steep and near vertical in places. An entire 600-m (1,970-foot) section of the pre-existing sedimentary rocks has been lifted about 30 m (100 feet) to form the south wall of the crater. It is well preserved, and has become a popular tourist attraction. There is no doubt about its origin – it was formed by the impact of a meteorite, which hit the Arizona Desert in prehistoric times, around 50,000 years ago.

The crater is circular, even though the impact occurred at an angle. When the meteorite struck, its kinetic energy

▼ False-colour, 3-D image from NASA's Terra satellite of the Barringer Meteorite Crater (Meteor Crater) in the arid sandstone of the Arizona Desert, south-west United States. When Europeans first discovered the crater, the plain around it was covered with more than 30 tons of meteoritic iron, scattered over an area 12–15 km (7–9 miles) in diameter. The meteorite was composed mostly of nickel-iron, suggesting it may have originated in the interior of a small planet. It was 150 ft (50 m) across, weighed roughly 300,000 tons, and traveled at a speed of 65,000 km/h (40,000 mph). It is named for Daniel Moreau Barringer.

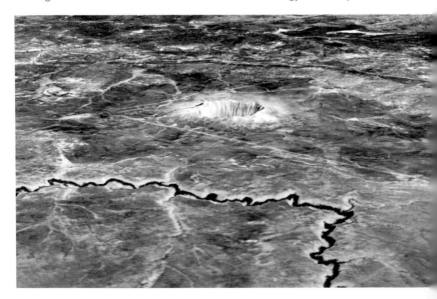

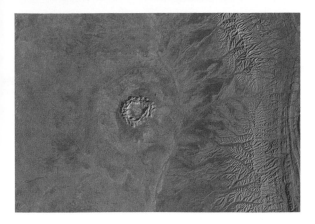

▲ NASA astronaut photograph of Gosse Bluff, an impact crater about 160 km (100 miles) west of Alice Springs in Northern Territory, Australia. Gosse Bluff is one of the most studied of Australia's impact craters. The impactor, an asteroid or comet, was probably about 1 km (0.6 miles) in diameter and crashed into the Earth about 142 million years ago. The isolated circular feature within the crater consists of a central ring of hills about 4.5 km (2.8 miles) in diameter. Australia is a very good place to observe and study impact craters. Much of Australia's surface is very ancient, so it has collected more impacts than many other parts of the world. Because of Australia's dry climate, the craters have not weathered away, nor are they been covered by dense vegetation.

converted into heat, and it became what was to all intents and purposes a powerful bomb. It is unlikely that anything remains of the impacting object, which would have been vapourized at the time of impact. Meteor Crater (or Arizona Crater or Barringer Crater) was the first crater on Earth to be recognized as being caused by meteorite impact. The feature first created interest in 1891, when large quantities of meteoritic iron were discovered on the surrounding plain. In 1905 boreholes and shafts were sunk in the centre of the crater in an attempt to find the main mass of the meteorite. After passing through crushed sandstone and rock flour, undisturbed rocks were found at a depth of 185 m (607 feet). In 1920 scientists concentrated their attention on the southern rim of the crater, but without success. It is now known that at times of such impacts, the meteorite is either vaporized or shattered to extents that depend on the characteristics of the particular event. It is almost certain that no large mass exists.

More than 30 tonnes of iron meteorite, known as Canyon Diablo, have been found around the crater. The fragments consist mainly of iron with slightly more than 7 percent nickel and 0.5 percent cobalt. In addition, oxidized iron shale balls were found intermingled with the local rock debris. Silica glass and very finely divided white sand (known as rock flour), together with high-pressure forms of quartz such as coesite and stishovite, all point to the structure having been formed by meteoritic impact. Studies of the distribution of the meteoritic material around the crater have led to the conclusion that the object responsible for the crater was travelling from north-northwest to south-southeast. This is consistent with the evidence gained from studies of the tilt of the rock layers forming the rim. Many attempts have been made to ascertain the age of Meteor Crater. Early findings suggested 2,000 to 3,000 years; current estimates give an age of about 50,000 years.

A smaller, but essentially similar, impact crater is Wolf Creek in Western Australia. There are various local legends about it. The Kjaru Aborigines call it *Kandimalal*, and describe how two rainbow snakes made sinuous tracks across the desert, forming Wolf Creek and the adjacent Sturt Creek, while the crater marks the spot where one of the snakes emerged from below the ground. It is much older than Meteor Crater, probably around 2 million years old. Wolf

METEORITES/COMETS

Creek is more difficult to reach than Meteor Crater, and the road from the nearest settlement, Halls Creek, is usually open for only part of the year, but it has now been extensively studied since aerial surveys first identified it in 1947. The wall rises at an angle of 15 to 35°, and the floor is flat 55 m (180 feet) below the rim and 25 m (80 feet) below the level of the surrounding plain. The diameter of the crater is 675 m (2,215 feet). Meteoritic fragments found in the area leave no doubt that it is of cosmic origin. Australia also hosts other impact craters, including one at Boxhole and a whole group at Henbury, both in Northern Territories. Equally intriguing is Gosse Bluff, also in Northern Territories. This is at least 50,000 years old and highly eroded, although there is the remnant of a central structure and indications of the old walls.

More than 165 impact craters have now been identified, including structures in North America, Arabia, Argentina, Estonia and elsewhere, but one must be wary of jumping to conclusions; for example, independent geologists who have made careful studies of the Vredefort Ring, near Pretoria, South Africa, are unanimous in finding that it is of internal origin. It is linked with local geology, and the form is not characteristic of collision. It should also be noted that no crater is associated with the giant Hoba West meteorite. The Hoba West meteorite is the largest individual meteorite yet discovered, weighing about 60 tons and measuring 2.95 by 2.84 m (9.7 by 9.3 feet). It crashed to Earth less than 80,000 years ago, landing near Grootfontein, northern Namibia.

The effects on our planet should it be struck in the future by a large object from space will be devastating. Sixty-five million years ago, at the end of the Cretaceous Period, a 10 km (6 mile) -wide comet or asteroid struck the Earth, and this caused such a change in the Earth's climate that about 60 percent of all species became extinct, including the dinosaurs. The impact site has now been located buried

▼ *On January 31, 1996, Japanese amateur astronomer Yuji Hyakutake discovered a long-period comet. On March 25, 1996, Comet Hyakutake made a remarkably close passage (0.10 AU) to Earth, and was easily visible by the naked eye in the night sky. Reaching a peak brightness of −1 in March 1996, the comet was particularly noticeable for its strong bluish ion trail stretching for up to 70° through Ursa Major. The comet tail is by far the longest yet found, measuring more than 570 million km (350 million miles). Comet Hyakutake, possible making its first visit to the inner Solar System from the Oort Cloud, has an orbital period of about 14,000 years.*

▶ In August 1993, the Galileo spacecraft examined the main-belt asteroid (243) Ida. As this image shows, Ida is elongated in shape and heavily cratered from impacts by smaller bodies. Ida measures about 56 × 24 × 21 (35 × 15 × 13 miles). It is composed largely of metal-rich silicates. Galileo images revealed Ida to be accompanied by a small moon, Dactyl.

▼ Satellite image of the 70 km (45 mile) -diameter Manicougan impact crater in Québec, south-eastern Canada. The feature was formed by an asteroid impact about 212 million years ago, toward the end of the Triassic period. Some scientists believe the impact may have been responsible for the mass extinction of 60 percent of all species that occurred at about this time.

beneath Mexico's Yucatán Peninsula, where geophysical surveys have revealed the existence of the huge 180 km (110 mile) -diameter Chicxulub Crater. There is no doubt that the Earth will be struck again many times in the future, forming new craters. There are plenty of potential impactors moving in the closer part of the Solar System, and although the chances of a major collision are slight, they are not zero, which is partly why constant watch is now being kept to identify wandering bodies. It is even possible that if one of these bodies could be seen during approach, we might be able to divert it by nuclear warheads carried on ballistic missiles – though whether we would be given enough advance warning is questionable.

In January 2000, the British government set up a special committee to look into the whole question of the danger of impact from asteroids or comets. Other governments and the United Nations are doing the same. If there is such an impact, let us hope that we cope with the situation better than the dinosaurs did.

Great Extinctions

Numerous extinction events have been recorded throughout geological time, each of which destroyed many species and allowed new players to enter the scene. Many of the mass extinctions appear to have been the result of changes in the Earth's geography, such as reductions in the areas of shallow tropical ocean that killed off species that required warm and shallow marine waters. Many vertebrate species were killed at the end of the Permian period, 251 million years ago, while many species of mammals and all the dinosaurs plunged into extinction at the end of the Cretaceous period, 65 million years ago.

Causes of mass extinctions are currently a very hot topic, and arguments rage, in particular, about what caused the great Permian and Cretaceous extinctions. At the end of the Permian, the uniting of the continents, sea-level fall, climatic changes, the change in the composition of the ocean waters, and the outpouring of vast amounts of lava in the form of the flood basalts, and a major impact event have all been implicated in the extinction level event. One model proposes that the sea-level fell because less molten rock material was being generated at the mid-ocean spreading centres, thus increasing the volumetric capacity of the ocean basins. Shorelines retreated from the continents by as much as 1,900 km (1,200 miles), reducing the area of shallow seas and forcing more species into extinction. Because the African and South American continental landmasses were joined there was less shoreline exposed to the climatic effects of the oceans. The result was a dryer climate. Alternative explanations that are gaining credence are that great outpourings of lava in Siberia, or a collision with a large comet or asteroid, or possibly both, changed the climate sufficiently to wipe out 90 percent of all life.

New species evolved in the millions of years following the close of the Permian only to be knocked back by another great extinction at the end of the Cretaceous period, almost 200 million years later. Major losses occurred in bony fishes, sponges, foraminifera, snails, clams, mammals, reptiles, and all of the dinosaurs. Once again, a number of candidates have been proposed to have caused the extinction, including long-term changes in climate and sea level, flood basalt volcanism in the Indian subcontinent, and collision with a large comet. In truth, the effects of the last event alone would have been sufficient to explain the observed loss of species.

The location of the impact event at the end of the Cretaceous has now been identified and has been the subject of study for over a decade. The collision produced the Chicxulub crater on Mexico's Yucatán Peninsula, identified – but not recognized – by oil prospectors in the 1950s, who encountered shattered rock about 2 km (1 mile) below the surface. Subsequent geophysical surveys showed that

▶ Planet Earth coalesced from a cosmic cloud about 4,600 million years ago, but it took hundreds of millions of years for conditions to stabilize enough for organic molecules to accumulate. Earth's early atmosphere was devoid of oxygen, made up mostly of hydrogen, ammonia, methane, and water vapour. This thin layer was no shield against the Sun's powerful radiation. Lightning storms, volcanic eruptions, and meteorite impacts were commonplace, and all provided energy vital to the evolution of life.

◄ ▼ The history of life on Earth has been puncuated by several mass extinctions. Perhaps the best-known example was the demise of the dinosaurs at the end of the Createceous period (65 million years ago). The demise of dinosaurs such as the kronosaurus (left) and the iguanodon (below) was due to a dramatic cooling of Earth's climate, most likely caused by the impact of a giant meteorite, which threw up clouds of dust into the atmosphere.

the impact crater has a diameter of 180 km (110 miles), consistent with an impact in the 10 km (6 miles) size range resulting in a blast of the order of 100 million megatonnes.

The magnitude and precise details of the worldwide effects of this impact remain a topic of hot scientific debate. Certainly the impact would have created a monumental earthquake and a possible tsunami in the Gulf of Mexico. It also would have created a cloud of vaporized water and rock that rose high into the Earth's stratosphere. What is further hypothesized is that this cloud of debris blocked the incoming rays of the Sun for many months creating a cosmic winter. Plants that rely on sunlight to build themselves by photosynthesis would have suffered greatly. Even after the dust had settled, gases would have remained aloft creating a greenhouse effect and years of higher temperatures. Such severe climatic disruption would have played havoc with both plant and animal life and is the leading candidate implicated in the demise of the dinosaurs.

The fossil record also documents the extinction of large animals during the advances and retreats of the continental glaciers during the Ice Ages in the past 1.5 million years. The earliest humans that migrated to the Americas 13,000 years ago found many species of large land mammals that are extinct today, such as the mammoth elephants, the short-faced bear, and the sabre-toothed cat. Except for Africa, extinctions appeared to follow the arrival of human habitants. It is sobering to realize that the greatest mass extinction is occurring today, with human activities currently wiping out between 3,000 and 30,000 species a year, from an estimated total of just ten million. Up to 30 percent of flowering plants may be at risk, while between 25 percent and 50 percent of all animal species may have vanished by the time the 22nd century dawns. We are truly living in a time of great extinction.

Further Reading

Abbott, P.L. Natural Disasters (McGraw Hill, 4th edition, 2002)

Alexander, David Natural Disasters (UCL Press, 1998)

Allaby, Michael Hurricanes (Facts on File Inc., 2003)

Bell, Fred Geological Hazards (Spon Press, 1999)

Bishop, Victoria Hazards and Responses (Collins Educational, 2nd edition, 2001)

Bolt, Bruce Earthquakes (W.H. Freeman & Co., 4th edition, 1999)

Bryant, Edward Tsunami: The Underrated Hazard (Cambridge University Press, 2001)

Burroughs, William J. Climate Change (Cambridge University Press, 2001)

Clark, C. Natural Disasters (Kendall Hunt Publishing, 2002)

Decker R. & Decker, B. Volcanoes (W.H. Freeman & Co., 3rd edition, 1997)

Dregne, H.E. Desertification of Arid Lands (Harwood, 1983)

Francis, Peter Volcanoes – a Planetary Perspective (Clarendon Press, 1993)

Gross, M.G. Oceanography (Prentice Hall, 7th edition, 1996)

Intergovernmental Panel on Climate Change (IPCC) Working Group II Climate Change 2001: Impacts, Adaptations and Vulnerability (Cambridge University Press, 2001)

Keller, E. Introduction to Environmental Geology (Prentice Hall, 2nd edition, 2002)

Longshore, David Encyclopedia of Hurricanes, Typhoons and Cyclones (Facts on File Inc., 2000)

Lutgens, F.K. & Tarbuck, E.J. The Atmosphere (Prentice Hall, 2000)

McGuire, Bill Apocalypse: A Natural History of Global Hazards (Cassell, 1999)

McGuire, Bill Raging Planet: Earthquakes, Volcanoes and the Tectonic Threat to Life on Earth (Apple Press, 2002)

McGuire, Bill, Mason, Ian, and Kilburn, Christopher Natural Hazards and Environmental Change (Arnold, 2002)

Murck, Barbara, et al. Dangerous Earth: an Introduction to Geologic Hazards (Wiley, 1996)

Press, F., Siever, R., Grotzinger, J. & Jordan, T.H. Understanding Earth (W.H. Freeman & Co., 4th edition, 2003)

Reynolds, R. Guide to Weather (Philip's, 2002)

Sigurdsson, Haraldur et al. Encyclopedia of Volcanoes (Academic Press, 1999)

Smith, Keith Assessing Risk and Reducing Disaster (Routledge, 3rd edition, 2001)

Steel, Duncan Target Earth (Readers Digest, 2000)

Zebrowski, E., Jr. Perils of a Restless Planet: Scientific Perspectives on Natural Disasters (Cambridge University Press, 1997)

Websites

When you are entering an address in a web browser, it should be prefixed by 'http://'. In most browsers, this is automatic if the address begins 'www'. We have carefully selected the following sites for the quality of their information on natural hazards.

www.volcano.si.edu
www.volcanoworld.org
www.tsunami.org
www.avalanche.org
www.geocities.com/hurricanene
www.wildweather.com
www.nhc.noaa.gov/
earthobservatory.nasa.gov
www.benfieldhrc.org
www.who.int
www.ifrc.org
www.unicef.org
www.reliefweb.int
www.disasterrelief.org
www.cred.be/emdat
www.usgs.gov
www.fema.gov
www.noaa.gov
www.environment-agency.org.uk
www.met-office.gov.uk
www.ocipep.gc.ca
www.greenpeace.org

The editors would like to acknowledge the assistance of EM-DAT: The OFDA/CRED International Disaster Database - www.cred.be/emdat - Université Catholique de Louvain, Brussels, Belgium, in compiling some of the tables of disaster statistics that appear in Guide to Global Hazards.

Picture Credits

9 Dave Saville/FEMA News
10 Bob McMillan/FEMA News
12–13 NGDC/NOAA
21 Derrell Jones/Corbis
24–25 Bettmann/Corbis
26 Roger Ressmeyer/Corbis
27 Baldev/Corbis Sygma
28 Peter Turnley/Corbis
29 top: Michael S. Yamashita/Corbis, bottom: Peter M. Wilson /Corbis
30 Dr. Roger Hutchison/NGDC/NOAA
32 Bisson Bernard/Corbis Sygma
33 Corbis
39 J.D. Griggs/Hawaiian Volcano Observatory/USGS
41 K. Segerstrom/USGS
42 J.D. Griggs/USGS
43 Jonathan Blair/Corbis
44 top: JSC/NASA, bottom: Roger Ressmeyer /Corbis
45 Gary Braasch/Corbis
47 top: Cees J. van Western/USGS, bottom: R. P. Hoblitt/USGS
48 J.D. Griggs/Hawaiian Volcano Observatory/USGS
50 D.A. Swanson/Hawaiian Volcano Observatory/USGS
51 J.D. Griggs/Hawaiian Volcano Observatory/USGS
53 Langevin Jacques/Corbis Sygma
54 LRC/Aerosol Research Branch/NASA
54 R.S. Culbreth/US Air Force/NGDC
55 top: Roger Ressmeyer/Corbis, bottom: Roger Ressmeyer/Corbis
56 top: R.S. Culbreth/US Air Force/USGS, bottom: LRC/NASA
58 James A. Sugar/Corbis
59 top: JPL/NASA, bottom: Roger Ressmeyer /Corbis
60 Roger Ressmeyer /Corbis
61 Michael P. Doukas/USGS/CVO
65 Lloyd Cluff/Corbis
67 Jose C. Borrero/USGS
68 Keith Dannemiller/Corbis Saba
69 Hugh Davies/NOAA
71 News Ltd/Austral/Corbis Sygma
70 Pacific Tsunami Museum Archive/Yasuki Arakaki collection/Cecilio Licos
73 Hugh Davies/NOAA
76 Joel W. Rogers/Corbis
78 Bettmann/Corbis
80 Hulton-Deutsch Collection/Corbis
84 Royalty free/Corbis
88 Wolfgang Kaehler/Corbis
92 Alan Hawes/Corbis Sygma
93 Jesse Allen/GSFC/NASA
96 David Turnley/Corbis
97 Jacques Descloitres/MODIS/NASA
98 Bettmann/Corbis
99 Ted Spiegel/Corbis
104 David Saville/FEMA News
105 FEMA News
107 Hubert Stadler/Corbis
108 Hal Pierce/GSFC/NASA
113 RSD/GSFC/NASA
114 Prensa Nicaragua/Corbis Sygma
118 Jim Zuckerman/Corbis
122 David Hies/Corbis Sygma

123 Andrea Booher/FEMA News
124 Adam duBrowa/FEMA News
126 NOAA/GSFC/NASA
130 Historic NWS Collection/Boston Globe/NOAA/Department of Commerce
132 Aaron Horowitz/Corbis
134 SeaWiFS/GSFC/NASA/ORBIMAGE
135 James Leynse/Corbis Saba
136 Galen Rowell/Corbis
141 PICIMPACT/Corbis
145 USGS
146 Kike Arnal/Corbis Sygma
149 London Aerial Photo Library/Corbis
153 Steve McCurry/Magnum
155 Landsat 7/NASA
156–157 Landsat/USGS
159 Rex
163–164 Chris Rainier/Corbis
165 GSFC/NASA
167 Andrea Booher/FEMA News
169 JSC/NASA
170 Timothy Liu and Hua Hu/JPL/QuickScat/NASA
171 Justin Domeroski/FEMA News
172–173 Raymond Gehman/Corbis
174 Raymond Gehman/Corbis
175 Numerical Terradynamic Simulation Group/UMT/NASA
175 Andrea Booher/FEMA News
177 NASA
178 GSFC/NASA
180 John McColgan/Alaska Forest Service
189 Ron Boardman/Frank Lane Picture Agency/Corbis
190 Seibert Carl/Corbis Sygma
196 Space Imaging
197 Gallo Images/Corbis
198 Greg Shirah/GSFC/NASA
201 JSC/NASA
203 Ted Spiegel/Corbis
207 Judyth Platt/Ecoscene/Corbis
208 Jacques Descloitres/MODIS/GSFC/NASA
210 Bettmann/Corbis
214 LBA-ECO Project/NASA
216–217 Landsat Project/USGS
225 Paul Hardy/Corbis
228 JPL/NASA
231 JSC/NASA
233 R. Batalon, US Air Force/NGDC
234 Safari project/NASA
235 NCAR and University of Toronto MOPITT Teams/NASA
237 Gregory W. Shirah (and others)/GSFC/NASA
241 James A. Sugar/Corbis
242 Vince Streano/Corbis
243–244 JPL/NASA
245 Don Davis/NASA
246 NASA
247 JSC/NASA
248 H. Weaver (ARC), HST Comet Hyakutake Observing Team and NASA
249 top: NASA, bottom: Landsat/NASA

Index

Number in bold type points to major reference
Asterisk (*) next to number indicates illustration